The Comprehensive Plan

The practice of comprehensive planning is changing dramatically in the 21st century to address the pressing need for more sustainable, resilient, and equitable communities. Drawing on the latest research and best practice examples, *The Comprehensive Plan: Sustainable, Resilient, and Equitable Communities for the 21st Century* provides an in-depth resource for planning practitioners, elected officials, citizens, and others seeking to develop effective, impactful, comprehensive plans, grounded in authentic community engagement, as a pathway to sustainability. Based on standards developed by the American Planning Association to provide a national benchmark for sustainable comprehensive planning, this book provides detailed guidance on the substance, process, and implementation of comprehensive plans that address the critical challenges facing communities in the 21st century.

David Rouse, FAICP, ASLA, is a consultant, educator, researcher, and author with over 40 years of experience in urban and regional planning and design. From 2013 to 2019, he served as Managing Director of Research and Advisory Services for the American Planning Association (APA). As Research Director, David co-led APA's Comprehensive Plan Standards for Sustaining Places Initiative with the late David R. Godschalk. Prior to joining APA he was a principal at the planning and design firm Wallace Roberts & Todd in Philadelphia, where many of his projects were recognized with professional awards for excellence. David's areas of expertise include comprehensive planning, parks and open space planning, green infrastructure, and planning for emerging technologies.

Rocky Piro, PhD, FAICP, is Executive Director of the Colorado Center for Sustainable Urbanism at the University of Colorado Denver. He also serves as Associate Professor in the College of Architecture and Planning. Previously he was the Manager for Planning and Community Development in Denver and Program Manager for Growth Management at the Puget Sound Regional Council in Seattle. He is a member of the Board of Directors for the International Urban Planning and Environment Association, and past chair for the Regional and Intergovernmental Planning Division of the American Planning Association. Dr. Piro earned a doctorate in Urban Design and Planning at the University of Washington. He is a recipient of the Myer Wolfe Award for Excellence in Planning and was inducted in the College of Fellows of the American Institute of Certified Planners.

APA Planning Essentials

APA Planning Essentials books provide introductory background information aligned to planning curricula, with textbooks meant for graduate students to be used in urban planning courses, and continuing education purposes by professional planners.

Titles in the Series

Basic Quantitative Research Methods for Urban Planners
Edited by Reid Ewing and Keunhyun Park

The Comprehensive Plan: Sustainable, Resilient, and Equitable Communities for the 21st Century
David Rouse and Rocky Piro

The Comprehensive Plan

Sustainable, Resilient, and Equitable Communities for the 21st Century

David Rouse
and
Rocky Piro

Routledge
Taylor & Francis Group

NEW YORK AND LONDON

Cover image: © Getty Images

First published 2022
by Routledge
605 Third Avenue, New York, NY 10158

and by Routledge
4 Park Square, Milton Park, Abingdon, Oxon, OX14 4RN

Routledge is an imprint of the Taylor & Francis Group, an informa business

© 2022 Taylor & Francis

Library of Congress Cataloging-in-Publication Data
A catalog record for this title has been requested

ISBN: 9780367903992 (hbk)
ISBN: 9780367897550 (pbk)
ISBN: 9781003024170 (ebk)

DOI: 10.4324/9781003024170

Typeset in Adobe Garamond Pro
by codeMantra

This book is dedicated to David R. Godschalk, 1931–2018

Contents

Figures

Tables

Foreword

The seeds of this book were planted at the World Urban Forum in Rio de Janeiro in 2010, when the American Planning Association (APA) announced the *Sustaining Places* initiative. Through this initiative, APA committed to improve local planning practice to advance more sustainable human settlements. APA created a task force of leading practitioners and appointed Dr. David Godschalk of the University of North Carolina as co-chair. Godschalk was the ideal person to serve in this position, having had a distinguished career as a scholar, a practicing planner and architect, an appointed and elected official, and a teacher and mentor.

The task force's mission was to develop best practice standards to guide the development of the comprehensive plan as the leading local policy document to help communities of all sizes achieve sustainable outcomes. The task force's work culminated in a landmark report, *Comprehensive Plan Standards for Sustaining Places* (Godschalk and Rouse 2015). The standards have had a substantial impact on comprehensive planning practice. Numerous local jurisdictions across the nation have applied them to updates of existing plans and development of new ones.

Rouse and Piro use the Comprehensive Plan Standards as a foundation, extending them to offer an in-depth exploration of 21st-century planning practice. They provide an impressive array of examples that demonstrate how the principles and best practices defined by the standards have been applied in comprehensive plans adopted by diverse communities across the United States. A strong base of research supports the use of core principles that may otherwise seem theoretical and unrelated to the day-to-day challenges facing communities. Rouse and Piro skillfully draw on knowledge from planning theory, contemporary planning practice, and findings from empirical research to address this void.

We are excited about the benefits this book will bring to the practice of meaningful planning by local planners, decision-makers, and community members, as well as to the academic analysis of planning and its impacts. The structure of the book provides a much-needed update to the literature about how planning should be performed. Its examples and practical suggestions will give planners and community members the guidance they need to tailor their processes, plans, and implementation so they can successfully achieve a community's particular vision for its future. It will also help students learn the approaches and tools that today's planning must apply to address a range of difficult, uncertain, and often controversial topics, and to build community engagement throughout the planning process.

The book offers a comprehensive framework for creating the plan, including steps for identifying a community's values, articulating a vision and goals for the future, and defining how to achieve the vision and goals through policy and action. The book also addresses how process and substance come together in a final comprehensive plan that can be successfully implemented. Contemporary innovations are presented, including how to ensure the internal consistency of the comprehensive plan, coordinate it with other plans, and enhance communication of the plan to diverse stakeholders and the public.

A major contribution of this book is the application of a *systems approach* to the comprehensive plan. In contrast to the traditional comprehensive planning model, which addresses functional systems such as land use and transportation as stand-alone elements, a systems approach emphasizes interactions among issues in the plan and its implementation. Rouse and Piro persuasively demonstrate how systems thinking is crucial to overcoming the grand challenges that confront 21st-century communities around the world in order to achieve sustainable, resilient, and equitable outcomes.

Issues such as environmental degradation, climate change, technological disruption, and stark disparities in the distribution of resources and engagement of low income and minority communities are complex and seemingly intractable to address. The practice and study of planning have experimented with ways of addressing these issues in the face of current realities (limited resources, polarized viewpoints, expectations of immediate results, and more) that make action on a grand scale seem all but impossible. This book provides the inspiration and the insights that will enable planners and communities to use a familiar document – the comprehensive plan – in new ways to have a meaningful impact on the grand challenges of our times.

Philip Berke and Karen Walz

Philip Berke, PhD, is a professor of planning at the University of North Carolina Chapel Hill and a long-time colleague of David Godschalk. They collaborated with two other authors on *Urban Land Use Planning: Fifth Edition,* a classic planning text. Over the past 25 years, Berke has conducted research and authored numerous publications on plan evaluation. His research contributed to the formulation of the principles defined by APA's Comprehensive Plan Standards.

Karen Walz, FAICP, Principal with Strategic Community Solutions, is a planner and consultant with more than 40 years of experience working with diverse communities to create and implement long-range plans. She participated in developing the Comprehensive Plan Standards framework and continues to use the standards to educate community members about the ways a 'best practice' comprehensive plan can help them address the challenges they face.

Reference

Godschalk, David and David Rouse (2015). *Sustaining Places: Best Practices for Comprehensive Plans*, APA Planning Advisory Service 578. Chicago, IL: American Planning Association.

Acknowledgments

I would like to acknowledge my wife, Beverly, who encouraged me to take on this book project. In addition, I would also like to acknowledge our family – Andrew, Emily, Brad, Ryan, Kristin and Kristin, and Taylor – who provided support and enthusiasm throughout. Finally, my thanks to countless friends and colleagues who have been a great source of motivation and joy.

– Rocky Piro

I would like to thank countless friends and colleagues I have worked with and learned from over the years. I would particularly like to acknowledge my colleagues and clients at Wallace Roberts & Todd, where I learned the art of comprehensive planning, as well as all those whom I worked with and supported me while I was Research Director for the American Planning Association. Special thanks go to my wife, Amy, and daughter, Hana, for their love and support throughout my career and while Rocky and I were writing this book in the midst of a global pandemic.

Finally, Rocky and I would like to acknowledge the enormous debt of gratitude we and the planning profession owe to David Godschalk, the great scholar, researcher, practitioner, and long-time professor at the University of North Carolina-Chapel Hill. Dave (as all called him) was the driving force behind the development of the American Planning Association's Comprehensive Plan Standards for Sustaining Places, which are the foundation of this book. He is sorely missed.

– David Rouse

Chapter 1

Introduction

The 21st century is a time of unparalleled progress and unprecedented challenges for humankind. People around the globe enjoy a standard of living unimaginable to those who came before us, made possible by rapid technological change that promises to help solve many of civilization's most intractable problems. But technological advancements have come at a heavy price: a changing climate driven by fossil fuel emissions; degradation of natural resources caused by population growth and development; and the growing divide between rich and poor. The effects of climate change are evident in the increasing frequency and severity of floods, droughts, wildfires, heat waves, and other natural disasters, which disproportionately impact poor and vulnerable populations.

According to a global assessment of biodiversity and ecosystem services, the rate of change in nature during the last 50 years is unprecedented: up to 1 million of the estimated 8 million plant and animal species on Earth are at risk of extinction, many of them within decades (IPBES 2019). Technological innovations such as automation and artificial intelligence threaten to disrupt the workforce and displace workers, compounding the effects of globalization and other macroeconomic trends on local communities. While globalization has raised living standards for over a half a billion people and reduced inequality between the developing and developed world, inequality within the United States and nations around the globe is increasing (Bourguignon 2015). Socioeconomic inequality is reflected in stark differences in life expectancies between nearby zip codes, as chronic illnesses associated with lifestyle-related conditions like obesity and stress have replaced infectious diseases as the leading cause of death in most industrialized and many developing countries.

The comprehensive plan is the leading policy document guiding the long-range development of counties, cities, towns, and other local jurisdictions across the United States.[1] Just as communities need to adapt to the forces of environmental, economic,

DOI: 10.4324/9781003024170-1

social, and technological change, comprehensive planning practice needs to evolve to help communities navigate those changes in an increasingly uncertain world.

In the 20th century, comprehensive plans focused on land use and the physical development of communities. The typical plan consisted of elements such as land use, transportation, and housing, each with its own goals, objectives, and policies. While this model persists today, a new approach has emerged over the past several decades. Contemporary plans engage community members and articulate their shared values through a collaborative process; organize plan content around cross-cutting themes; connect values and vision for the future to a defined action agenda; address issues that transcend jurisdictional boundaries; and use alternatives to paper documents to communicate the plan to different audiences (Rouse, Chandler, and Arason 1999). In doing so, they go beyond the roots of comprehensive planning in physical development to address social dimensions of community, such as equity, public health, and human investment.

As planning practice continues to evolve, how can the comprehensive plan – an invention of the first half of the 20th century, with a mixed track record of implementation – position communities to deal with the magnitude of challenges confronting them in a world of accelerating change? How can its outcomes improve community health, livability, and sustainability while addressing global problems like climate change? To help answer these questions, this book provides a resource and guide to comprehensive planning practice for professional planners, elected officials, citizens, and others seeking to create sustainable, resilient, and equitable 21st-century communities. Drawing on research and best practice examples of plans from across the United States, it covers the comprehensive planning process, the content and attributes of the plan, and plan implementation with the overarching goal of creating sustainable, resilient, and equitable communities. While geared toward comprehensive planning as it is practiced by local jurisdictions in the United States, the principles and practices it elucidates can be adapted for use at different scales (for example, neighborhood, region, and megaregion) and by communities worldwide.

While the authors were writing this book in 2020, the United States absorbed two major shocks that brought the magnitude of the challenges that communities face to the forefront. The first was the loss of life and economic impacts caused by the global COVID-19 pandemic. The second was the deaths of George Floyd and other Black Americans at the hands of law enforcement officers, which sparked anger and protests across the nation. Both were symptomatic of deep-seated structural disparities in the nation's society and economy. COVID-19 disproportionately affected minority communities and people with underlying conditions, such as obesity and diabetes, that relate to the social determinants of health. Its economic effects were experienced most severely by workers in the service economy, many of whom live from paycheck to paycheck, rather than by those who could work remotely using digital technology. Violence against Blacks is a manifestation of institutionalized racism to which planning practice has contributed. Although reversing systemic inequality requires a sustained, broad-based societal commitment, the authors believe that the comprehensive plan can and must be part of the solution.

Sustainability, Resilience, and Equity

Sustainability, resilience, and equity – the overarching themes of this book – are distinct but interrelated concepts. The Brundtland Report defines sustainable development as "development that meets the needs of the present without compromising the ability of future generations to meet their own needs" (World Commission on Environment and Development 1987). Building on that definition, the Institute for Sustainable Communities defines a sustainable community as one that "manages its human, natural, and financial capital to meet current needs while ensuring that adequate resources are available for future generations" (Institute for Sustainable Communities n.d.).

The Rockefeller Foundation's *100 Resilient Cities* initiative defines resilience as "the capacity of individuals, communities, and systems to adapt, survive, and grow in the face of stresses and shocks, and even transform when conditions require it" (Arup n.d.). Stresses are chronic challenges to natural and human systems such as the long-term effects of climate change and entrenched poverty. Shocks are acute natural and human-caused disasters such as extreme weather events and severe economic disruptions.

The American Planning Association (APA) defines equity as "just and fair inclusion into a society in which all can participate, prosper, and reach their full potential. Unlocking the promise of the nation by unleashing the promise in us all" (American Planning Association 2019). According to the U.S. Environmental Protection Agency, equitable development is "an approach for meeting the needs of underserved communities through policies and programs that reduce disparities while fostering places that are healthy and vibrant. It is increasingly considered an effective place-based action for creating strong and livable communities" (U.S. Environmental Protection Agency n.d.).

The American Institute of Certified Planners *Code of Ethics and Professional Conduct* implicitly charges professional planners with the ethical responsibility to help the communities they serve become more sustainable, resilient, and equitable (American Institute of Certified Planners 2016). The aspirational principles (ideals to which they are committed) contained in the Code call for certified planners to:

- Have special concern for the long-range consequences of present actions.
- Pay special attention to the interrelatedness of decisions.
- Give people the opportunity to have a meaningful impact on the development of plans and programs that may affect them.
- Seek social justice by working to expand choice and opportunity for all persons, recognizing a special responsibility to plan for the needs of the disadvantaged and to promote racial and economic integration.

Systems Approach

A fundamental premise of this book is that a systems approach is necessary for the comprehensive plan to yield truly sustainable, resilient, and equitable outcomes. A system can be defined as an interconnected set of elements that are coherently organized in a way that achieves something; in other words, it has a function or purpose (Meadows 2008). A system is part of (nested within) a larger system and, in turn, comprises smaller subsystems (a concept referred to as system hierarchy). From this perspective, a community such as a city or town is a complex system that is both part of a larger system (the region) and an aggregate of smaller subsystems. Community subsystems include geographic subareas (for example, neighborhoods) and functional components such as land use, transportation, and housing, which themselves are systems comprising subsystems. For example, transportation is a multimodal system whose subsystems accommodate vehicles, bicyclists, pedestrians, public transit, and other ways that people and goods move through a community. In contrast to the traditional comprehensive planning model, which addressed functional systems like transportation and land use as siloed elements, a systems approach accounts for interactions between them in the plan and its implementation.

Systems demonstrate characteristic behaviors that reveal themselves over time. From a systems perspective, the real-world impacts of the comprehensive plan result from altering the behavior of multiple systems to create desired change.[2] The following are examples of how a systems approach can help a community become more sustainable, resilient, and equitable:

- Land use and transportation system behavior can be changed to increase energy efficiency and reduce fossil fuel consumption (sustainability).
- An enhanced urban forest as a subsystem of a community-wide green infrastructure system can ameliorate the urban heat island effect while absorbing and reducing stormwater runoff (resilience).
- All such interventions can be designed to increase access and opportunity for poor and underserved populations (equity).

A Brief History of the Comprehensive Plan

The origins of comprehensive planning date back to the City Beautiful movement, embodied by the 1893 Columbian Exposition in Chicago and the 1902 McMillan Commission's plan for the monumental core of Washington, DC (Kelly 2010). In 1912, the American Society of Landscape Architects published *A Brief Survey of Recent City Planning Reports in the United States*, which identified 28 planning reports published during the prior two years, by cities such as Baltimore, New Haven, and St. Louis and authors such as Daniel Burnham, John Nolen, and Frederick Law Olmsted, Jr. (Kimball 1912). Reflecting the influence of the City Beautiful movement (Burnham led the Columbian Exposition and both Burnham and Olmsted served on the McMillan Commission), these reports emphasized the physical development of the city, for example through park and boulevard systems.

The formal foundation for urban planning as it is practiced today was established by *A Standard State Zoning Enabling Act (SZEA)*, published by the U.S. Department of Commerce in 1926, and *A Standard City Planning Enabling Act* (SCPEA), published in 1928. The SZEA called for zoning regulations to "be made in accordance with a comprehensive plan" in order to, among other purposes, "facilitate the adequate provision of transportation, water, sewerage, parks, and other public requirements." Intended to complement the SZEA, the SCPEA directed the planning commission to "make and adopt a master plan for the physical development of the municipality" and elaborated on the purpose, contents, and legal status of the plan (also referred to as the comprehensive or official plan). All 50 states adopted versions of the SZEA and many have adopted elements of the SCPEA (Meck 1996).

The post-World War II era was a time of rapid growth and development for the United States following the Great Depression and World War II. Section 701 of the *Housing Act of 1954* provided a major boost to comprehensive planning practice by making funding available to smaller communities that lacked resources for planning. Federal appropriations from 1955 to 1981 (when the 701 program was rescinded) totaled over $1 billion, enabling thousands of local jurisdictions to prepare comprehensive plans (Feiss 1985). The program contributed to widespread acceptance of planning as a local governmental function and of comprehensive planning as a core planning activity.

First published in 1964, *The Urban General Plan* by T.J. Kent provided a guide to comprehensive planning practice in the post-World War II era. Kent defined the general plan as:

> ...the official statement of a municipal legislative body which sets forth its major policies concerning desirable future physical development; the published general-plan document must include a single, unified general physical design for the community, and it must attempt to clarify the relationships between physical-development policies and social and economic goals.
>
> (Kent 1990)

Kent asserted that the general plan should be long-range, comprehensive, and general in nature; should focus on physical development; and should provide a policy guide for decision making rather than a detailed implementation program. He identified the city council (the elected representatives of the people) as the client of the general plan. While Kent referred to the role of the general plan in "providing an opportunity for citizen participation," he did not specify such participation as part of the plan preparation process.

Throughout much of the 20th century, comprehensive plans were prepared using a top-down process referred to as the *rational model.* Public participation in shaping the plan was limited. In the latter part of the century, this model began to change, influenced by societal trends such as the civil rights and environmental movements of the 1960s and trends in planning practice, such as advocacy planning and community visioning.

Two plans – *Toward a Sustainable Seattle* and *FOCUS Kansas City* – illustrate how comprehensive planning practice was changing at the dawn of the new millennium. *Toward a Sustainable Seattle* was one of the first comprehensive plans that identified sustainability as a fundamental goal (Godschalk and Anderson 2012). While organized into elements as required by Washington's *Growth Management Act*, the plan identified four overarching values (themes) based on citizen engagement in the planning process: community, environmental stewardship, economic opportunity and security, and social equity. Recognizing climate change as a global challenge, the plan set targets for greenhouse gas emission reductions with the goal of making Seattle carbon neutral by 2050.

FOCUS Kansas City was prepared using a values-driven planning process with extensive citizen and stakeholder participation (Rouse 1998; Figure 1.1).[3] The process was led by a steering committee and included 12 perspective groups representing different interests and viewpoints, as well as work teams for seven interrelated component plans (alternatives to traditional elements). The component plans addressed physical development (for example, the *Citywide Physical Framework* and *Urban Core Plans*), and topics not previously addressed by comprehensive plans (governance and human investment). Plan implementation was structured around 12 *Building Blocks*, such as Citizen Access and Communication, FOCUS Centers, and Moving About the City, that form "the foundation for building the new model for a connected city."

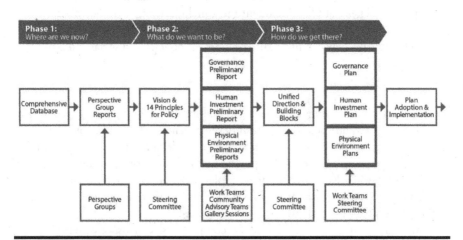

Figure 1.1 FOCUS Kansas City Planning Process
Source: Rouse (1998).

Comprehensive Plan Standards for Sustaining Places

The *Comprehensive Plan Standards for Sustaining Places* (Standards) are widely recognized as a benchmark for excellence in comprehensive planning practice. The Standards are a product of the *Sustaining Places Initiative*, launched by the American Planning Association (APA) in 2010 to define the role of planning in addressing the sustainability of human settlement. As part of this initiative, APA established the Sustaining Places Task Force to explore how the comprehensive plan can help local communities achieve sustainable outcomes. The task force's work culminated in publication of the Planning Advisory Service (PAS) Report *Sustaining Places: The Role of the Comprehensive Plan* (Godschalk and Anderson 2012).

Following publication of the PAS Report, APA formed a working group to develop a framework (the Standards) that local communities can use in creating new comprehensive plans and to evaluate existing plans against a national benchmark. The framework consists of six principles, two processes, and two attributes (Table 1.1). Best practices that communities should incorporate into their plans are identified for each of these ten components. The Standards are presented in a second PAS Report, *Sustaining Places: Best Practices for Comprehensive Plans* (Godschalk and Rouse 2015).[4]

Organization of this Book

The Comprehensive Plan Standards for Sustaining Places were based on research of best practices found in leading comprehensive plans and the planning literature. As such, they encapsulate the changes in comprehensive planning practice as it has evolved from its 20th-century antecedents to the present day. This book uses the Standards as a foundation and departure point to provide a guide to comprehensive planning in the 21st century, with the goal of creating more sustainable, resilient, and equitable communities. Examples from contemporary plans of local jurisdictions across the United States are provided throughout (see Appendix B for a complete list of the comprehensive plans cited). The book is organized into three major sections:

Part I: The Planning Process. This section covers the methodology to create a comprehensive plan that leads to sustainable, resilient, and equitable outcomes. Its chapters address how to design the comprehensive planning process; assess current conditions, trends, and issues; articulate a community vision and goals for the future; and develop policies and actions to achieve the vision and goals.

Part II: The Substance of the Plan. This section covers the substantive contents of the comprehensive plan that results from the process described in Part I, based on the six principles defined by the Comprehensive Plan Standards for Sustaining Places. It explores the

Table 1.1 Comprehensive Plan Standards for Sustaining Places: Principles, Processes, and Attributes

Principles	
Livable Built Environment	Ensure that all elements of the built environment, including land use, transportation, housing, energy, and infrastructure, work together to provide sustainable, green places for living, working, and recreation, with a high quality of life.
Harmony with Nature	Ensure that the contributions of natural resources to human well-being are explicitly recognized and valued and that maintaining their health is a primary objective.
Resilient Economy	Ensure that the community is prepared to deal with both positive and negative changes to its economic health and to initiate sustainable urban development and redevelopment strategies that foster green business growth and build reliance on local assets.
Interwoven Equity	Ensure fairness and equity in providing for the housing, services, health, safety, and livelihood needs of all citizens and groups.
Healthy Community	Ensure that public health needs are recognized and addressed through provisions for healthy foods, physical activity, access to recreation, health care, environmental justice, and safe neighborhoods.
Responsible Regionalism	Ensure that all local proposals account for, connect with, and support the plans of adjacent jurisdictions and the surrounding region.

Processes	
Authentic Participation	Ensure that the planning process actively involves all segments of the community in analyzing issues, generating visions, developing plans, and monitoring outcomes.
Accountable Implementation	Ensure that responsibilities for carrying out the plan are clearly stated, along with metrics for evaluating progress in achieving desired outcomes.

Attributes	
Consistent Content	Ensure that the plan contains a consistent set of visions, goals, policies, objectives, and actions that are based on evidence about community conditions, major issues, and impacts.
Coordinated Characteristics	Ensure that the plan includes creative and innovative strategies and recommendations and coordinates them internally with each other, vertically with federal and state requirements, and horizontally with plans of adjacent jurisdictions.

Source: Godschalk and Rouse (2015).

range of topics covered by a robust comprehensive plan, organized into natural, built environment, social, and economic systems. The last two chapters address community health and regional connections in the comprehensive plan, respectively.

Part III: Forward to Implementation. This section addresses how process and substance come together in a final comprehensive plan that is successfully implemented. It covers the components of a successful implementation program; the attributes of a final plan that can be effectively communicated to the public; and the ongoing process of using and updating the plan following its adoption.

The concluding chapter in Part III provides the authors' speculations on what the future of the comprehensive plan may be, given accelerating change and the major challenges facing communities in the 21st century. We believe that a new generation of comprehensive plans is needed to address these challenges, and we hope that this book helps point the way forward.

Notes

1 Some jurisdictions refer to the comprehensive plan as the general plan (for example, in California) or the community master plan (for example, in New Jersey).

2 Donella Meadows identified 12 leverage points, or places to intervene in a system, ranked in order of their relative effect on system behavior (Meadows 2008, pp. 145–165). For example, changing numbers (constants and parameters such as taxes, subsidies, and standards) ranked the lowest in terms of its potential impact while changing paradigms (the mindset out of which the system arises) ranked the second highest, after transcending paradigms. An example of the former might be to change level-of-service standards for a transportation system that prioritizes efficient movement of vehicles. An example of the latter might be to change the system priority to providing mobility and accessibility for people.

3 Values-driven planning was developed in the 1990s by the firm Wallace Roberts & Todd as a methodology to understand and articulate community values through the planning process as the basis for the goals, policies, and implementation strategies of the plan (Rouse 1998).

4 The complete set of principles, processes, attributes, and best practices is provided in Appendix A.

References

American Institute of Certified Planners (2016). *Code of Ethics and Professional Conduct.* Chicago, IL: American Institute of Certified Planners.

American Planning Association (2019). *Planning for Equity Policy Guide.* Chicago, IL: American Planning Association.

Arup, supported by the Rockefeller Foundation (n.d.). *City Resilience Index.* Accessed at https://www.cityresilienceindex.org/#/

Bourguignon, Francois (2015). *The Globalization of Inequality*. Princeton, NJ: Princeton University Press.

Feiss, Carl (1985). "The Foundations of Federal Planning Assistance: A Personal Account of the 701 Program," *Journal of the American Planning Association*, 51:2. Chicago, IL: American Planning Association. pp. 175–184.

Godschalk, David and David Rouse (2015). *Sustaining Places: Best Practices for Comprehensive Plans* (PAS Report 578). Chicago, IL: American Planning Association.

Godschalk, David and William Anderson (2012). *Sustaining Places: The Role of the Comprehensive Plan* (PAS Report 567). Chicago, IL: American Planning Association.

Institute for Sustainable Communities (n.d.). What is a Sustainable Community? Accessed at https://sustain.org/about/what-is-a-sustainable-community/

Intergovernmental Science-Policy Platform on Biodiversity and Ecosystem Services (IPBES) (2019). *Global Assessment Report on Biodiversity and Ecosystem Services of the Intergovernmental Science-Policy Platform on Biodiversity and Ecosystem Services*. Eduardo Brondizio, Josef Settele, Sandra Díaz, and Hien Thu Ngo (eds.). Bonn, Germany: IPBES secretariat.

Kelly, Eric Damien (2010). *Community Planning: An Introduction to the Comprehensive Plan*, Second Edition. Washington, DC: Island Press.

Kent, T.J., Jr. (1990). *The Urban General Plan*. Chicago, IL: American Planning Association. First published in 1964 by Chandler Publishing Company.

Kimball, Theodora (1912). "A Brief Survey of Recent City Planning Reports in the United States" in *Landscape Architecture Magazine*, 2:3. Washington, DC: American Society of Landscape Architecture, pp. 111–126.

Meadows, Donella, edited by Diana Wright (2008). *Thinking in Systems: A Primer*. White River Junction, VT: Chelsea Green Publishing.

Meck, Stuart (1996). "Model Planning and Zoning Enabling Legislation: A Short History," in Meck, Stuart (general editor), *Modernizing State Planning Standards: The Growing Smart Working Papers*, Volume 1 (PAS Report 462/463). Chicago, IL: American Planning Association, pp. 1–18.

Rouse, David (1998). *A Values-Driven Approach to Comprehensive Planning*. Paper presented at APA's National Planning Conference, Boston, MA.

Rouse, David, Michael Chandler, and Jon Arason (1999). *The 21st Century Comprehensive Plan*. Paper presented at APA's National Planning Conference, Seattle, WA.

United States Environmental Protection Agency (n.d.). Equitable Development and Environmental Justice. Accessed at https://www.epa.gov/environmentaljustice/equitable-development-and-environmental-justice

World Commission on Environment and Development, Gro Harmon Brundtland, Chair (1987). *Report of the World Commission on Environment and Development: Our Common Future*. General Assembly Resolution 42/187, United Nations. Oxford, England: Oxford University Press.

THE PLANNING PROCESS

DOI: 10.4324/9781003024170-2

Creating a comprehensive plan that leads to sustainable, resilient, and equitable outcomes begins with the process used to develop the plan. When embarking on a comprehensive planning process, it is useful to consider the basic purpose of the plan, which is to define a common direction for the future to guide plans, programs, investments, and other local governmental activities. More specifically, the comprehensive plan provides:

- A statement of community values and aspirations (future vision).
- A reference point for decision-making (goals and policies).
- Priorities for action (implementation program).

Part I of this book describes the components of a successful comprehensive planning process that fulfills the above purpose. It is organized into four chapters:

> *Chapter 2: Setting the Stage.* This chapter describes how to conduct project scoping and design the comprehensive planning process, a step that is critical to its success.
>
> *Chapter 3: Where Are We Now and Where Are We Headed?* This chapter covers the first major phase of the process, which includes assessment of existing conditions and trends; identification of community values and issues; and projection of future conditions and trends.
>
> *Chapter 4: Where Do We Want to Go?* This chapter addresses the second phase of the process – articulation of a shared vision and goals for the future through robust community engagement.
>
> *Chapter 5: How Do We Get There?* This chapter covers development of policies and actions to achieve the community vision and goals, including the role of scenario planning, in the third phase of the process.

The comprehensive planning process described in these chapters reflects a number of planning models or theories that evolved over the course of the 20th century, including rational planning, incremental planning, advocacy planning, vision planning, and communicative planning.

Rational planning. Rational planning emerged as the predominant planning paradigm in the post-World War II era (Brooks 2002). A rational planning process uses a sequence of logical steps to develop the plan, for example: scoping of issues and topics; setting of goals and objectives; evaluation of alternatives; and selection of a preferred alternative for implementation. The prevalent model used in practice throughout much of the 20th century, rational planning is a top-down process in which planners use their technical knowledge to analyze and synthesize data and present choices to decision-makers.

Incremental planning. Incremental planning (referred to as the "science of muddling through" by Charles Lindblom) was proposed in the 1950s as an alternative to rational planning (Lindblom 1959). In contrast to the latter's comprehensive, long-range scope (which Lindblom believed was costly and ineffective in responding to unforeseen changes), its approach is to implement incremental policy changes over time to address issues as they arise.

Advocacy planning. Advocacy planning was developed in the 1960s to give voice to low-income and minority groups that were excluded from the rational planning process (Davidoff 1965). In advocacy planning, the planner's role shifts from "value-neutral" expert to one of advocating pluralistic community interests and promoting substantive solutions. Advocacy planning also calls on planners to go beyond their traditional focus on physical planning to address socioeconomic issues and causes.

Vision planning. Vision planning emerged in the 1980s as a process to engage the whole community in defining a desired future (20 or so years from the present) and determining strategies and actions to achieve it. It differed from rational planning in its emphasis on the normative values of citizens and from advocacy planning in its comprehensive, future-oriented approach.

Communicative planning. Planning scholars identify communicative planning as a new planning paradigm that emerged in the 1990s (Goodspeed 2016). Also referred to as collaborative planning theory, it focuses on deliberation among community members who may be affected by the outcome of the planning process, with planners acting as facilitators to build shared understanding and consensus for solutions to problems.

Comprehensive planning practice in the 21st century contains strands of these different schools of thought. The rational model is reflected in the sequence of phases and tasks in the typical planning process, albeit transformed by practices such as the emphasis on community engagement and replacement of alternatives analysis by scenario planning techniques. The legacy of incremental planning is evident in plans that focus implementation on actionable steps and call for monitoring of progress and adjustment as conditions change. Advocacy planning's influence is evident in the importance of equity and concern for engaging underrepresented groups in the process, which assumed new urgency in the aftermath of the tragic events of 2020. Vision planning is at the core of most contemporary comprehensive planning processes. Finally, building consensus for action by engaging diverse community groups and interests in the process reflects communicative planning theory.

A Note on Terminology

Terms such as goals, objectives, policies, strategies, and actions have various meanings as used in planning theory and practice. In this book, we define these terms as follows, as they pertain to the comprehensive plan:

- *Goal:* A general outcome the community seeks to achieve in order to realize its vision of the future. Benchmarks, targets, and indicators are used to measure progress in achieving desired outcomes.
- *Objective:* A specific and measurable condition that must be attained in order to accomplish a goal.

- *Policy:* A statement of principle or criteria to direct decision-making and operations. Effective policies have official standing bestowed by the governing body.
- *Strategy:* An organized set of steps to achieve a goal or goals.
- *Action:* A task carried out within a specified time frame as part of the strategy to achieve a goal or goals.

References

Brooks, Michael P. (2002). *Planning Theory for Practitioners*. Chicago, IL: Planners Press.

Davidoff, Paul (1965). "Advocacy and Pluralism in Planning," *Journal of the American Institute of Planners*, 31. Chicago, IL: American Planning Association, pp. 277–296.

Goodspeed, Robert (2016). "The Death and Life of Collaborative Planning Theory," *Urban Planning*, 1:4. Lisbon, Portugal: Cogitatio Press, pp. 1–5.

Lindbloom, Charles A. (1959). "The Science of 'Muddling Through'" in *Public Administration Review*, 19:2. American Society for Public Administration. Hoboken, NJ: Wiley-Blackwell, pp. 79–88.

Chapter 2

Setting the Stage

Comprehensive planning is a continuing process rather than a one-time endeavor that ends with plan adoption. Following adoption, the process should include ongoing implementation actions, monitoring and annual progress reviews, and an update every five to ten years at the most (see Chapter 16). However, many jurisdictions update the comprehensive plan infrequently, so that when an update is undertaken it essentially requires creation of a new plan. Whether updating an existing comprehensive plan or preparing a new one, the planning process needs to be carefully conceived and organized if it is to be successful. This chapter covers key steps in the initial project scoping that should be undertaken before the comprehensive planning process begins. These steps include: (1) define responsibilities and available resources; (2) determine the community engagement process; (3) characterize community values and issues; (4) collect relevant mandates, plans, and initiatives; (5) compile data sources; and (6) develop the scope framework.

While the chapter describes these steps in the order listed, they can be conducted concurrently. For example, reviewing relevant plans and initiatives (step 4) can inform characterizing community values and issues (step 3), and vice versa. The end product developed in step 6 defines the overall scope (phases and work tasks), timeline, responsibilities, methods of community engagement, products, and other components of the process to be undertaken to create the plan.

Define Responsibilities and Available Resources

A comprehensive plan is by definition the responsibility of the local governmental jurisdiction. While different jurisdictions have different organizational structures, and rural counties and small towns have less capacity and resources than larger cities, the planning department is normally charged with leading the comprehensive plan,

DOI: 10.4324/9781003024170-3

in keeping with its role as the agency that supports the planning commission or its equivalent.[1] Given the level of effort required for a comprehensive planning process, it is critical to determine responsibilities and available resources at the beginning of the process. Basic questions include:

- What is the in-house capacity to take on the comprehensive planning project given other work responsibilities and commitments? Who will be the project manager? What support will that person have? How will other departments be involved?
- What is the project budget? Is it adequate to support a robust community engagement process? Does it allow for consultant assistance?
- If the budget will support consultant assistance, in what role(s) will the consultant(s) operate? Will a consultant/consultant team lead the entire process? Or will the process be led by the planning department, with consultants selected for specific roles?
- Can outside partners and resources be enlisted to augment the capacity of the local jurisdiction? If so, what will be their role in the process and relationship to the project management team?

While it is assumed that the planning department is the lead agency for the comprehensive plan, it should be noted that new models for collaboration and partnerships are emerging in contemporary practice. As comprehensive planning has evolved from its original focus on land use and physical development into a multidisciplinary practice, the process may require new relationships among planners and staff from other departments and agencies to ensure a truly comprehensive effort.

It is important to establish upfront whether to prepare the comprehensive plan in-house, retain an outside consultant, or combine the two approaches, as it will affect overall project management and design of the planning process. Larger jurisdictions with sufficient staff capacity may choose to prepare the plan in-house (possibly contracting out specific tasks). Small to mid-sized jurisdictions with less capacity may rely on consultant support if adequate funding is available. If funding for outside assistance is not available, the planning team must be creative in designing a process that matches available capacity and resources while delivering a final comprehensive plan that meets community needs and expectations.

A consultant can be retained in the scoping phase to help design the planning process or be brought on board through a *request for qualifications* and/or *request for proposals* (RFQ/RFP) solicitation after this phase is complete. Considerations in selecting and effectively using a consultant include:

- Defining the roles of consultant and staff and designating adequate funding to support consultant responsibilities.
- Preparing a RFQ/RFP that concisely and accurately describes the community and its major issues, the project objectives and scope, and the role and expectations of the consultant.

■ Conducting a fair and transparent request process that results in the selection of a consultant or consultant team that is the best fit for the project.

■ Establishing a good working relationship with the consultant throughout the process, including clear lines of communication, a project schedule with milestones to work from, and provisions for efficient review of and feedback on consultant work (Kelly 2013).

Determine the Community Engagement Process

The comprehensive plan expresses a community's shared values and aspirations in the form of a vision and goals for the future. It is essential that initial project scoping define how a diverse range of participants across generations, racial and ethnic groups, and incomes will be involved in the process of developing the vision, goals, and strategies to achieve them. In practice, it can be challenging to engage all interests and voices in identifying issues that need to be addressed, evaluating implications of conditions and trends, developing a future vision and goals, and defining preferred outcomes. Too often, the process is put in the hands of a limited group of stakeholders. For example, the volunteer working group that provides guidance, review, and input throughout the process (referred to in this book as a community advisory committee) may comprise persons who are actively involved in local governmental affairs and lack more diverse, outside perspectives. Traditional public meetings can be dominated by self-selected individuals with time and points of view to advocate while broader representation is missing. The result is a lack of transparency and buy-in from the larger community, leading to a final plan that has limited long-term impact.

Two measures during initial project scoping are key to avoiding the above pitfalls. The first is to identify people and groups representing all segments of the community to engage in the comprehensive planning process. The second is to define means of engagement that will most effectively involve these people and groups.

Determining the community engagement process should start from the perspective of its users, including people who will directly engage in the process and others who may choose not to participate but whose lives will be impacted by plan outcomes. The concept known as *human-centered design* is a useful frame of reference for engaging and communicating with the public from the beginning of the process through to plan adoption and implementation. This concept has been described as:

> ...a creative approach to problem solving that starts with people and ends with innovative solutions tailored to meet their needs. When you understand the people you're trying to reach and then design [plan] from their perspective, not only will you come up with unexpected answers but you will come up with ideas that they will embrace.
>
> (IDEO.org n.d.)

Identifying People and Groups to Engage

Given the comprehensive plan's broad scope and potential impact, the range of community groups is likely quite complex. A genuine and authentic planning process provides opportunities for all people and groups to participate in meaningful ways. For the purposes of determining the process for meaningful engagement, these groups fall into three major categories: community members, community leaders, and opinion leaders (McElvaney and Foster 2014).

Community members comprise by far the largest group, comprising residents, business owners, and others who have an interest in or will be affected by the outcomes of the comprehensive plan. From a diversity standpoint, they include people with different perspectives and life experiences, as reflected in racial and ethnic background, gender, income, age, and ability. They also encompass the following sectors with different perspectives on the future of the community:

- Civic (residents, neighborhood associations, civic organizations)
- Private (real estate developers, investors, businesses, and membership organizations)
- Private nonprofit (advocacy, interest, and professional organizations)
- Governmental (local, regional, state governmental agencies and quasi-governmental organizations)

While online and other community engagement techniques have expanded the reach of contemporary planning, it is unrealistic to expect that all or most community members will be involved in the process. Nevertheless, all should be provided with ample opportunities to participate throughout the process, with the overall goal of obtaining input from persons representing the full spectrum of community interests.

Community leaders include elected and appointed officials, representatives of organizations and interests in the above sectors, and others responsible for making decisions that affect their constituencies. While they may not hold positions of formal leadership, *opinion leaders* exercise powerful influence as trusted voices and communicators within different participant groups (McElvaney and Foster 2014). Community and opinion leaders should be identified during initial project scoping and consulted regarding their potential engagement and roles in the process. These roles can include serving on working committees, participating in interviews and focus groups, and facilitating outreach to and engagement of their constituencies.

A core working group (community advisory committee) that represents and can participate on behalf of all constituencies is vital to provide a forum for ongoing community interaction. It is particularly important to ensure that groups typically excluded from political and decision-making processes (for example, low-income, minority and youth populations) are represented on the committee and otherwise provided opportunities for meaningful participation in the process.

Additional community representation can be provided by forming subcommittees or work groups with different perspectives and interests to address important themes or issue areas. Technical advisory committees comprising staff and subject matter experts from departments other than the planning department, as well as from agencies and organizations outside the local government, are often established to provide technical information and input to the planning process. Involving staff from internal departments and external agencies is important to build understanding of the importance and relevance of the comprehensive plan to their work programs as the plan moves forward to implementation.

Because the local political environment will influence the impact and outcomes of the comprehensive plan, it is important to define the involvement of local political leaders, such as city council members or county commissioners, in the planning process. Will they be directly represented on the committee or (more common practice) receive regular progress briefings? Will a member of the governing body serve as liaison to the committee? How much influence will the governing body have over the composition of the committee?[2] What are the major issues motivating different political leaders? How will they be provided opportunities for input to the process on behalf of the constituencies they represent? Such questions should be considered in designing a process that is most likely to succeed.

Determining the Means of Community Engagement

Having identified the people and groups to involve in the process, the next step is to define the means (how and when) to effectively engage them. The International Association of Public Participation (IAP2) has identified five levels of public participation – *inform, consult, involve, collaborate, and empower* – based on increasing impact on decision-making (Table 2.1). In the rational planning model of the 20th century, the first two levels (inform and consult) were the predominant means of public participation. Since the 1990s, comprehensive planning processes have increasingly expanded the spectrum by engaging the public in articulating values and aspirations (involve) and identifying solutions (collaborate).[3] Examples of truly empowering citizens to make final decisions (the fifth level) are limited or non-existent in comprehensive planning practice at present.

Methods to involve community members have become more sophisticated with the proliferation of digital communication tools and development of alternative formats to supplement or replace traditional public meetings. Accelerated by the COVID-19 pandemic in 2020, a number of tools are available for online community deliberation and dialogue. Many have customizable formats to facilitate engagement. Examples include information-sharing modules, document-sharing resources, collective databases, breakout groups, and polling functions. Some tools are designed specifically for governments and other agencies to collect public comment and feedback. Others focus on equity and inclusivity to ensure that all voices are included.

Table 2.1 Spectrum of Public Participation

Level	Public Participation Goal
Inform	Provide the public with balanced and objective information to assist them in understanding the problem, alternatives, opportunities, and/or solutions
Consult	Obtain public feedback on analysis, alternatives, and/or decisions
Involve	Work directly with the public throughout the process to ensure that public concerns and aspirations are consistently understood and considered
Collaborate	Partner with the public in each aspect of the decision including the development of alternatives and the identification of the preferred solution
Empower	Place final decision-making in the hands of the public

Source: International Association of Public Participation (n.d.)

Online engagement can increase community participation by reaching people who would not normally attend in-person events, particularly as society becomes more comfortable with remote communication. However, virtual participation comes with its own set of challenges (first and foremost, the digital divide) and should be supplemented by traditional outreach and engagement opportunities throughout the process. Examples include providing a call-in option for all digital meetings, using telephone and mail outreach, and partnering with local community organizations and trusted leaders to reach vulnerable groups and individuals (Salt Lake City Civic Engagement Team 2020).

As a rule, community engagement tools should be geared toward the needs of the people and groups the process seeks to involve. For example, open houses, community events, and online forums can be used to make the public aware of the purpose of the comprehensive plan, the planning process, and opportunities for people to get involved. Public roundtables, surveys, and focus groups can be used to solicit input on community values and priority issues from a range of participants early in the process. In-person and online workshops and charrettes can be used to engage community members in exploring alternatives and developing strategies to address the issues.

Opinion leaders and community advisory committee members can help identify appropriate methods to reach different constituencies. Considerations include, among others, scheduling in-person meetings in locations and at times that are convenient for community members; addressing needs such as childcare and transportation; providing translation services for non-English speakers; and providing equivalent participation opportunities for persons who lack access to digital technology.

The Role of the Community Advisory Committee

The comprehensive planning process should be structured to seek input from community members at key points during the process, such as identifying core values and issues, articulating a vision for the future, and exploring scenarios to realize the vision. As surrogates for the broader community, the community advisory committee meets regularly throughout the process to provide review, feedback, and guidance.[4] Its role should be clearly defined to ensure an open, transparent process. For example, Sausalito, California defined the role of the advisory committee in developing its General Plan Update as follows:

- Facilitate, in concert with city staff, consultants, and the public, the update of the *Sausalito General Plan.*
- Supplement the community input provided at public workshops and provide feedback and guidance throughout the process.
- Provide feedback and direction to the project consultant and city staff, with the goal of developing policies and objectives that are responsive to community input, conditions, goals, and vision.
- Refine the approach taken for each major step in the process, provide feedback through interim steps, review reports, and review policy alternatives to select preferred policies.
- Provide guidance at key project milestones.
- Communicate information about the General Plan Update to Sausalito community members and encourage all interested parties to participate in the process.
- Make a recommendation to the planning commission and the city council on the adoption of the General Plan Update (Sausalito n.d.)

Preparing the Public Participation Plan

Having determined who to engage in the planning process and the means to be used to engage them, a public participation plan should be prepared to define how they will be engaged over the course of the planning process. The plan should include the following:

- Community engagement goals and desired outcomes.
- An overview of the engagement process, including key milestones, opportunities for community input, and how the community's input will be incorporated into plan development.
- Methods to be used to communicate with the public during the process.
- How materials developed during the process will be transmitted to elected officials and decision-makers, what form these materials will take, and how the public will be engaged after transmittal has occurred.

The public participation plan should incorporate existing community engagement principles or processes established by the jurisdiction, adapted for the purposes of the comprehensive plan. The plan should be incorporated into the scope framework, which is the product of project scoping described at the end of this chapter.[5]

Characterize Community Values and Issues

Community values (common ground on which different groups can agree) are at the heart of the comprehensive plan, providing the foundation for articulating a shared vision and goals for the future. While values and issues affecting them are identified through community engagement in comprehensive plan development, an initial assessment of the priorities of community groups in project scoping is useful to inform design of the overall process. This assessment can be accomplished by asking basic questions of the identified opinion leaders and community group representatives, for example: What do you and the people you know value most about our community? What are the most important issues to address in the comprehensive plan? Reviewing public input received during previous planning efforts can also provide insights regarding important community values and issues.

As part of this task, the planning team can conduct an initial scan of internal and external trends, issues, and implications for the comprehensive planning process. Various models are available for this purpose. *A Strengths, Weaknesses, Opportunities, and Threats* (SWOT) analysis, a technique developed for strategic planning processes, is the most commonly used by planners. A SWOT analysis identifies key internal (strengths and weaknesses) and external (opportunities and threats) factors that may affect the community's future.

A *Social, Technological, Economic, Ecological, and Political* (STEEP) analysis, which is used in business and marketing to assess external factors that may impact an organization, is another tool that can be adapted for comprehensive planning. A STEEP analysis explores societal trends that are driving or may drive change in five categories: social, technological, economic, environmental, and political. This analysis is particularly germane given the accelerating pace of change in the 21st century and the long-range orientation of the comprehensive plan.

Collect Relevant Mandates, Plans, and Initiatives

A fundamental purpose of the comprehensive plan is to provide a common direction for all local plans, programs, and initiatives. Lacking this common direction, plans and programs are developed and implemented separately and can work at cross purposes rather than synergistically. Large jurisdictions typically have many adopted plans and policy directives, as well as in-progress planning projects and related initiatives, when they begin the comprehensive planning process. Smaller jurisdictions may have fewer plans and initiatives but still need to consider those developed by other entities, such as adjacent municipalities or the regional planning agency. All such materials should be collected as part of the information baseline for the comprehensive plan.

Collecting applicable local plans begins with the jurisdiction's previous comprehensive plan. Even if many years may have passed since its adoption, it is worthwhile to review the previous plan and pose questions such as: What were the key issues at the time? How successfully was the plan implemented? How have conditions changed? Were demographic or other projections in the plan accurate? What new issues have arisen that were not foreseen in the previous plan? In circumstances where a previous comprehensive plan does not exist, a review of other relevant plans, policies, and initiatives can fulfill a similar purpose.

The more recent the previous plan is, the more relevant it is to the current comprehensive planning effort. Additional questions to consider include: What information can be updated and incorporated into the new inventory and analysis? What policies and action recommendations are still valid? Where are the gaps and how can they be filled?

Other local governmental plans and programs to catalogue during project scoping include functional plans, subarea plans, and policy and program directives (for example, the capital improvements program) adopted by the local governing body. Functional plans address community systems such as mobility, parks and recreation, and housing. Subarea plans address geographic areas such as the downtown or other districts, neighborhoods, and corridors.

External plans and initiatives of interest should also be documented as a basis for building consistency and coordination through the comprehensive planning process (see Chapter 14). Examples include:

- Comprehensive and other plans prepared by adjacent jurisdictions.
- Plans prepared by the metropolitan planning organization or other regional agency, such as regional mobility plans.
- Plans prepared by quasigovernmental agencies, such as water, sewer, and housing authorities and special districts.
- Plans and programs of nonprofit organizations, such as institutions, community foundations, and interest groups.

State legislative requirements or guidance related to the comprehensive plan are important to document during project scoping. According to a 2018 survey, 49 states have legislation referencing local comprehensive plans or the equivalent, 35 require preparation of local plans by municipalities and/or counties (in many states, this requirement applies if they have a planning commission), and 40 specify or suggest plan elements (American Planning Association 2019). California and Pennsylvania are examples of states that specify elements to be contained in the comprehensive or general plan. California's seven required elements are land use, circulation, housing, conservation, open space, safety, and noise. Elements required by the *Pennsylvania Municipalities Planning Code* include land use, housing, movement of people and goods, community facilities and utilities, and protection of natural and historic resources. Pennsylvania's code includes an energy conservation plan as an optional element, while California's guidance for general plans suggests economic development and healthy communities, among others, as elements that can be included in the general plan (Shirazi et al. 2017).

The traditional comprehensive planning model organizes plan content around elements that are required or suggested by state legislation. However, states that specify elements to be included in the plan generally provide flexibility to deviate from this model as long as the required content areas are addressed. For example, California's general plan guidance states that "a jurisdiction may organize its general plan in any format, including consolidated elements, so long as all of the relevant statutory issues are addressed" (Shirazi et al. 2017). At this stage, it is most important to document applicable legislative requirements and policy guidance to ensure that all bases are covered. The ultimate organization of the plan will be determined by the issues and themes that emerge during the planning process.

Compile Data Sources

A solid baseline of information providing an understanding of past, current, and likely future conditions and trends (such as population, housing, and employment) is essential to the comprehensive planning process. Planning departments generally maintain planning information systems with data on land use, transportation, and natural resources, and other community systems. Additional information is available from various sources, such as federal, state, and regional agencies.

During the scoping phase, the planning team should inventory available data sources, organize relevant information in accessible formats, and develop a strategy to address any identified data gaps. In today's world of big data accessible via the Internet, the problem is likely to be too much or not the right kind of information available rather than too little. The planning team should use its judgment in determining the appropriate level of detail for the comprehensive plan, keeping in mind the plan's role as a strategic guide for the community's future rather than a more detailed area or functional plan. The team should ensure that information is available to elucidate the community values and issues identified through the initial assessment described above. As the process moves forward, community values will be clarified and additional issues will emerge, which may merit additional targeted data collection efforts.

Develop the Scope Framework

Project scoping concludes with development of a scope framework that defines the process, work program, and management structure to be used to develop the comprehensive plan. Key components include:

- The plan for public participation.
- The roles of the community advisory committee and other committees or work groups.
- The overall schedule and milestones.
- Tasks, subtasks, work products, and outcomes for each of the major phases.
- Responsibilities for managing and carrying out the work.

Summary findings of other project scoping steps (community values and issues, relevant plans, and data sources) can be included in the scope framework document.

The scope framework provides direction and sufficient detail for allocation of resources over the time period required to complete the plan.[6] It also incorporates flexibility to adapt to circumstances that may arise during the process (for example, the need to reach out to groups that have not been sufficiently engaged). It defines the role of consultants (unless the plan is to be prepared entirely in-house), informs preparation of the RFQ/RFP, and provides the basis for the scope of work to be negotiated with the selected consultant team.

It is useful to include a diagram of the comprehensive planning process in the scope framework as a visual aid for understanding the process. Figure 2.1 illustrates a model planning process that can be adapted to fit the local context and circumstances. The process begins with the initial project scoping (Setting the Stage) described in

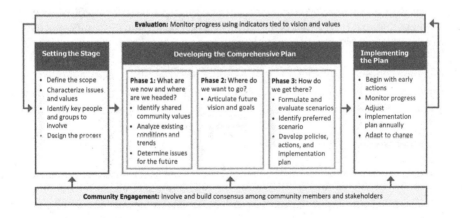

Figure 2.1 Model Comprehensive Planning Process

Source: Rouse and McElvaney (2016).

this chapter. The three major phases of comprehensive plan development correspond to the three basic questions that the process asks and answers:

1. Where are we now and where are we headed?
2. Where do we want to go?
3. How do we get there?

As shown in Figure 2.1, an effective comprehensive planning process extends beyond plan adoption into implementation. Ongoing implementation activities include monitoring, evaluation of progress, and periodic course adjustments, until the process begins again by setting the stage for the next major plan update (see Chapter 16).

Summary

Careful preparation before the planning process begins is necessary to lay the groundwork for a successful comprehensive plan. Key components of project scoping include establishing responsibilities and resources to carry out the process; determining how the community will be engaged; gaining an initial understanding of community values and issues to be addressed; and assembling relevant plans and data sources to inform comprehensive plan development.

The comprehensive planning effort must be tailored to the resources available. These can vary widely based on a range of factors, such as staff capacity, budget, and size of the jurisdiction. Responsibilities within the lead agency (typically the planning department), involvement of other departments, and consultant roles and relationships need to be clearly defined. To ensure that all segments of the community contribute to the comprehensive plan, project scoping identifies people and groups to involve, the methods to be used to effectively engage them, and when during the planning process engagement activities will occur. As representatives of the range and diversity of the community-at-large, community advisory committee members play an important role in the process.

Additional scoping activities include conducting an initial scan of community values and issues; cataloguing relevant mandates, plans, and initiatives; and collecting sources of information on existing conditions and trends. Tools such as a SWOT or STEEP analysis can be used to help understand the potential implications of internal and external trends and issues for the community's future.

The final step in project scoping is to develop a scope framework defining the process to be used to develop the comprehensive plan. A model comprehensive planning process consists of three major phases that are described in Chapters 3–5, respectively.

Notes

1 This role can be traced back to the *Standard State Zoning Enabling Act* and *Standard City Planning Enabling Act* of the 1920s, which specifically mention the local planning commission or its equivalent as the entity responsible for comprehensive planning.

2 Direct appointment of committee members by the local governing body, which has been the practice in some communities, can result in limited participation and the lack of representation of diverse perspectives.

3 The values-driven planning process used for the FOCUS Kansas City Comprehensive Plan is an example (see Chapter 1). This process made extensive use of collaborative work teams comprising participants representing different community perspectives.

4 Community participation in an open process that typically falls under the "consult" and "involve" levels of IAP2's spectrum of public participation (Table 2.1). The community advisory committee and supporting subcommittees or work groups provide the opportunity for community representatives to collaborate in comprehensive plan development because of the ongoing nature of the involvement.

5 The civic engagement plan prepared by the Minneapolis Department of Community and Economic Department prior to the start of the *Minneapolis 2040* comprehensive planning process is a good model (Minneapolis 2016). The plan's five chapters address (1) engagement goals, (2) key audiences, (3) how these audiences will be engaged in the phases of the planning process, (4) engagement methods, and (5) the committee structure and decision-making process.

6 A typical time frame from project kickoff to plan adoption is from 18 to 24 months. This time frame can be shorter for smaller and longer for large, complex jurisdictions.

References

American Planning Association (2019). *Survey of State Land Use and Natural Hazards Laws.* Chicago, IL: American Planning Association.

IDEO.org (n.d). What is Human-Centered Design? Accessed at https://www.ideo.org/tools

International Association of Public Participation (n.d.). *Public Participation Pillars: Internationally Recognized Principles for Making Better Decisions Together.* Accessed at https://cdn.ymaws.com/www.iap2.org/resource/resmgr/Communications/A3_P2_Pillars_brochure.pdf

Kelly, Eric Damian (2013). *Working with Planning Consultants* (PAS Report 573). Chicago, IL: American Planning Association.

McElvaney, Lisa A. and Kelleann Foster (2014). "Enhancing Stakeholder Engagement: Understanding Organizational Design Principles for Geodesign Professionals," Chapter 20 in Lee, Danbi, Eduardo Dias, and Henk Scholten (eds.), *Geodesign by Integrating Design and Geospatial Services.* Cham, Switzerland: Springer International Publishing, pp. 315–329.

Minneapolis, Minnesota (2016). *Minneapolis 2040: Civic Engagement Plan.* Minneapolis, MN: Department of Community Planning and Economic Development.

Rouse, David and Shannon McElvaney (2016). *Comprehensive Planning and Geodesign* (PAS Memo). Chicago, IL: American Planning Association.

Salt Lake City Civic Engagement Team (2020). *Practices for Engagement in the Time of COVID.* Salt Lake City, UT. Accessed at https://www.slc.gov/can/wp-content/uploads/sites/8/2020/04/Best-Practices-for-Engagement-During-COVID-19.pdf

Sausalito, California (n.d.). The Role of the General Plan Advisory Committee. Accessed at https://www.sausalito.gov/city-government/special-committees/general-plan-advisory-committee

Shirazi, Shahar, Elizabeth Baca, Michael McCormick, and Seth Litchney, principal authors (2017). *State of California General Plan Guidelines.* Sacramento, CA: Governor's Office of Planning and Research.

Chapter 3

Where Are We Now and Where Are We Headed?

The purpose of Phase 1 of the comprehensive planning process is to understand the community's past, where it is today, and what it may become in the future. In technical terms, this involves conducting an inventory and analysis of existing conditions and trends and making reasonable forecasts of what the future will bring if present trends continue. Values and issues (what people care about) identified through community engagement provide context and direction for the inventory and analysis. The results of Phase 1 provide the foundation for developing a future vision, goals, policies, and implementing actions in subsequent phases of the planning process.

Where Have We Been?

A community is a dynamic system that is constantly evolving. Its present state (or existing conditions) reflects the interplay of people and place over time, shaped by larger social, economic, and technological trends. At a fundamental level, a community's identity and sense of place are the product of its local history and cultural development. Understanding how the community became what it is today can inform how it may evolve and what levers of change are available to shift direction in the future.

Typical comprehensive plans briefly summarize the community's history as part of the context for planning. Some provide more elaborate descriptions and timelines, particularly for places with longer historic legacies. While these are interesting and informative, the most insightful analyses will connect the past to the present by asking:

DOI: 10.4324/9781003024170-4

- What historic qualities (for example, cultural resources and natural advantages that spurred the community's development) can be maintained and built on for the future?
- What historic forces (for example, economic changes that have caused population and job losses) must be addressed to forge a positive path to the future?

The first question is perhaps easier to answer because it speaks to local assets such as a traditional downtown, historical narrative tied to place, or waterfront location that can be leveraged for quality of life and community enrichment. The second question is more challenging because it is the product of forces that are beyond the purview of localities and regions. Consider, for example, the profound effects on local communities of two major societal trends: institutional racism and automobile-oriented development.

Institutional Racism

The history of racism against Blacks is well documented, as is the role of planning in the institutional structures that perpetuated it. For example, segregation ordinances, which prohibited Blacks from purchasing homes in white areas, were an early zoning application in many American cities (Rothstein 2017).[1] In 1926, the Court's landmark decision in *Village of Euclid v. Ambler Realty Co.* upheld the Village's zoning ordinance that prohibited industrial, commercial, and multi-family (apartment) uses in a single-family use district. Also in 1926, the U.S. Department of Commerce published *A Standard State Zoning Enabling Act*, which led to nearly universal adoption by local municipalities of ordinances based on the principle that different uses should be separated (so-called Euclidean zoning). Exclusionary single-family zoning with minimum lot size and setback requirements, typically in suburban neighborhoods, was widely used as a tool to exclude Black individuals and families, along with other minority and ethnic groups, and remains a root cause of segregation and inequality in metropolitan regions across the United States today. Systemic racism and discriminatory planning practices have impacted other racial and ethnic groups as well, for example, Latinos, Asians, Jews, and European immigrants.

Planning's contribution to institutional racism and discrimination is evident in the effects of 20th-century federal housing policy. Established in 1933 as a New Deal program to assist homeowners who were threatened with foreclosure, the Home Owners' Loan Corporation developed the practice known as "redlining" to assess mortgage risk. Research demonstrates that racial segregation and economic inequality caused by the lack of access to financial resources in redlined neighborhoods persists today (Mitchell and Franco 2018). Other examples of racist policies include restrictive covenants, the siting of unwanted land uses in minority communities, and infrastructure investments that have disproportionately harmed disadvantaged neighborhoods, while benefitting affluent communities. This history is important to understand communities as they exist today and should be documented in the inventory and analysis.

Automobile-Oriented Development

Today's built environment reflects the various time periods during which it developed. Typical characteristics of pre-World War II urban neighborhoods and districts include grid-like street networks, compact development, and a fine-grained mix of uses, all of which facilitated walking or transit use to access destinations. A confluence of forces in post-World War II era (federal mortgage programs, the construction of the interstate highway system, and Euclidean zoning) caused a fundamental shift in this development paradigm. The result was metropolitan expansion, decline of central cities, and the rise of suburban landscapes comprising separated uses such as residential subdivisions, commercial strip corridors, and office parks. Transit usage also declined, replaced by a preference for roadway systems designed exclusively for automobiles.

Suburban, automobile-oriented development offered an unprecedented level of lifecycle choice and mobility for middle-class Americans. It has come, however, with a host of unintended consequences: loss of open space, degradation of natural resources, socioeconomic inequality, traffic congestion, and increased costs of infrastructure and services. Recent decades have witnessed a resurgence of interest in traditional neighborhoods and downtowns and walkable, mixed-use environments. Even more recently, metropolitan areas have experienced a proliferation of warehousing and distribution uses driven by e-commerce.

The takeaway for the inventory and analysis is that land use and development patterns are a product of evolution over time and continue to change due to socioeconomic forces. Conventional land-use maps and zoning classifications do not account for the dynamics of change or the physical character of the built environment. Additional analysis and mapping of factors such as historic development patterns, susceptibility to change, community form, and typology of place are needed to understand how the community became what it is today and how it might evolve in the future.

Memphis 3.0 Comprehensive Plan: Accounting for the Past in Planning for the Future

> Memphis is a city of *Equity and Opportunity*. Through actions, investments, and citizen-led neighborhood interventions, historically disadvantaged communities must gain greater access to resources and opportunities to succeed and prosper.

Equity and Opportunity is one of three values (guiding principles) of the Memphis 3.0 Comprehensive Plan, around which the plan elements, goals, objectives, and actions are organized. The plan begins with a timeline of the city's first 200 years from its founding in 1819 on a bluff overlooking the Mississippi River in western Tennessee. Key historic trends over the years have included:

- Outward expansion via annexation.
- The legacy of slavery and segregation, urban renewal in the 1950s and 1960s, and the struggle for racial equality.
- The rise and decline of manufacturing and Memphis' emergence as a transportation and logistics hub.
- The end of the annexation era with state legislation in 2013 and 2014, followed by a new strategy to "strategically shrink the city's footprint" via deannexation.

The plan's overarching vision – *build up, not out* – captures this fundamental change in direction for the city's next 100 years. The Equity and Opportunity principle addresses Memphis's legacy of segregation and disinvestment. It is supported by goals, objectives, and actions addressing access to quality jobs, education, affordable healthy and housing, and more for all.

What Do We Care About?

Community engagement in Phase 1 focuses on identifying shared values and issues. Values are the qualities that community members (residents and others who will be affected by comprehensive plan outcomes) consider most important and which define their attachment to the place. They capture both current conditions (what people think is best about the community) and conditions that people would like to exist (McElvaney and Foster 2014). Because people tend to resist change, values can also express qualities they believe existed in the past but are currently under threat. Issues are problems that they feel need to be addressed in order for the community to become a better place in which to live. These often relate to personal experience (for example, mobility challenges and traffic congestion from lack of alternatives to driving alone) or to threatened values (for example, loss of open space and natural resources).

As described in Chapter 2, characterizing community values and issues begins in the initial scoping stage. In Phase 1, a range of community members should be engaged to determine shared values and important issues, including participants representing the community's diversity (age, gender, race, ethnicity, and socio-economic status) and interests (civic, business, environmental, and philanthropic). Engagement should be structured to elicit responses to a common set of questions, allowing the results to be compared across participant groups.

Determining Shared Values: Austin, Texas; Memphis, Tennessee; and Minneapolis, Minnesota

The comprehensive plans for Austin, Memphis, and Minneapolis are examples of engaging community members in the planning process to identify shared values and issues:

Imagine Austin Comprehensive Plan. Austin used community forums, surveys, and meetings-in-a-box to ask three questions: What are Austin's strengths? What are our challenges? How can the city be improved in 2039 (its 200th anniversary)? The results informed development of a vision statement in Phase 2 of the planning process.

Memphis 3.0 Comprehensive Plan. Memphis used public meetings and online surveys to ask the public what they considered to be the city's strengths, weaknesses, and opportunities for the future (a type of SWOT analysis). The results were synthesized into 10 common themes that provided the basis for the vision and goals developed in Phase 2.

Minneapolis 2040 Comprehensive Plan. Minneapolis engaged community members in a variety of venues, such as street fairs, cultural festivals, and community dialogues, during Phase 1 of the planning process. Participants were asked a series of "big questions" addressing topics such as transportation, jobs, and the environment (including climate change), as well as their vision of the "ideal Minneapolis" in 2040. The results were used by city staff to develop 14 overarching goals for the comprehensive plan.

Particularly in large, diverse communities, it is unlikely that all groups will agree on what is important. Building consensus is an iterative process that collects, analyzes, and synthesizes community input; shares the findings with community members; and makes adjustments based on the feedback received. In Phase 1, this means identifying values and issues identified by the most people, those on which there are differing perspectives, and establishing priorities based on community dialogue. As representatives of diverse community interests, community advisory committee members have an important role to play in assisting the planning team in this process.

Smaller communities have their own dynamics, which include deeply held values and attachment to place as well as divergent beliefs among different groups. Developed by the Orton Family Foundation, *Community Heart & Soul* is an example of an engagement process that helps small cities and towns shape their future based on shared values: "the unique character of the place and the emotional connection of the people who live there" (Orton Family Foundation n.d.). Steps in this process include:

- Conduct a community network analysis to understand the people of the place and how best to reach them.
- Gather stories and articulating Heart & Soul Statements that reflect what matters most to the community.
- Collect and prioritize ideas for action guided by the statements.

Community Heart & Soul **Example: Essex, Vermont**

Essex is a community of about 22,000 residents in the northwestern part of Vermont. It comprises the Town of Essex and the Village of Essex Junction, each with its own distinctive character and interests. A Community Heart & Soul process was used to engage Essex residents in identifying six core values shared by people with a wide range of opinions: (1) local economy, (2) health and recreation, (3) community connections, (4) education, (5) thoughtful growth, and (6) safety. Heart & Soul Statements were developed for each core value. For example, the Health and Recreation statement is:

> We value public places for outdoor and indoor recreation for all ages and abilities. We treasure Indian Brook reservoir, neighborhood parks and the chance to connect by bicycle or on foot. Community institutions provide education and programs to support healthy lifestyles.
>
> (Heart and Soul of Essex 2014)

The process "created a culture of collaboration and participation" that contributed to a subsequent school district merger, establishment of a shared town manager position, and consolidation of finance departments (Orton Family Foundation n.d.). The Heart & Soul Statements were subsequently incorporated into the *Essex Town Plan*, the community's comprehensive plan under the *Vermont Planning and Development Act*.

As evidenced by the Community Heart & Soul methodology, creative alternatives to standard public participation methods can be used to identify shared values and issues. For the *Minneapolis 2040 Comprehensive Plan*, the city issued a *Call for Artists* for three different projects (social practice artist, happenings project, and mobile engagement tool) to engage traditionally underrepresented communities in the planning process. The Community Heart & Soul process for Victor, Idaho used a technique called *value mapping* to translate qualitative values identified through community engagement into quantitative measures (weighted value scores). These measures were used to evaluate alternative future scenarios generated by the GIS application CommunityViz (Rouse and McElvaney 2016).

Asset mapping is a community development approach that could be adapted for the comprehensive planning process, particularly in smaller communities. Typically applied at the neighborhood level, asset mapping engages community members in identifying local strengths and resources that can be leveraged to build capacity for change (Kretzmann and McKnight 1993). Examples include organizational assets such as neighborhood associations and community development corporations; institutional assets such as schools and libraries; and physical places such as parks and gathering spaces.[2] Asset mapping could be used in Phase 1 to create an inventory of resources (referred to by practitioners as an asset directory) that community members value.

Inventory and Analysis

The inventory and analysis form the substantive core of Phase 1 of the planning process, necessary to establish a baseline for policy and action to effectuate desired change. The inventory presents spatial, demographic, and other characteristics of the community, its major systems, and how these characteristics have changed over time (for example, population growth or decline, land use conversions, and shifts in employment sectors). The analysis considers why this information is important for the community's future, providing key takeaways that can be framed in various ways, for example as themes, trends, and indicators; strengths and weaknesses; or opportunities and constraints.

The conventional planning approach organizes the inventory and analysis into elements tied to available data sets and (where applicable) state legislative requirements. The following is a representative list of elements:

- Population (Demographics)
- Land Use
- Transportation
- Community Facilities and Services
- Economy
- Housing
- Parks, Recreation, and Open Space
- Natural Resources
- Cultural and Historic Resources

In contemporary practice, some of these elements have been reconceptualized (for example, transportation as mobility; parks, recreation, and open space as green infrastructure) and new ones have been added (for example, community health, resilience, and community form). More importantly, there is growing awareness that the conventional approach does not account for the interrelationships between topical elements that in reality function as interdependent, dynamic systems. Land use, mobility, and housing, for example, cannot be effectively planned as discrete elements by separate disciplines (as has been common in conventional practice).

As an alternative to the conventional approach, the inventory and analysis can be structured in ways that make sense for the community context, address the issues its people care about, and account for the connections between different community systems. Part II of this book (Chapters 6–12) provides guidance on inventory and analysis needs for different community systems. Other texts provide more detail on information needs and sources.[3]

Existing conditions and trends information is readily available in the era of big data. The challenge is to identify relevant data sets; organize and analyze the data at a level of detail appropriate for comprehensive planning purposes; and make the findings accessible to different audiences. Some additional research may be needed to fill gaps and address values and issues identified through community engagement. Identifying key statistical indicators is useful to summarize where the community stands relative to issues and trends; the indicators can be used later in the process to compare the performance of alternative future scenarios. In constructing the inventory and analysis, it is useful to consider how the data will be maintained and updated on an ongoing basis after plan adoption, including indicators that can be used to monitor plan implementation progress.

Inventory and Analysis Examples: Lancaster County, Pennsylvania and Boston, Massachusetts

Lancaster County and the City of Boston offer examples of comprehensive plan inventories and analyses conducted in rural and urban contexts. *Lancaster County: A Changing Place, 2000–2015* (the inventory and analysis report for the *places2040* comprehensive plan) is organized into six thematic chapters "to stimulate informed discussion and innovative thinking about where we're headed and how we're going to get there" in subsequent steps of the planning process. The chapters cover:

- Who we are (demographics, education, and health)
- Where we live (residential development and housing)
- Where we work (workforce, economy, and land use)
- How we invest in our communities (water and sewer infrastructure, emergency services, and community amenities)
- How we move people and goods
- How we protect treasured resources (farmland, natural lands, environment, and historic resources)

The report provides key statistics, changes from 2000 to 2015, and conclusions for planning. It makes extensive use of infographics to summarize and communicate information to readers.

Imagine Boston 2030: A Plan for the Future of Boston includes a context chapter that provides an overview of Boston's rich history as the "City of Ideas." It then organizes the discussion of existing conditions around six interconnected trends:

- Productive economy
- Growing population
- Inequality
- Affordability
- Changing climate
- Transformative technology

These trends connect Boston's past, present, and future and set the context for policy and action. For example, Boston's population declined significantly from 1950 to 1980, followed by sustained growth and increasing diversity resulting from immigration and the emergence of the "knowledge economy." However, enduring racial inequities tied to Boston's legacy of redlining, busing, and urban renewal limit a significant portion of the population from sharing in economic and social opportunities, underscoring the need to address past and present disparities in planning for the future.

Where Are We Headed?

The inventory and analysis provide a snapshot of community conditions that are the product of past and current trends and dynamics. Given the role of the comprehensive plan as a guide for managing future change, it is equally important to develop reasonable forecasts of future conditions. The standard approach is to project future population and employment levels assuming present trends continue and then estimate demand for different types of land uses, likely environmental and fiscal impacts, and the public infrastructure and services needed to support them.

Various methodologies are used to estimate future population, including straight line projection (the simplest and crudest method), cohort survival, and calculations incorporating assumptions regarding fertility, mortality, and migration. Often referred to as the baseline or *trend growth scenario*, this approach is best suited for growing communities that are experiencing demand for conversion of undeveloped land to other uses. It is less useful for predominantly built-out communities with limited capacity for new development, as well as those experiencing slow growth or declining population. In such cases, a *susceptibility to change analysis* can be conducted to identify areas most likely to change character. Because local population and economic change are influenced by what is happening in the region and beyond, projections developed at the regional and state levels should be taken into consideration in developing future scenarios.

Forecasting the future is an inherently uncertain exercise that has become even more so in the 21st century given the accelerating pace of change and its potential effects on communities. For example, how many forecasts of development activity in the early 2000s anticipated the impacts of the Great Recession of 2008? How reliable are projections of commercial, office, and industrial land uses based on criteria such as employees per acre or disposable household income given trends such as telecommuting and e-commerce, as well as disruptive events such as the COVID-19 pandemic? To help deal with uncertainty, the forecast can set a range (that is, low, medium, and high) rather than fixed projections, for use as scenarios to characterize the implications of different growth trajectories.

Accelerating change in the 21st century further suggests that forecasting future conditions should consider how larger (societal and global) trends may impact the local community and region. Figure 3.1 provides examples of social, technological, economic, and environmental drivers of change (Hitchings and Rouse 2020).

Trends such as those shown in Figure 3.1 will interact in complex ways and their impacts will vary according to local conditions, assets, and vulnerabilities. For example, automation (the substitution of work performed by machines for human labor) is facilitated by technological advances in artificial intelligence. A Brookings Institution study concluded that jobs in office administration, production, transportation, and food preparation are at the highest risk (more than 70 percent) of replacement (Muro, Maxim, and Whito 2019). The least vulnerable jobs are (1) high-paying professional and technical roles with advanced educational requirements and (2) low-paying service work involving non-routine activities or requiring social and emotional intelligence (such as personal care). Implications for communities

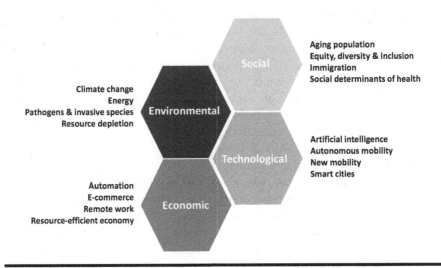

Figure 3.1 Drivers of Change Examples

Source: Hitchings and Rouse (2020).

will be determined by factors such as the employment sector mix and workforce education and skill levels.

The planning team can begin exploring the community implications of drivers of change in initial project scoping (see Chapter 2). Exercises such as a STEEP analysis can be incorporated into Phase 1 to engage community members in considering how they may affect the community's future. Potential questions to ask include:

- How are drivers of change affecting (or likely to affect) community systems such as land use, mobility, and housing?
- Is the community vulnerable to certain drivers (for example, reliance on jobs in sectors susceptible to automation or natural disasters likely to be exacerbated by climate change)?
- What are the community's assets and capacity to address negative impacts and realize potential positive effects of change?

Imagine Boston 2030 is an example of a comprehensive planning process that considered the implications of drivers of change for the city's future. Informed by public input, trends identified in the context chapter of the plan include increasing diversity and socioeconomic inequality (immigration and racial inequities), climate change (sea-level rise and extreme weather), and transformative technology (broadband communications, smart utilities, and new mobility).

Summary

The purpose of Phase 1 of the comprehensive planning process is to understand shared community values and issues, existing conditions, and likely future trends, providing the basis for developing vision, policies, and actions in subsequent phases of the process. Existing conditions reflect the community's past and broader social, economic, and technological forces that influenced its evolution into what it has become today. Assessing this legacy is important to understand both community assets and structural issues (for example, historic development patterns and institutional racism) that should be accounted for in the plan.

To understand shared values and issues, public participation should be designed to engage a range of participants who reflect the community's socioeconomic diversity and range of interests. Using a standard set of questions (for example, what are the community's strengths, weaknesses, and opportunities for the future?) facilitates identification of common responses across participant groups. The inventory and analysis of existing conditions and trends should be targeted to address the identified community priorities.

The conventional planning approach organizes the inventory around topics such as land use, transportation, and housing, often corresponding to elements required by state legislation. Contemporary plans use a more integrated approach that addresses the interrelationships between different community systems, as demonstrated by inventories organized around cross-cutting themes that emerged from the public input.

Building on where the community has been and what it is today, Phase 1 includes a forecast of what it is likely to become in the future if current trends continue. The standard approach is to project future population and employment levels, their spatial distribution, and the resulting impacts on land use, infrastructure, natural resources, and so on. In response to the accelerated pace and uncertain impacts of global change, forecasts can also characterize how social, technological, economic, and environmental drivers of change may affect the community. In addition to helping the community understand the implications of change drivers for community values and aspirations for the future, such assessments can inform scenario development in Phase 3 of the planning process.

Notes

1 This practice was deemed unconstitutional by the U.S. Supreme Court in 1917 on the basis that racial zoning ordinances interfered with private property rights. However, many border and southern cities continued to enact segregation ordinances or other forms of racial zoning after this decision (Rothstein 2017).

2 The City of Boise, Idaho uses an asset-mapping approach in its *Energize Our Neighborhoods* program, "a collaboration between the city and neighborhoods to guide the future of Boise's neighborhoods" (Boise n.d.). Among other activities, this program develops neighborhood plans that support *Blueprint Boise*, the city's comprehensive plan.

3 See, for example, Berke et al. (2006), Early (2015), and Kelly (2010).

References

Berke, Philip R., David R. Godschalk, and Edward J. Kaiser, with Daniel A. Rodriguez (2006). *Urban Land Use Planning*, Fifth Edition. Urbana, IL and Chicago, IL: University of Illinois Press.

Boise, Idaho (n.d.). "Community Asset Mapping" in *Energize Our Neighborhoods*. Accessed at https://www.cityofboise.org/programs/energize/energize-toolkit/worksheets/community-asset-mapping/

Early, David (2015). *The General Plan in California*. Point Arena, CA: Solano Press Books.

Heart and Soul of Essex (2014). *Project Summary*. Accessed at http://www.heartandsoulofessex.org/uploads/6/7/8/8/67881087/project-summary-2.21.14.pdf

Hitchings, Benjamin and David Rouse (2020). *Proact Now: Planning Effectively in a Rapidly Changing World*. Smart Growth Network and Maryland Department of Planning Webinar. Accessed at https://smartgrowth.org/proact-now-planning-effectively-in-a-rapidly-changing-world/

John P. Kretzmann and John L. McKnight (1993). *Building Communities from the Inside Out: A Path toward Finding and Mobilizing a Community's Assets*. Evanston, IL: Institute for Policy Research.

Kelly, Eric Damien (2010). *Community Planning: An Introduction to the Comprehensive Plan*, Second Edition. Washington, DC: Island Press.

McElvaney, Lisa A. and Kelleann Foster (2014). "Enhancing Stakeholder Engagement: Understanding Organizational Design Principles for Geodesign Professionals," Chapter 20 in Lee, Danbi, Eduardo Dias, and Henk Scholten (eds.), *Geodesign by Integrating Design and Geospatial Services*. Cham, Switzerland: Springer International Publishing, pp. 315–329.

Mitchell, Bruce and Juan Franco (2018). HOLC *"Redlining" Maps: The Persistent Structure of Segregation and Economic Inequality*. National Community Reinvestment Coalition. Accessed at https://ncrc.org/wp-content/uploads/dlm_uploads/2018/02/NCRC-Research-HOLC-10.pdf

Muro, Mark, Robert Maxim, and Jacob Whito (2019). *Automation and Artificial Intelligence: How Machines Are Affecting People and Places*. Washington, DC: Brookings Institution Metropolitan Policy Program.

Orton Family Foundation (n.d.). *Community Heart & Soul*. Accessed at https://www.communityheartandsoul.org/

Rothstein, Richard (2017). *The Color of Law: A Forgotten History of How Our Government Segregated America*. New York, NY: Liveright Publishing Corporation.

Rouse, David and Shannon McElvaney (2016). *Comprehensive Planning and Geodesign* (PAS Memo). Chicago, IL: American Planning Association.

Chapter 4

Where Do We Want to Go?

Having determined existing conditions, trends, and the likely future trajectory of the community, the next phase of the planning process is to determine what people want their community to become as an alternative to current trends. While communities use different approaches to represent a desired future, common components include a vision statement, principles, and goals that provide a framework for achieving the vision. Themes identified through community engagement can be used to organize and integrate these components.

Vision Statement

The vision statement depicts the desired future conditions and qualities of the community – physical, environmental, and social – based on shared values and priority issues identified in Phase 1.[1] The statement sets the overarching direction for the plan's goals, policies, strategies, and implementing actions and provides a guide for the community to understand what the plan seeks to achieve (Godschalk and Rouse 2015).

Private, nonprofit, and public sector organizations develop visions through strategic planning processes to describe what they seek to become in the mid- or long-term future, as a guide for strategy and decision-making. Community vision statements have different motivations, engagement processes, and time horizons and typically deal with a more complex environment than those developed for individual organizations. Nevertheless, characteristics of organizational vision statements are relevant to developing effective community vision statements (Table 4.1).

DOI: 10.4324/9781003024170-5

Table 4.1 Shared Attributes of Organizational Vision Statements

Attribute	Definition
Brevity	A vision statement should be brief but definitive.
Clarity	A vision statement should be clear and precise so that it is understood.
Future Orientation	A vision statement should focus on the long-term perspective of the organization and the environment in which it functions.
Stability	A vision statement should be general enough to not be affected by short-term changes in the market or technology.
Challenge	A vision statement should motivate the organization to work toward a desirable outcome.
Abstractness	A vision statement should represent a general idea as opposed to a specific achievement that can be met and then discarded.
Desirability or Ability to Inspire	A vision statement should express an ideal that the organization find worth working toward.

Source: Adapted from Kantrabutra (2008).

Vision planning for communities emerged in the final two decades of the 20th century, in large part as a reaction to the top-down, rational planning model. The National League of Cities developed *The Community Visioning and Strategic Planning Handbook* as a guide for communities to apply a collaborative, consensus-based planning and decision-making process it termed "a new model of citizen democracy" (Okubo 2000). The steps in the process are to: (1) conduct an environmental scan; (2) assess community capacity (referred to as civic infrastructure); (3) develop a community vision statement; (4) select key performance areas to guide action to achieve the vision; and (5) define an action strategy and implementation agenda. The handbook identifies seven ingredients of a quality vision statement:

- Positive, present tense language.
- Qualities that provide the reader with a feeling for the region's uniqueness.
- Inclusiveness of the region's diverse population.
- A depiction of the highest standards of excellence and achievement.
- A focus on people and quality of life.
- Addresses a time period 15–20 years in the future.
- Language that is easily understood by all (Okubo 2000).

An effective vision statement is concise, memorable, and lends itself to being widely cited and disseminated in different formats (such as online, video, and print) to reach all segments of the community. It incorporates diverse perspectives in an expression of shared aspirations, inspiring a sense of ownership among all segments of the community. Public input received in Phase 1 provides the basis for the vision statement. A transparent, replicable methodology should be used to distill multiple forms and points of input into key ideas that resonate with diverse audiences. While the planning team or consultant is normally responsible for drafting the vision statement, the community advisory committee has a key role to play in an iterative process to ensure that the end result most accurately reflects community input. This process includes sharing the draft vision statement with the public, asking them the question – "did we get it right?" – and then revising the draft based on the input received.

Contemporary comprehensive plan vision statements vary widely in format, from a sentence or a few bullets to a narrative two pages or more in length. (Table 4.2

Table 4.2 Vision Statement Examples

Comprehensive Plan	Vision Statement
Plan Salt Lake City Salt Lake City, Utah	Salt Lake City is a *Regional Capital City*, a social, cultural, and religious center, and a model of open government.
	Salt Lake City's *Neighborhoods* are diverse, exciting, safe, well maintained, and supportive of families and young people.
	Salt Lake City's *Urban Design* is aesthetically appealing, reflects excellent standards, diversity of influence, and a commitment to making people the focus of development decisions.
	Salt Lake City's *Economic Base* is strong and diverse, providing excellent wages and benefits for our citizens.
	Salt Lake City's *Transportation System* is integrated and multimodal. The focus first is on pedestrian and bicyclists, second on mass transit, and third on single-occupant automobiles.[2]
Memphis 3.0 Memphis, Tennessee	*In our third century, Memphis will build up, not out.* Memphis will be a city that anchors growth on strengths of the core and neighborhoods; a city of greater connectivity and access; a city of opportunity for all.
Build One Portsmouth Portsmouth, Virginia	*Thriving:* We draw from our rich history to promote healthy individuals, local economies, regional collaboration, and vibrant neighborhoods with strong identities.
	Resilient: We prepare for long-term prosperity by thoughtfully creating adaptable structures, systems, and practices to prepare for opportunities and to meet challenges.
	Evolving: We embrace the future and respond positively to emerging opportunities to care for the people and places we love by balancing historic preservation with thoughtful reinvestment and redevelopment.
	Equitable: We cultivate a vibrant city where equality is evident as we meet the needs of all our citizens in ways that are fair, meaningful, and empowering.

provides several examples.) No single approach is correct; shorter vision statements can communicate intent to a general audience in a concise and memorable way, while longer ones can be more comprehensive in their coverage of the desired future attributes of the community. As the touchstone for policy and action, the vision statement can be organized around themes that carry through to other plan components. For example, the *Build One Portsmouth* comprehensive plan vision consists of four themes that provide the organizing structure for the plan goals, strategies, and tactics.

A vision statement is aspirational in nature, depicting the ideal future conditions that the community wishes to achieve. As such it expresses potential – something to strive for – rather than a literal end state. The National League of Cities handbook refers to an impactful vision as a "stretch," inspiring people to work toward making it happen despite the challenges involved (Okubo 2000). Given the rapid pace of change in the 21st century, the vision statement (along with other plan components) should be periodically reviewed and modified as necessary to keep it up to date.

Visual images, maps, and diagrams can be used in combination with text to communicate the intent of the vision statement. For example, Hillsborough County, Florida's *Imagine 2040 Comprehensive Plan* has a four-bullet vision statement, a vision map (described as a "general plan for guiding future growth"), and text and photos illustrating the character of "areas of opportunity" for growth shown on the vision map. The statement serves as a common framework for the comprehensive plans of the County's four local governments (Hillsborough County and the cities of Plante City, Tampa, and Temple Terrace), which were updated simultaneously.

Principles

Principles (also referred to as guiding, core, or community principles) are used in various ways, from guiding plan development during the comprehensive planning process to supplementing or replacing the vision statement in the plan itself.[3] They are defined here as providing strategic direction for policy and action to achieve the vision statement. For example, the *Imagine Austin Comprehensive Plan* identifies six core principles for action:

- Grow as a compact, connected city.
- Integrate nature into the city.
- Provide paths to prosperity for all.
- Develop as an affordable and healthy community.
- Sustainably manage water, energy, and other environmental resources.
- Think creatively and work together.

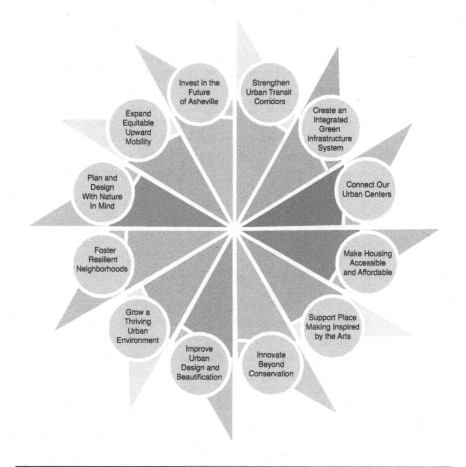

Figure 4.1 Guiding Principles: *Living Asheville Comprehensive Plan*
Source: City of Asheville, North Carolina.

Principles can be general in nature (similar to *Imagine Austin*) or targeted toward more specific topics or themes that emerge through the community engagement process. For example, the *Living Asheville Comprehensive Plan* for Asheville, North Carolina, identifies 12 guiding principles that provide strategic direction for action across community systems (Figure 4.1). According to the plan:

> (These principles) will require synergistic implementation between departments and disciplines, whose outcomes can…improve livability in numerous ways…(They) reflect the vision which emerged throughout the planning process and they have been used as a framework to help inform the plan's themes, goals, and strategies.

Goals

Goals define the long-term outcomes that the jurisdiction seeks to achieve through implementation of the comprehensive plan. In the traditional comprehensive planning model, goals are set for discrete elements addressing standard planning topics such as land use, transportation, and housing. While this model is still in use, particularly where topical elements are specified by state legislation, alternative approaches have emerged in contemporary practice. Examples include organizing goals and other plan components around cross-cutting themes or topics identified through the planning process. The comprehensive plans for the cities of Aurora, Colorado, Burlington, Vermont, and Manitou Springs, Colorado provide examples of these approaches:

> *Aurora, Colorado.* The *Aurora Places Comprehensive Plan* organizes goals under seven community principles that were determined through public input. The principles are: (1) Strong Economy, (2) Diverse and Equitable City, (3) Housing for All, (4) Healthy Community, (5) Thriving Environment, (6) Easy Mobility and Active Transportation, and (7) Authentic Aurora.
>
> *Burlington, Vermont.* The City of Burlington's *planBVT* organizes goals around four themes distilled from previous plans and community input during the planning process. These themes are intended to guide the city's growth as a dynamic, distinctive, inclusive, and connected city. The plan states that "each theme is meant to complement the others, in order to demonstrate the interrelatedness of individual planning actions."
>
> *Manitou Springs, CO.* An integrated community master plan and hazard mitigation plan, *Plan Manitou* is organized around 13 elements. These elements address both conventional planning topics (for example, land use and the built environment and transportation and mobility) and others, such as arts and culture, education, and municipal governance and community engagement.

Table 4.3 provides examples of goals from each of these plans.

Goals reflect community values and aspirations and address priority issues identified through public engagement. They set the direction for realizing the vision statement through policy and action. As such, they should incorporate ambition (the "stretch" referred to by the National League of Cities) rather than focusing solely on feasibility. Businesses and organizations often use the acronym SMART (*Specific, Measurable, Achievable, Relevant, and Time-bound*) as a tool to develop goals that can be effectively implemented.[4] Table 4.4 shows how the criteria defined by this tool could be adapted for use in setting comprehensive plan goals. In so doing, it is important to consider the differences between a community – a complex, large-scale system comprising interacting subsystems – and the organizations to which it is typically applied. The role of the comprehensive plan goals is to guide the evolution of the community in an uncertain future world to achieve its potential as expressed in the vision statement.

Table 4.3 Comprehensive Plan Goal Examples

Plan	Plan Component	Goal Example
Aurora Places Aurora, Colorado	A Diverse and Equitable City	Embrace and promote multiculturalism in education, communication, celebration, and commerce.
planBVT Burlington, Vermont	Burlington as a Dynamic City	Make tangible efforts to reduce greenhouse gas emissions and become a *Net Zero Energy* community by 2030.
Plan Manitou Manitou Springs, Colorado	Health, Human Services, Food Access, and Well-Being	Enhance access to affordable, healthy, local foods and promote public investment in a sustainable, resilient food system.

Table 4.4 "SMART" Criteria for Comprehensive Plan Goals

Criterion	Definition
Specific	The goal should be general in nature while defining a domain for which more specific policies and actions can be developed.
Measurable	Progress in achieving the goal should be trackable over time using indicators, benchmarks, or targets. These measures can be specified in objectives or performance metrics for each goal.
Ambitious + achievable	The goal should be both ambitious in its reach and feasible to implement through manageable action steps.
Relevant	The goal should be derived from and address issues identified through community engagement.
Time-bound	The goal should have a defined time period, including an end date (that is, the plan time horizon) and a timeline for actions to implement the goal (typically defined in an implementation component of the plan).

Minneapolis 2040: **Integrating Vision, Goals, Policies, and Action**

The *Minneapolis 2040 Comprehensive Plan* is an example of integrating vision, goals, and polices to set the direction for action. Fourteen interrelated goals provide the foundation of the plan. Identified through community engagement in the early phases of the planning process, these goals were adopted by the city council to provide direction to staff in developing comprehensive plan policies that reflect community aspirations. Toward that end, each goal expresses an outcome the city seeks to achieve by 2040. For example, the first goal (*Eliminate Disparities*) states:

> In 2040, Minneapolis will see all communities fully thrive regardless of race, ethnicity, gender, country of origin, religion, or zip

code having eliminated deep-rooted disparities in wealth, opportunity, housing, safety, and health.

The 14 goals collectively serve as the plan vision statement. According to *Minneapolis 2040*, "the goals are intended to state the plan's intent as clearly as possible, so that we as a city know what we are working to accomplish through the policies of the comprehensive plan." The plan identifies 100 policies "intended to guide city decision-making in a manner that achieves the Comprehensive Plan goals." Each policy supports multiple goals and includes specific action steps. The plan's web-based format facilitates navigation between goals and related policies.[5] Table 4.5 lists *Minneapolis 2040's* 14 goals with randomly selected examples of relevant policies for each goal.

Table 4.5 *Minneapolis 2040* **Goals and Policy Examples**

Goals	Policy Examples
Eliminate disparities	Affordable Housing Production and Preservation, Educational and Economic Access, (39 total)
More residents and jobs	Access to Housing, Human Capital and a Trained Workforce, Technology in the Economy (26 total)
Affordable and accessible housing	Affordable Housing Production and Preservation, Housing Displacement, Innovative Housing Types (22 total)
Living-wage jobs	Healthy Pre-K Development, Human Capital and a Trained Workforce, Supporting Small Businesses (18 total)
Healthy, safe, and connected people	Aging, Food Access, Healthy Housing (28 total)
High-quality physical environment	Place-based Neighborhood Engagement, Public Realm, Tree Canopy and Urban Forest (25 total)
History and culture	Cultural Districts, Quality of Life, Stewarding Historic Properties (11 total)
Creative, cultural, and natural amenities	Artists and Creative Workers, New Parks, Public Realm (17 total)
Complete neighborhoods	Access to Commercial Goods and Services, Complete Streets, Shared Mobility (21 total)
Climate change resilience	Climate Resilient Communities, Energy Efficient and Sustainable Buildings (21 total)
Clean environment	Air Quality, Soil Health, Sustainable Water System Management (19 total)
Healthy, sustainable, and diverse economy	Educational and Economic Access, Value of Arts and Culture, Innovation Districts (27 total)
Proactive, accessible government	Access to Health, Social, and Emergency Services, Public Safety, Technology in the City Enterprise (7 total)
Equitable civic participation system	Arts and Culture in Community Development, Place-based Neighborhood Engagement, Social Connectedness (8 total)

Summary

Defining where to go as a community is a critical step in the comprehensive planning process. The vision statement is an expression of potential: the ideal future that the community seeks to achieve. Principles provide strategic direction for efforts to realize the vision statement, while goals define the long-term outcomes that will result from successful implementation. The vision statement, principles, and goals are based on shared values and priorities identified through community engagement in Phase 1 of the planning process, informed by findings of the inventory and analysis. They should be reviewed and confirmed with the public in Phase 2 by asking the question: Did we get it right?

As illustrated by the examples provided in this chapter, the vision, principles, and goals can be organized and framed in different ways so long as they express the collective aspirations of the community for the future. As opposed to the traditional approach of organizing goals around topical elements, contemporary plans use cross-cutting themes to integrate these various components into a framework for policies and actions to implement the plan (addressed in Chapter 5, How Do We Get There?).

Notes

1 While this text assumes that the vision statement is developed as part of the comprehensive planning process, it can be developed through a separate process that informs comprehensive plan development. For example, Asheville, North Carolina used *City Council Vision 2036* (adopted in 2016) as the vision statement for the *Living Asheville* Comprehensive Plan (Asheville 2018).

2 This is a slightly condensed version of the "common community vision" developed through the *Creating Tomorrow Together* process (Salt Lake City Futures Commission 1998). *Plan Salt Lake City*, the city's current comprehensive plan, continues to reference and embrace this vision.

3 For example, Butte County, California identified 13 Guiding Principles early in the planning process for *General Plan 2030*. According to the General Plan, these principles "describe how Butte County intends to grow and develop" through plan implementation. *Aurora Places*, the comprehensive plan for Aurora, Colorado, expresses the plan vision as seven Community Principles (Aurora 2018).

4 The origins of the SMART criteria date back to goal-setting theory developed by Edwin Locke and Gary Latham, and colleagues (Locke and Latham 1990).

5 *Minneapolis 2040*'s web-based format also provides an option to navigate the policies by topic (land use & built form, transportation, housing, and so forth).

References

Godschalk, David and David Rouse (2015). *Sustaining Places: Best Practices for Comprehensive Plans* (PAS Report 578). Chicago, IL: American Planning Association.

Kantrabutra, Sooksan (2008). "What Do We Know About Vision?" Littleton, CO: *The Journal of Applied Business Research*, 24:2, pp. 127–138.

Locke, Edwin A. and Gary P. Latham (1990). *A Theory of Goal Setting & Task Performance*. Englewood Cliffs, NJ: Prentice Hall, Inc.

Okubo, Derek, Principal Author and Editor (2000). *The Community Visioning and Strategic Planning Handbook, Third Printing*. Denver, CO: National Civic League Press.

Salt Lake City Futures Commission (1998). *Creating Tomorrow Together (Common Community Vision)*. Salt Lake City, UT. Accessed at https://www.yumpu.com/en/document/view/30659462/creating-tomorrow-together-final-report-of-the-salt-lake-

Chapter 5

How Do We Get There?

Having defined the desired future that the community wishes to achieve (Phase 2 of the comprehensive planning process), the purpose of the third and final phase of the process is to determine how to turn potential into reality through action. Long-range planning in a rapidly changing world is an uncertain undertaking that defies easy answers or linear solutions (for example, the notion that sequential steps can be followed over time to realize the vision statement). The inevitable resource constraints will limit how much the community can take on, highlighting the need to prioritize catalytic actions that can leverage further progress. Because our reality is one of constant flux in which the unforeseen can quickly become routine (witness the effects of the COVID-19 pandemic), the flexibility to adjust course as conditions change is paramount.

Comprehensive plans of the past typically contained a future land-use map (intended to guide zoning and development decisions), general policies organized by element, and only limited guidance for implementation. While contemporary plans have more robust implementation sections, they often consist of lists of unprioritized actions. Effective plans are comprehensive and visionary in their scope and reach, as well as strategic, focused, and adaptable in their approach to implementation.

Effective implementation of the comprehensive plan is addressed in Chapter 13. This chapter covers the role of community engagement in setting the direction and priorities for plan implementation; the use of scenario planning to explore paths to realizing the vision and goals; and how to develop a framework for policy and action. It concludes with a section on the future land-use plan – the mainstay of 20th-century comprehensive plans – as it is evolving in 21st-century practice.

DOI: 10.4324/9781003024170-6

The Role of Community Engagement

Authentic and robust engagement is critical throughout the planning process to ensure that the final plan accurately reflects community aspirations for the future. Community engagement in Phase 3 is a continuation of the iterative, consensus-building process used in Phases 1 and 2. (In Phase 1, the process identifies shared community values and issues. In Phase 2, the process develops a vision and goals for the future based on the input received in Phase 1.) In Phase 3, community engagement sets the direction for policy and action to realize the vision and goals and address community-identified issues. A key step is to involve community members in constructing future scenarios, evaluating their performance relative to the vision and goals, and selecting a preferred scenario to guide development of policies and actions.

The public participation plan developed in project scoping will define the community engagement methods used in Phase 3. Online survey platforms are available to supplement more traditional methods such as public workshops. These platforms can be used to engage community members in activities such as ranking alternative scenarios, prioritizing issues and strategies to address them, and exploring budget allocations and revenue sources.

Community Engagement Examples: Las Cruces (New Mexico), Memphis, (Tennessee), and Minneapolis (Minnesota)

The City of Las Cruces structured community engagement for the *Elevate Las Cruces Comprehensive Plan* around public open house series and online surveys in each of the three phases of the planning process. The input received in Phase 3 was used to prioritize proposed implementation strategies. Additional, more targeted input on proposed strategies and actions was provided by subcommittees established for the three overarching plan themes: *Community Prosperity*, *Community Livability*, and *Community Environment*.

In Phase 3 of the *Memphis 3.0* comprehensive planning process, community members were invited to explore tradeoffs between three citywide future growth scenarios in a series of workshops, other engagement events, and online and paper surveys. The input was used to refine the vision and goals developed in Phase 2 and establish a preferred growth scenario for the next 20 years. City staff then worked with community members in 14 districts to develop place-specific visions, strategies, and actions to implement the preferred growth scenario.

Phase 3 of the *Minneapolis 2040* comprehensive planning process engaged community members in the development of a policy framework to implement the 14 overarching goals for the city's future developed from public input in Phase 2 (see Table 4.5). According to the *Minneapolis 2040* website, engagement questions centered on equity (including the city's enduring legacy of systemic racism) and access to housing, jobs, and transportation. Two rounds of engagement were conducted to increase participation opportunities. Creative engagement methods included a mobile engagement tool (designed in collaboration with local artists), an online story-telling tool, and an online mapping tool.

Scenario Planning

Simply stated, a scenario is a plausible story of the future. Scenario planning involves constructing narratives about how the world may turn out, with the purpose of helping organizations recognize and adapt to changing external conditions in a world of uncertainty (Schwartz 1991). In the comprehensive planning process, scenario planning is used to generate and evaluate possible futures to frame choices and inform community decision-making on how to realize the vision and goals. It is well suited for this role given the uncertainty of future change over the long-range time horizon of the plan, which suggests that communities should prepare for and adapt to a range of possible future outcomes.

Scenario planning engages community members in exploring different choices for the future and their consequences, with the underlying purpose of building consensus for a preferred scenario or strategic direction that best moves the community toward the vision. Workshops and small group exercises are often used to enable participants to construct spatial representations of future land use and development (the growth scenario approach described below) and consider their implications for the vision and goals developed earlier in the process. Geographic information system (GIS) applications can be used to generate scenarios and evaluate their impacts. The use of sophisticated software is not mandatory; many communities have used manual "chip" exercises or other non-digital techniques to engage the public in scenario planning.

Scenario planning is a complex field, but researchers from different disciplines have identified three general types: normative, predictive, and explorative. *Normative* scenario planning addresses one or more visions of the future (what *should* be). *Predictive* scenario planning constructs futures based on forecasts (what *will* be). *Exploratory* scenario planning considers futures that may occur as a result of external influences and strategic responses (what *can* be). While comprehensive planning processes can incorporate elements of all three types, we distinguish between two overall approaches – growth scenarios and strategic scenarios – described below. Both take the vision developed in Phase 2 (what we say we want to be) and explore environments in which the community will act to achieve the vision (become what we say we want to be) (Smith 2007). Used in this way, scenario planning provides direction for policy and action to implement the comprehensive plan.

Online scenario planning tools will likely be used to supplement or replace in-person engagement as patterns of public participation change (for example, as a response to the COVID-19 pandemic). Given accelerating change and increasing uncertainty about the future, exploratory scenario planning to explore community responses to several possible futures (referred to below as strategic scenarios) is emerging as an alternative to the standard growth scenarios approach. Regardless of the approach, it is important to ensure that scenario planning provides meaningful participation opportunities for all segments of the community, including those who cannot easily access digital technology. Scenario planning can address the role of land use and development patterns shaped by past planning practices in reinforcing and exacerbating social and racial inequalities. For example, the trend growth and alternative scenarios can be evaluated through an equity lens to consider implications for minority and historically underserved communities.[1]

Growth Scenarios

This approach starts with a baseline or trend growth scenario that projects the spatial distribution of projected future growth if current development trends continue. Alternative scenarios are then constructed to characterize different ways the community could develop in the future. Population, employment, and other forecasts of future conditions developed in the inventory and analysis provide the basis for the scenarios. The relative performance of alternative scenarios is compared against the baseline and a consensus or preferred scenario identified that best fulfills the community vision and goals. Growth scenarios are the most commonly used approach in comprehensive planning and are most applicable to growing communities in which development trends can be readily extrapolated.

Growth Scenario Examples: Las Cruces (New Mexico) and Austin (Texas)

The *Elevate Las Cruces Comprehensive Plan* is an example of the growth scenarios approach. Population and household forecasts were developed to estimate the amount of land required to accommodate estimated residential growth through 2045. The city's consultant team used GIS software (CommunityViz) to develop three growth scenarios for the plan horizon year: (1) trend, (2) alternative – compact centers, and (3) alternative – centers and corridors. Generalized future land-use categories (Place Types) were incorporated into each scenario to depict Las Cruces' development footprint at build-out. The scenarios were then evaluated for the degree to which they "would promote the community's long-term vision of fiscal, environmental, and social sustainability." A *scenario dashboard* characterizing probable development outcomes for eight indicators (for example, environmental stewardship, proximity to destinations, and public facilities and services) provided the basis for the evaluation. A consensus scenario incorporating input from City Council and the Comprehensive Plan Advisory Committee was used to generate the Future Development Map and Major Thoroughfare Map for the *Elevate Las Cruces Comprehensive Plan.*

In another example, the city of Austin engaged citizens in interactive chip exercises to spatially allocate projected future growth of approximately 750,000 new residents and 300,000 new jobs over the 30-year time horizon of the *Imagine Austin Comprehensive Plan.* The results were synthesized by city staff and the consultant team into five alternative scenarios that were assessed against indicators derived from the vision statement (for example, acres developed, greenhouse gas emissions, and cost of public infrastructure). The scenarios were then reviewed with the public to select a preferred scenario for development into a Growth Concept Map that supports the components of the *Imagine Austin* Vision Statement.

Strategic Scenarios

The growth scenarios approach can be characterized as a combination of the predictive (growth forecasts) and normative (implications of forecasts for the community vision) types of scenario planning. Trend forecasts are inherently uncertain because they cannot account for the impacts of disruptive future conditions (for example, technological advances such as automation and artificial intelligence) and events (for example, economic shocks and pandemics). Moreover, growth scenarios are not well suited for mature communities with stable or declining populations.

The strategic scenarios approach considers the implications of plausible future conditions for the community vision, thus combining elements of exploratory and normative scenario planning. Its purpose is to position the community to strategically adapt to future change in ways that support its vision and goals. While planners increasingly use exploratory scenario planning to anticipate the effects of emerging trends such as climate change and autonomous vehicles, there has been limited use of strategic scenarios in comprehensive planning practice. Such an approach could: (1) identify social, technological, economic, or environmental trends that are particularly relevant to the community; (2) construct narratives (scenarios) of how those trends might play out within the time horizon of the comprehensive plan; (3) and develop strategic responses under different scenarios (which may involve adapting the vision statement and implementation program).

Strategic Scenarios Example: Sahuarita, Arizona

Aspire 2035, the general plan for the Town of Sahuarita, Arizona, is an example of the use of scenario planning in conjunction with a comprehensive planning process to address future uncertainty. Sahuarita is a community of approximately 30,000 residents located 15 miles south of Tucson. Staff from the Sonoran Institute conducted an exploratory scenario exercise with participants in the town's comprehensive planning process (Marlow et al. 2015). The purpose of the exercise was to consider how different future conditions might affect implementation of the plan (which was then in draft form) and its vision of Sahuarita being a "stand-alone" community (that is, "…a place where people choose to live and where businesses choose to locate"). Participants in a scenario workshop identified what they considered to be the most important drivers of future change, which included availability of water supply, availability of state land for future growth, ability to attract workforce, availability of high-quality recreation amenities, and willingness to create municipal financial tools. A series of possible futures combining opportunities and threats posed by combinations of these drivers were identified and developed into four narrative storylines of potential futures:

- Low Support for Public Financing
- Constrained Water Resources
- Overcoming all Barriers
- The Best Bedroom Community

The following is the narrative for The Best Bedroom Community scenario:

> The community has had little success in attracting new employers or skilled workforce due to market competition or changing workplace requirements. There has been little development of state trust land resulting from either weak market conditions or political barriers. There are no new water resources available for acquisition as a result of statewide drought and/or climate change. The community has decided to change its initial objectives of being a stand-alone community, opting to focus on becoming a sustainable, high-quality bedroom community.
>
> (Marlow et al. 2015)

Participants in a second workshop (selected to represent expertise in different areas of community planning and management) then evaluated draft plan goals and strategies for their effectiveness in addressing the issues posed by the four scenarios. Recommendations for the final general plan included, among others: (1) identify robust strategies that would work across a range of possible futures; (2) undertake incremental and flexible implementation of strategies that could be adapted as conditions change over time; and (3) utilize "hedge" strategies to prepare for undesirable future outcomes.

From Vision to Policy and Action

Scenario planning enables the community to determine a preferred scenario with strategic directions to realize its vision for the future. The next step in Phase 3 of the planning process is to develop these directions into policies and actions to implement the plan.[2] Goals, policies, and actions are typically organized into a framework consisting of elements or other components that form the substantive core of the plan.[3]

The framework can be organized in various ways. As previously discussed, the traditional approach (particularly where state legislation specifies the elements included in a comprehensive plan), is to develop elements addressing standard planning topics such as land use, transportation, and housing. Developing these elements separately, however, does not account for synergies and connections between related topics. This approach can also create difficulties aligning the elements with a unifying vision statement and incorporating actions from separate elements into an integrated implementation program.

In practice, even states with mandated elements provide flexibility in how the comprehensive plan is organized as long as it covers the required content. For example, the *Envision Stockton 2040 General Plan Update* for Stockton, California combines elements required by state legislation, optional elements from the city's previous general plan, and priority topics identified by the community during the planning process into four consolidated chapters: Land Use, Transportation, Safety, and Community Health (Figure 5.1).

Alternatives to organizing the comprehensive plan into conventional elements can be divided into two broad categories or approaches:

■ The *topical* approach organizes the plan around substantive planning topics. It differs from the traditional approach in that the topics are identified through the planning process rather than corresponding to standard plan elements.[4] Plans that are organized around community systems (and which consider the interrelationships between them) are a variation of the topical approach.

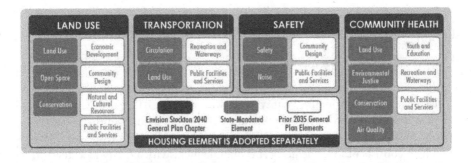

Figure 5.1 Envision Stockton 2020 Plan Framework
Source: City of Stockton, California.

- The *thematic* approach, which has become prevalent in 21st-century practice, organizes the comprehensive plan around themes that cut across planning topics and systems.

Table 5.1 provides examples of comprehensive plans that fall into these two categories. More detail on two of the plans is provided following the table.

Table 5.1 Topical and Thematic Approach Examples

Plan	Organization
Topical Approach	
Albany 2030 Albany, New York	Eight systems (for example, Natural Resources, Community Form, and Economy)[5]
Vision 2030 Allentown, Pennsylvania	Five systems (see box below)
Imagine Austin Austin, Texas	Seven building blocks (for example, Conservation and Environment, Society, and Creativity)
Focus Kansas City Kansas City, Missouri	Twelve building blocks (for example, Citizen Access and Communication, FOCUS Centers, and Moving About the City)
Thematic Approach	
Living Asheville Asheville, North Carolina	Six themes (principles defined by the *Comprehensive Plan Standards for Sustaining Places*)
Elevate Las Cruces Las Cruces, New Mexico	Three overarching themes (Elevate Our Community Environment, Elevate Our Community Prosperity, and Elevate Our Community Livability)
Build One Portsmouth Portsmouth, Virginia	Four vision themes (Thriving, Resilient, Evolving, and Equitable)
Stearns 2040 Stearns County, Minnesota	Five vision pillars (Agriculture, Living, Nature, Business, and Connectivity)

Examples: Allentown (Pennsylvania) and Stearns County (Minnesota)

The *Allentown Vision 2030 Comprehensive Plan and Economic Development Plan* uses a systems approach as an alternative to structuring the plan around elements specified in the Pennsylvania Municipalities Planning Code. The plan is divided into three main sections: executive summary, urban systems, and area planning. The Executive Summary defines the city's vision for 2030, which consists of four themes: (1) economic inclusivity, (2) city as a steward, (3) diversity and inclusion, and (4) empowerment and collaboration. The Urban Systems section addresses five urban systems as "a comprehensive way to understand the City of Allentown…and encompass many different forces and factors that make up the systems of the city." The five systems are: economic development, housing, accessibility and connectivity, services and amenities, and living systems. An overall goal, principles, and catalytic actions are identified for each system. The Area Planning section applies the citywide recommendations of the Urban Systems section to meet community needs and improve quality of life in the four geographic areas of the city.

The *Stearns 2040 Comprehensive Plan* is an example of the thematic approach. Stearns County is a predominantly rural community, located in Minnesota about 60 miles northwest of Minneapolis-St. Paul. The county's vision for the year 2050 is expressed as five pillars: (1) agriculture, (2) living, (3) nature, (4) business, and (5) connectivity. According to the plan,

> the Pillars look to the current values and character of the County to help define the priorities and directions for future decisions. The Pillars also serve as an umbrella for structuring the comprehensive plan into five cohesive areas that cover a wide spectrum of topics.

The substantive core of the plan consists of five chapters, one for each pillar. These chapters identify goals, focus areas (important directions for the county's future related to the pillar), and policies for the focus areas.

The Evolving Future Land-Use Map

A key component of the traditional comprehensive planning model, the future land-use map designates different land uses as a guide for land-use policy and decision-making (including zoning). This model has two key limitations. From a historic perspective, the separation of different uses and housing types has been translated into zoning ordinances that promote land-consumptive, automobile-dependent development and reinforce racial segregation. Moreover, the future land-use map is a static tool that does not account for three-dimensional form, the dynamics of land-use change, or the quantity, quality, and character of public realm elements such as streets and public spaces (Hinshaw 2017).

While many contemporary comprehensive plans have future land-use maps, new ways of spatially representing the desired future are emerging to address the limitations of the conventional model. These can be broadly characterized as the conceptual growth, place-based, and strategy-based approaches.

Conceptual Growth Approach. Particularly well suited for communities with undeveloped land, experiencing growth pressures, this approach establishes a spatial framework to guide future development to achieve more sustainable outcomes than projected trend growth. For example, the *Imagine Austin Comprehensive Plan* replaces the future land map with a growth concept map developed from the pre-ferred scenario. This map is organized around centers (regional, town, and neighbor-hood); corridors (activity, high-capacity transit, and highway); and environmental resources and open spaces.

Place-Based Approach. This approach defines desired development based on characteristics such as form, character, and scale. Visual images such as photos and renderings are used to communicate the intent. *Aurora Places*, the comprehensive plan for Aurora, Colorado, is an example of the place-based approach. It substitutes a *Placetype Plan* for the traditional future land use plan, accompanied by a matrix showing how the Placetypes relate to typical land-use categories (Figure 5.2).

Strategy-Based Approach. Particularly well suited for mature communities that may or may not be experiencing redevelopment pressures, this approach delineates areas for the implementation of different strategies to realize the vision and goals. For example, the *Our Future Land Use* section of *planBVT*, the comprehensive plan for Burlington, Vermont, is structured around three maps. These maps identify areas to conserve (natural areas, open space, and working land), sustain (residential neighborhoods), and grow (neighborhood centers, major thoroughfares, regional center, and special areas). The text describes how these areas support plan vision and provides links to relevant policies and actions.

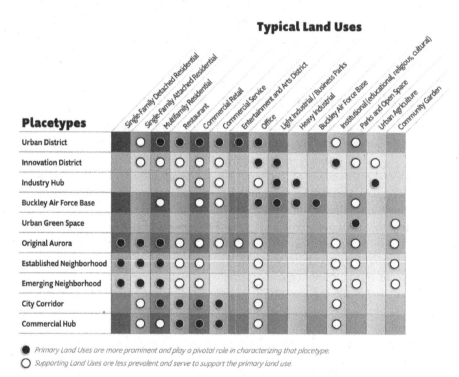

Figure 5.2 Aurora Places Placetypes and Land Uses

Summary

Phases 1 and 2 of a successful comprehensive planning process identify community values and issues; characterizes present conditions, trends, and the likely future if trends continue; and defines a vision and goals that the community will direct its efforts to achieve, all with robust community engagement. Phase 3 of the planning process (the focus of this chapter) develops a framework for policy and action to realize the vision and goals. By evaluating the implications of possible futures, scenario planning enables the community to determine a preferred scenario and strategic directions to guide plan implementation. The growth scenario approach, which defines a preferred development pattern as an alternative to trend (projected) growth, is most commonly used in practice. Given an increasingly uncertain future, strategic scenarios that explore the implications of drivers of change for the plan vision and goals are emerging as an alternative to the standard approach.

The traditional comprehensive planning model organizes policies and actions around separate elements that address standard planning topics such as land use, transportation, and housing, often specified by state legislation. Alternatives to the traditional model have emerged in contemporary practice, as evidenced by plans organized around topics identified through the planning process, community systems, or cross-cutting themes (often derived from the vision statement). Contemporary plans go beyond the traditional focus on land use and physical development to address broader community and societal issues such as equity, health, and resilience.

New approaches to spatially representing the community's desired future are similarly emerging to replace the traditional future land-use map. These approaches establish a spatial framework to guide future development (conceptual growth approach); define desired development based on characteristics such as form, character, and scale (place-based approach); or delineate areas for the implementation of different strategies to realize the vision and goals (strategy-based approach).

Notes

1 Robert Goodspeed discusses how to use scenario planning to address racial and social inequalities (Goodspeed 2020, pp. 187–191).
2 As illustrated by the examples provided in this chapter, comprehensive plans use various terms to refer to policies, actions, and similar concepts. Definitions for these terms used in this book are provided in the introduction to Part I.
3 Chapters 6–12 address community systems and particular planning topics that can be covered by this framework. Contemporary plans usually contain a separate section that describes how the policies and actions will be implemented (Chapter 13).
4 *Envision Stockton 2040* can be characterized as a hybrid between the traditional and topical approaches.
5 Interconnections between the eight systems were identified and used to priority actions in the implementation section of the *Albany 2030 Comprehensive Plan* (Godschalk and Anderson 2012).

References

Godschalk, David and William Anderson (2012). *Sustaining Places: The Role of the Comprehensive Plan* (PAS Report 567). Chicago, IL: American Planning Association.

Goodspeed, Robert (2020). *Scenario Planning for Cities and Regions: Managing and Envisioning Uncertain Futures*. Cambridge, MA: Lincoln Institute of Land Policy.

Hinshaw, Mark L. (2017). *True Urbanism: Living in and Near the Center*. London and New York: Routledge (first published by the American Planning Association in 2007).

Marlow, Joe, Hanna Oliver, Ray Quay, and Ralph Marra (2015). *Integrating Exploratory Scenario Planning into a Municipal General Plan Update*, Working Paper WP15JM1. Cambridge, MA: Lincoln Institute of Land Policy.

Schwartz, Peter (1991). *The Art of the Long View: Planning for the Future in an Uncertain World*. New York, NY: Bantam Doubleday Bell.

Smith, Erik (2007). "Using a Scenario Approach: From Business to Regional Futures," Chapter 5 in Lewis D. Hopkins and Marissa A. Zapata (eds.), *Engaging the Future: Forecasts, Scenarios, Plans, and Projects*. Cambridge, MA: Lincoln Institute of Land Use Policy, pp. 79–101.

THE SUBSTANCE OF THE PLAN

DOI: 10.4324/9781003024170-7

Building on Part I, which covers the process for creating the comprehensive plan, Part II focuses on the substantive contents of the plan that results from the process. Five of its seven chapters cover the core community systems (natural, built environment, social, and economic) addressed by the comprehensive plan. The sixth chapter addresses an overarching theme – community health – that cuts across all of these systems. The final chapter explores the connections of community systems to the larger region, emphasizing the importance of regional coordination and collaboration. Each chapter covers a series of planning topics that relate to its focus. Illustrative policy directions, applications, and examples from contemporary comprehensive plans are provided throughout the chapters.

The chapters are based on the six principles defined by the American Planning Association's *Comprehensive Plan Standards for Sustaining Places*: Harmony with Nature (Chapter 6), Livable Built Environment (Chapters 7 and 8), Interwoven Equity (Chapter 9), Economic Resilience (Chapter 10), Healthy Community (Chapter 11), and Responsible Regionalism (Chapter 12).[1] The chapters incorporate material from and expand upon these principles and associated best practices defined by the standards.

Systems Approach

As noted in Chapter 1, a fundamental premise of this book is that systems thinking is necessary for the comprehensive plan to yield sustainable, resilient, and equitable outcomes. Consistent with this premise, the Part II chapters incorporate a systems approach as an alternative to the 20th-century practice of organizing the comprehensive plan around discrete plan elements. Chapters 6–10 each address a major community system (for example, Chapter 6 addresses the natural environment) and the subsystems that comprise it (for example, land, water, air, and flora and fauna). Applying a systems approach allows for interrelationships among the different community systems and subsystems to be more fully expressed in the comprehensive plan policies and actions. Community health, the focus of Chapter 11, is both an overarching goal and an outcome of the interactions between the community systems and subsystems addressed in Chapters 6–10. Chapter 12 reflects systems thinking across jurisdictional boundaries and scales of concern. From this perspective, a community and the systems that comprise it are nested within a larger system (the region), meaning that plan outcomes will be the result of systems change at both the local and regional levels. In short, systems thinking embraces recognizing and working with the interrelationships among multiple component parts (Figure II.1).

As described in Part I, the systems approach also provides flexibility for the comprehensive planning process to address community issues and priorities, as well as for the various ways in which the plan contents can be organized. One approach is to organize the chapters or sections of a comprehensive plan around community systems. Alternatively, the plan can be organized around cross-cutting issues defined through community engagement, with different issues and policy responses

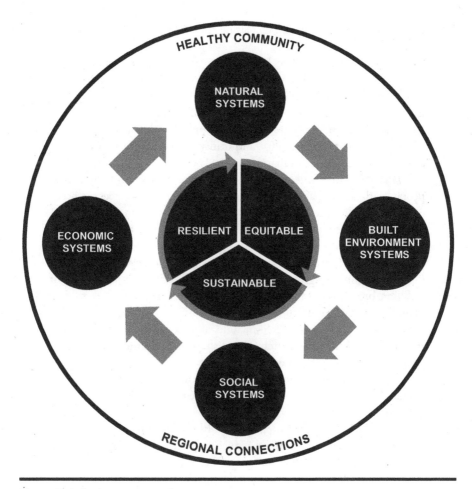

Figure II.1 Systems approach

integrated across systems. However, the plan is organized, it is important to reinforce the interrelationships these systems have with one another.

Overview of Chapters

Part II is organized into seven chapters, as follows:

Chapter 6: Natural Systems. This chapter emphasizes the importance of planning in harmony with nature to creating healthy and sustainable 21st century communities. It covers natural systems and resources that should be addressed in the comprehensive plan through an integrated ecosystem approach. The chapter concludes with a discussion of the role of the comprehensive plan in increasing community resilience to climate change.

Chapters 7 and 8: Built Environment Systems. These two chapters address the role of built environment systems in creating livable, complete communities in which all people can live, work, learn, play, and have their basic needs met. Major topics addressed by Chapter 7 include land use, development patterns, and community character. Chapter 8 addresses mobility, accessibility, and utility infrastructure systems, such as water, energy, and broadband.

Chapter 9: Social Systems. This chapter addresses systems that support people, with an emphasis on *planning with an equity lens* to meet the needs of all community members and groups. Topics covered include environmental justice, neighborhoods, social infrastructure, and housing.

Chapter 10: Economic Systems. This chapter addresses the evolution in planning practice from the 20th century economic development paradigm of maximizing growth as the primary objective to a new model of fulfilling broader community goals through the economy. Key themes include economic opportunity for all, economic resilience, and efficient use of resources. Topics covered include, among others, asset-based economic activity; the green, circular, and sharing economies; disaster preparedness and recovery; and fiscal sustainability.

Chapter 11: Healthy Community. In a return to the historic roots of the profession, health has become a major theme for 21st century planning. This chapter addresses the role of the comprehensive plan in creating healthy communities. It proposes a health in all policies approach to improve community health and reduce disparities in health outcomes. Topics covered include environmental health, access to healthy foods, and public safety.

Chapter 12: Regional Connections. This chapter highlights the importance of coordination and collaboration at the regional scale to improve the performance of systems that transcend jurisdictional boundaries. It addresses connections from local to regional natural, built environment, social, and environmental systems.

Chapter Organization

While there is variation in how the different Part II chapters are organized, they have the following common elements:

- Each chapter addresses the relationship of the chapter content to the three primary themes of this book: sustainability, resilience, and equity.

■ Each chapter introduces a theme that integrates the chapter contents. For example, the theme for Chapter 6 is an ecosystem approach, while regional coordination and collaboration is the theme for Chapter 12. Three interconnected themes (planning with a climate lens, planning with an equity lens, and health in all policies) underscore the importance of working across systems to achieve desired outcomes.

■ Each chapter covers a number of planning topics that are important to consider in developing the comprehensive plan. The identified topics are not intended to be definitive or exhaustive, and there may be additional ones to address in specific contexts.

■ Each chapter includes one or more sections titled *Inventory and Analysis*. These sections indicate information and data sources that are useful to understanding the system or topics covered by the chapter. Again, these sections are not definitive but are provided as guidance that may be useful in compiling the necessary information base and identifying issues for the comprehensive plan to address.

Tables with prototypical policy directions related to the planning topics, accompanied by examples of applications that might be used to implement the directions, are provided throughout the chapter. These materials are offered as possible models for developing policies and actions to address local circumstances.[2] As a rule, policies and actions included in the comprehensive plan should be unambiguous, use action verbs, and express clear directives that are easily understood by decision-makers, community members, and staff. Instances where flexibility is needed to account for the uncertainty of future change should be clearly and transparently stated.

Reference

Godschalk, David and David Rouse (2015). *Sustaining Places: Best Practices for Comprehensive Plans* (PAS Report 578). Chicago, IL: American Planning Association.

Chapter 6

Natural Systems

Since prehistoric times, natural systems (land, water, biological communities, the atmosphere, and climate) have determined the suitability of places for human habitation. Natural systems are the foundation of and inextricably connected with built environment systems (addressed in Chapters 7 and 8). However, it has become commonplace to think of the built and natural environments as separate constructs. The built environment, encompassing buildings and supporting infrastructure such as roads and utilities, signifies where people live and work. Conversely, the natural environment connotes undisturbed landscapes, natural ecosystems, and other areas that have experienced minimal human impact. The 20th-century environmental movement reflected this worldview in its focus on protecting nature from human intrusion (Wapner 2010).

The built and natural environments are not separate and discrete, but rather are dynamic, interconnected systems comprising intersecting subsystems. Human settlement always occurs within a natural context. Homes, commercial buildings, road networks, and the like are not detached from the natural terrain on which they were developed. Natural features such as slopes, soils, watersheds, and vegetation continue to exist, even if altered or degraded by urban development. The built environment incorporates features such as parks, riparian corridors, and the urban tree canopy. Beyond the current limits of urbanization, natural areas are modified to provide food, fiber, and other resources to cities, towns, and urban regions. Healthy, functioning natural systems integrated with the built environment are essential to support healthy, sustainable communities.

This chapter applies an ecosystem approach to sustaining natural systems, processes, and the services and benefits they provide. It covers natural systems and resources that should be addressed in the comprehensive plan, including land, water, and air (the three natural systems that support life on the planet); flora and fauna;

DOI: 10.4324/9781003024170-8

Sustainability, Resilience, and Equity

Planning in harmony with nature is foundational to creating sustainable, resilient, and equitable communities. Each community developed in a natural setting that resulted from the interactions of land, water, flora and fauna, and climate over time. Human activities, such as urban development and farming, have extensively modified the preexisting landscape, but natural processes continue to sustain ecosystems and provide benefits for people. Maintaining healthy and functioning natural systems at the local and regional scales while reducing global impacts is key to fulfilling the definition of sustainability: meeting current needs while ensuring that adequate resources are available for future generations.

A resilient approach to planning in harmony with nature recognizes the hazards and risks that are inherent in the natural environment (for example, steep slopes, unstable soils, and flood prone areas) and the role of climate change in magnifying the effects of natural disasters. It calls for natural hazards and risks to be identified in the inventory and analysis and for plan policies and actions to be developed that minimize danger to people and buildings from natural disasters. Resilience also involves pre-disaster preparedness and recovery planning, both to minimize loss of life and property damage when a disaster strikes and to ensure timely and effective reestablishment of community well-being in its aftermath.

Finally, an equitable approach to planning in harmony with nature ensures that all segments of the community have access to the services and benefits provided by natural systems and are not adversely impacted by environmental damage such as polluted air, water, and soils, regardless of race, ethnicity, or socioeconomic status. Where such damage exists, steps to repair the affected resources and restore the healthy functioning of natural systems should be prioritized. Every neighborhood should be free of environmental pollutants and toxins, while having equitable access to parks, greenspaces, tree canopy, and other forms of green infrastructure.

and sensitive environmental resources. It concludes with a discussion of climate, natural hazards, and the role of the comprehensive plan in increasing community resilience to shocks and stresses that are being magnified by climate change.

Ecosystem Approach

Natural systems and processes interact with built environment systems to form *ecosystems*, that is communities of living entities (flora, fauna, and other organisms, including humans) and the physical (non-living) environment that surrounds them. The physical environment includes both natural elements – land, soil, water, and air – and human ones, such as buildings, roads, and utilities. Natural ecosystems (that is, relatively undisturbed by human activity) provide vital contributions to human well-being and quality of life known as ecosystem services (European Environmental Agency 2018). While built environment systems are dominated by human development and activities, natural systems provide important ecosystem services, such as stormwater flow, amelioration of temperature extremes, provision of food and water, and improved physical and mental health.

The harmony with nature principle can most effectively be realized through an *ecosystem approach* that holistically integrates physical, biological, social, and cultural patterns and processes while accounting for natural ecosystem structure, functions, and change over time. For planning purposes, the ultimate intent is to ensure that natural systems are healthy and functional, that development reinforces natural systems, and that human health and well-being are sustained through access to nature.

Table 6.1 Ecosystem Approach

Policy Directions

Use an integrated ecosystem approach to sustain the health of natural systems and the ecosystem services and benefits they provide.

Use best available science in planning for the natural environment, including information on soils, water, air and climate, and habitat for all decision-making.

Applications

Maintain a comprehensive database of natural resources and systems for use in planning and decision-making. Regularly update the database to reflect environmental changes and new information available.

Implement an ecosystem approach to decision-making that accounts for the effects of projects and programs on natural resources and systems. Apply this approach to the development review and approval process, public investments, initiatives, and partnerships.

Develop regulations, standards, and incentives to maintain and restore natural resources and systems.

Example: Stearns County, Minnesota

The *Stearns 2040 Comprehensive Plan* is an example of an ecosystem approach to planning. A key purpose of the plan is to protect, restore, and preserve the county's natural resources, including wetlands, surface and groundwater, prairie, woodlands, habitat corridors, scenic views, agricultural land, resource extraction areas, and other open land. The plan includes a *Natural Resource Manual*, which provides information on the county's natural resources, parks, open spaces, and trails and is the foundation for the natural resource overlay on the Future Land Use Plan map. A chapter of the plan is devoted to sustainable agricultural practices and the interface of rural areas with urban communities.

Ecosystem Components

Ecosystems include both inorganic and living components. Inorganic elements include minerals, water, air, sunlight, and more. All living forms – from single-celled organisms to more complex flora and fauna (including humans) – are members of ecosystems. Plants that convert light into chemical energy through photosynthesis and generate oxygen are the primary ecosystem producers. An ecosystem also includes organisms that receive their energy by consuming plants and other living creatures, as well as organisms that decompose organic materials and make nutrients available for plants.

From a planning standpoint, major ecosystem components that should be addressed in the comprehensive plan include land, water, the atmosphere (air and climate), flora and fauna, and environmentally sensitive areas (Figure 6.1).

Land

Land is the foundation of community; how it is used is key to the sustainability of human settlement and of all species on our planet. Throughout human history, many cultures have had a spiritual connection with land and the sense of place it engenders. In the modern era, the predominant paradigm has viewed land as a commodity for purchase and sale, or expendable for purposes such as resource extraction or waste disposal. The 20th-century environmental movement emerged largely in response to the degradation of natural resources that resulted from this viewpoint.

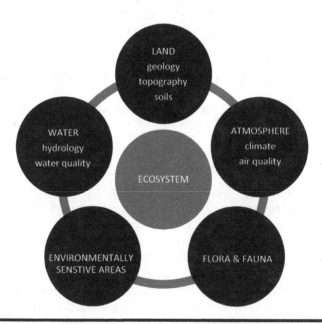

Figure 6.1 Ecosystem Approach

Land resource management continues to be a complex and challenging issue in the 21st century. Unsustainable practices result in adverse impacts such as soil contamination, erosion, and increased risk from natural hazards. By considering the community's physical base – its geology, topography, and soils – from the inventory and analysis through policy development to implementation – the comprehensive plan can set the direction for sustainable use of the land.

Inventory and Analysis

Topics to address in the inventory and analysis include surficial geology (landforms and the unconsolidated sediments that lie beneath them); topography (the slopes and contours of the land surface); and soils (organic and other materials at the surface that support plant growth). Landforms shape the physical setting of a community while topography and soils affect land suitability for different uses. Healthy soils and the microorganisms they contain are critical to support plant communities that provide essential ecosystem services and food and fiber production to meet human needs. Development constraints include steep slopes, susceptibility to landslides, hydric soils/depth to water table, shrink-swell potential, and depth to bedrock. Inventory information includes elevations, slopes, and soil types. This information

Table 6.2 Land

Policy Directions
Protect and preserve critical areas and environmentally sensitive lands from disturbance.
Conserve significant landforms (for example, hillsides, ridges, and lowlands) and viewsheds.
Maintain prime agricultural and resource lands.
Remediate and restore brownfields and other environmentally damaged sites.

Applications
Use land suitability analyses to guide policy and decision-making on the built environment.
Use techniques such as overlay zones and conservation development to conserve natural landforms.
Apply topographic and soils information to planning for public infrastructure and private development, in order to minimize adverse environmental impacts, decrease hazard risks, and lower construction costs.
Develop programs, regulations, and incentives to maintain resource lands, including prime agricultural soil and farmland.
Remediate and restore brownfields and other environmentally damaged sites.
Restrict human activity on contaminated sites, until such a time that the sites can be cleaned up and restored for productive uses.

can be overlaid with other natural factors such as wetlands, floodplains, and vegetation to indicate areas of the community that are more or less suitable for uses such as urban development, agriculture, and conservation.

Water

Water is essential for all life. The hydrologic cycle – the continuous movement of water above, below, and on the earth's surface – supports natural ecosystems and human needs such as potable water, irrigation, and industrial consumption (Figure 6.2). Human uses generate wastewater that is discharged to local waterways. Stormwater is the product of precipitation that flows overland as runoff rather than being absorbed into the ground. Flooding results when large volumes of runoff, typically from impervious surfaces such as streets and buildings, flow into rivers, streams, and adjacent low-lying areas.

Water quality became a national priority in the 1970s, following decades of discharging untreated wastewater, industrial pollutants, and other harmful substances into waterways. The *Clean Water Act* (1972, amended 1977, 1987) has created the basic structure for regulating discharges of pollutants into the waters of the United

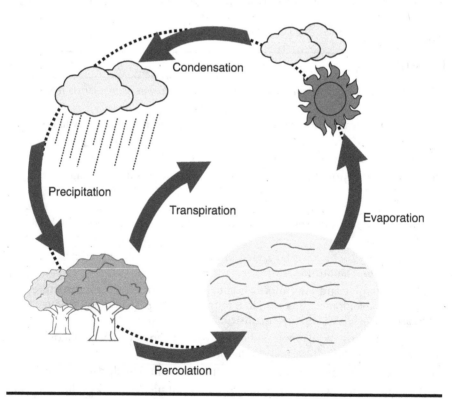

Figure 6.2 Hydrologic Cycle

States and established quality standards for surface waters. The *Flood Disaster Protection Act* (1973, amended 1982, 2004) has made the purchase of flood insurance mandatory for the protection of property located in special flood hazard areas.

Although water occurs naturally as a single, continuously circulating resource, its different manifestations and uses have traditionally been managed by separate professions and agencies, including water, wastewater, and stormwater utilities, natural resource managers, agricultural water districts, floodplain managers, and others. Water and land-use planning are highly interrelated but have often not been coordinated in practice. In recent years, an alternative paradigm has emerged called the *One Water* approach. This approach is based upon the idea that all water within a watershed is hydrologically interconnected and is most effectively and sustainably managed using an integrated approach (Cesanek, Elmer, and Graef 2017).

One Water Planning

The One Water framework embodies a holistic approach to planning for water, with the goal of improving, restoring, and maintaining watershed health and the ecosystem services provided by surface and groundwater resources (Figure 6.3). It emphasizes the need to coordinate land-use planning with water resource management. Having a full understanding of hydrologic conditions, including water availability, water reuse, and water discharges, is key to integrating One Water planning into the comprehensive plan (U.S. Water Alliance 2016). A typical One Water framework includes the following:

- Identification of the community's water resources (watersheds, waterways, water bodies, and groundwater).
- An assessment of whether water resources function in ways that support healthy people, habitats, and aquatic life.
- Information on and evaluation of water quality.
- Information on and evaluation of water quantity and demands for current and future water supply.
- Water conservation and opportunities for water reuse.
- Wastewater management and stormwater management, including an evaluation of the quality of water discharged into area waterways and natural ecosystems.

The One Water framework views water as a system that interacts with other systems addressed in the comprehensive plan, such as land use, built infrastructure, community facilities and services, parks and open space, and flora and fauna. It can be used to integrate policies, strategies, and implementation actions for different plan components to improve the health of people and ecosystems and achieve more sustainable, resilient,

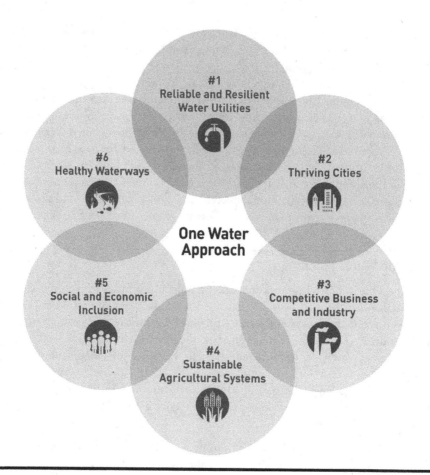

Figure 6.3 One Water Approach

and equitable outcomes. The One Water planning process is particularly useful in areas where sources of water are limited, such as arid parts of the American West, as well as in areas where water quality is compromised by urban runoff, wastewater discharges, or other sources of pollution (Lincoln Institute of Land Policy 2019).

Inventory and Analysis

Hydrologic conditions, including water quantity, quality, and availability, are critical for human health, commerce, and agriculture, as well as for ecological systems and habitats. Geospatial data is generally available for surface and groundwater resources at a level of data appropriate for comprehensive planning purposes. Watersheds are the basic unit of analysis for surface water hydrology. Surface water resources include rivers, streams, water bodies, and water supply reservoirs. Historic maps with stream location information can be used to determine natural hydrologic patterns in urban areas where waterways have been replaced with pipes and culverts. Areas susceptible to flooding can be determined from flood insurance rate maps or other sources (see discussion of *Natural Hazards and Resilience* below). Groundwater resources include underground aquifers, aquifer recharge areas, water supply wells (including surrounding areas of influence), and areas with a high groundwater table (which replenish natural ecosystems while presenting constraints to human uses such as development and agriculture).

Table 6.3 Water

Policy Directions

Protect and conserve water sources, including rivers and streams, shorelines and wetlands, floodplains and groundwater, and maintain infrastructure to ensure adequate facilities for clean water delivery and use.

Advance an integrated One Water approach to managing water resources in ways that respect natural hydrologic conditions and flows, maintain ecosystem health, and meet human needs for water.

Applications

Develop and implement an integrated, cross-disciplinary water resource planning and management strategy that addresses watershed and ecosystem health; water sources, supply, quantity, and quality; water conservation and reuse, and stormwater and wastewater management.

Reduce water use, especially for buildings and landscapes, through conservation practices and reuse.

Develop and implement a regulatory framework to support One Water planning actions and practices.

Example: Hillsborough County, Florida

Hillsborough County, located on Florida's west coast in the Tampa-Saint Petersburg metropolitan area, revised its comprehensive plan to include a One Water element. This new element integrates elements from previous plans that addressed topics such as stormwater management, potable water, and sanitary sewage. Recognizing the interrelatedness and importance of water planning issues, its purpose is to ensure that water is "provided, collected, treated, and managed" sustainably for community needs today and in the future. Plan strategies include protecting and preserving natural water systems, incorporating green infrastructure, conserving water, and responding to climate change. From an economic perspective, the plan advocates co-location of water facilities with other infrastructure, maintaining and maximizing existing water assets, and planning water infrastructure to encourage fiscal sustainability and the efficient use and redevelopment of land.

Air

Together with land and water, air (that is, the atmosphere, which is the envelope of gases surrounding the earth) is necessary to sustain all life on the planet. The atmospheric layer closest to the earth's surface, which is most affected by land uses and the emission of pollutants by human activities, is of particular concern for planning.

Air quality varies widely between rural areas, urban areas, and areas exposed to stationary and mobile sources of harmful emissions. Under the *Clean Air Act*, the U.S. Environmental Protection Agency has established *National Ambient Air Quality Standards* (NAAQS) for six air pollutants or groups of pollutants: sulfur dioxide, particulate matter, nitrogen dioxide, carbon monoxide, ground-level ozone, and lead. Exposure to air pollution can result in chronic ailments, such as cardiovascular disease, pulmonary disease (including lung cancer), asthma, and other respiratory conditions. Air pollution also contributes to developmental damage, increased susceptibility to infections, and early death (American Lung Association 2019). Moreover, greenhouse gas emissions to the atmosphere from local and regional sources contribute to global climate change. In addition to human health impacts, atmospheric pollutants (primarily sulfur dioxide and nitrogen oxide) from burning fossil fuels cause harm to natural ecosystems.

While pollution from industry, energy production, or processing activities are primary contributors to poor air quality, transportation-related activities and certain land-use patterns also are major factors. In many urban areas, transportation-related air pollution may account for more than half of the contaminants in the air.

Inventory and Analysis

The Environmental Protection Agency maintains information on the attainment status (conformance with air quality standards) of geographic areas within the United States (U.S. Chamber of Commerce 2010). This information should be documented in the inventory and analysis, along with the locations of stationary (for

Table 6.4 Air

Policy Directions
Improve and protect air quality to meet or be better than federal and state air quality standards.

Applications
Identify major emitters of air pollution, including mobile, area, and point sources. Develop strategies to reduce pollutants from each of these sources.
Identify local areas of concentrated air pollution, focusing on minority, poor, and other vulnerable communities. Develop strategies to mitigate effects, such as reducing transportation-related sources of pollution, filtering point source emissions, and expanding tree cover.

example, power plants and industrial districts) and mobile (for example, freeways and major arterials) sources of pollution. Juxtaposing this information with land-use data, prevailing wind directions, and tree canopy cover (which absorbs air pollutants and ameliorates the urban heat island effect) will reveal areas that are particularly sensitive to air pollution. Studies have demonstrated that poor and minority communities are disproportionately affected by air pollution relative to the overall population (Mikati et al. 2018).

Climate

Climate refers to the meteorological conditions in a region over an extended period of time (as opposed to weather, which reflects short-term fluctuations of the atmosphere). Climactic factors such as average and extreme temperatures, wind directions and velocity, amount and intensity of precipitation, and seasonal variations in these conditions shape the region's landforms, hydrology, native flora and flora, and its suitability for human habitation and uses.

Scientific evidence indicates that the global climate is changing due to increasing levels of carbon dioxide and other greenhouse gases in the atmosphere caused by fossil fuel emissions, deforestation, and other human activities. Observed effects include increasing temperature extremes and heavy precipitation events; shrinking glaciers, snow cover, and sea ice; sea level rise, ocean warming, and more frequent coastal flooding; changes in species habitat and migration patterns; and increasing wildfires. Implications for local communities include increasing frequency and severity of natural hazard occurrences (see Natural Hazards and Resilience below), declining human health, reduced economic productivity, and a host of other impacts. Low-income communities, communities of color, older adults, and children are particularly vulnerable to the negative impacts of climate change (U.S. Global Change Research Program 2018).

Addressing the causes of climate change through *mitigation* (reducing or preventing greenhouse gas emissions) and minimizing its effects through *adaptation* (increasing community resilience to climate-related impacts) is the defining challenge of the 21st century (Infield, Abunnasr, and Ryan 2018) (Figure 6.4). It is vitally important that all components of the comprehensive plan work together to meet this challenge. Policies related to land use and the built environment, for example, can reduce greenhouse gas emissions from the building and transportation sectors and reduce exposure to natural hazards (see Chapters 7 and 8). Policies related to social systems can address inequities that make segments of the community more vulnerable to climate change impacts (see Chapter 9). Policies related to public health can increase overall community resilience by increasing wellness and reducing health disparities between different populations (see Chapter 11).

Applying a *climate lens* in the planning process can promote a more cohesive approach to addressing climate change mitigation and adaptation. Examples of the wide range of practices that relate to climate change include reduced impervious surface coverage, water resource conservation, and maintenance of corridors for the migration of wildlife and plant species. Infrastructure Canada, a federal department, has developed a climate lens to address the climate change impacts of proposed infrastructure projects. This lens has two components: a greenhouse gas mitigation assessment and a climate change resilience assessment. The lens serves as a resource to increase knowledge about climate change, change behaviors, and promote consideration of green approaches to facilities and services (Infrastructure Canada 2019).

Table 6.5 Climate

Policy Directions

Reduce and mitigate sources and activities that contribute to greenhouse gas.

Adapt to changing climate conditions to minimize adverse effects on the environment, economy, and public health, especially to reduce impacts on vulnerable populations.

Applications

Develop greenhouse gas (GHG) emissions inventories and climate action plans to reduce or eliminate emissions.

Implement strategies to reduce carbon footprints from direct and indirect emissions (that is, from fossil fuel consumption, production, and transport of goods and services used by the community).

Expand the use of renewable energy and cleaner alternative forms of energy.

Develop and implement adaptation strategies to prevent or minimize the adverse effects of climate change.

Implement nature-based solutions to address climate change (for example, tree planting programs to sequester carbon and ameliorate the urban heat island effect).

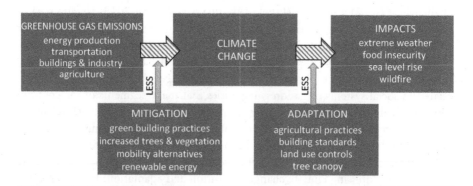

Figure 6.4 Climate Change Model

Example: San Diego County, California

The State of California has made a strong commitment to address the reduction of greenhouse gas emissions through legislation and executive orders. A number of these provisions are directed toward local general plans. San Diego County's General Plan prominently addresses climate change and emissions reduction. A guiding principle in the plan is to "maintain environmentally sustainable communities and reduce greenhouse gas emissions that contribute to climate change." Dozens of policies address climate change across all plan elements, including land use, mobility, conservation and open space, and housing. Examples of these policies include energy efficiency, reduced water consumption, preservation of green infrastructure, carbon-reducing landscaping, and education.

Flora and Fauna

Flora and fauna are the plant and animal populations that inhabit a particular region or were present in the region during a historic time period. Plant communities are associations of plant species that share a common environment in which they interact with each other, animal populations, and physical factors such as soil, hydrology, and climate. Native plant and animal species are adapted to the region's land, water, and climactic conditions, but their habitats have been extensively altered by human activities such as agriculture and urban development or supplanted by nonnative species introduced from other parts of the globe. While typically not providing the same level of ecosystem services as naturally occurring communities, most nonnative species have relatively benign environmental effects. Invasive species (including plants, animals, insect pests, and diseases), however, can cause serious ecological and economic damage, such as habitat disruption, resource competition that can lead to extinction of native plants and animals, reduced biodiversity, and impacts on local commercial activities. Climate change impacts such as warming temperatures, shifting seasons, and increasingly severe natural hazards (droughts, wildfires, floods, and so on) are stressing native habitats, facilitating the spread of invasive species, and expanding the range of vector-borne diseases that threaten human health.

Inventory and Analysis

The inventory and analysis should begin by understanding the flora and fauna that naturally occur in the region. Various classification systems divide the earth into biomes, ecoregions, and bioregions, which are large areas containing recurring, geographically distinct natural communities and species. Information on natural habitat areas, wetlands, and vegetative patterns (including tree canopy) is available from sources such as the *National Land Cover Database*, the *National Wetlands Inventory*, and satellite imagery. Information on ecologically valuable natural areas, plant and animal communities, and rare, threatened, and endangered species can be obtained from state natural heritage area programs (United States Geological Survey 2016; United States Fish and Wildlife Service 2020).

Table 6.6 Flora and Fauna

Policy Directions
Protect and restore native vegetation and species.
Discourage the use of nonnative plants that may become invasive.

Applications
Implement policies and programs to maintain and restore native plant communities and habitat for wildlife, including migration corridors.
Implement measures to regulate and control invasive species that threaten native vegetation and habitats.

> ### Example: Eugene, Oregon
>
> The state capital of Oregon, Eugene has developed a policy framework addressing native and invasive plant species. In recognition of the environmental and economic impacts of invasive species on native habitat, the policy framework prohibits the introduction of specified invasive plants and promotes the use of native vegetation, especially for city projects and programs. The city has developed plant lists to guide implementation of its policy framework. The lists identify exotic and invasive plants, as well as beneficial native plants (City of Eugene n.d.).

Environmentally Sensitive Areas

Environmentally sensitive areas contain land, water, and/or biological resources that are ecologically significant and easily disturbed by human activity. Examples include steep slopes and geologically unstable areas; wetlands, floodplains, and riparian corridors; and high-quality natural habitats. These areas provide important ecosystem services such as soil formation, nutrient cycling, and maintenance of biodiversity; natural regulation of water supply, quality, and flooding; moderation of climate and extreme weather; and cultural, aesthetic, and recreational benefits. Protecting and restoring environmentally sensitive areas helps maintain human and ecosystem health, mitigate climate change by sequestering carbon, reduce risks from natural hazards, and reduce the costs and impacts of development on natural systems.

Inventory and Analysis

Inventorying environmentally sensitive areas draws on the information developed for land, water, and flora and fauna to identify areas that have high ecological value (for example, priority habitat areas identified by a natural heritage program), are

Table 6.7 Environmentally Sensitive Areas

Policy Directions

Preserve and protect environmentally sensitive areas from harm by human disturbance and incompatible land uses.

Applications

Identify environmentally sensitive areas through the inventory and analysis process. Reassess environmentally sensitive areas prior to plan amendments or updates.

Use regulations and incentives such as overlay districts, transfer of development rights, and setback requirements to protect environmentally sensitive areas.

Prioritize environmentally sensitive areas for preservation through acquisition or conservation easements.

Restore the ecological functions of degraded resources (for example, steep slopes experiencing erosion due to the removal of vegetative cover).

Partner with nonprofit organizations and landowners to preserve and restore environmentally sensitive areas.

particularly vulnerable to human disturbance (for example, steep slopes), and/or at risk from natural hazards (for example, designated floodplain areas). These areas can be overlaid to identify priorities for open space and less intensive urban uses. Often following natural drainage patterns organized around watersheds and river and stream networks, they can provide the basis for designing a green infrastructure network that shapes land use, conservation, development at the community-wide scale.

The *Stearns 2040 Comprehensive Plan* for Stearns County, Minnesota (cited above) is a good example of a plan that addresses environmentally sensitive areas. It includes policies to preserve and restore critical natural areas and to avoid impairment of water resources.

Green Infrastructure

The term *green infrastructure* was first used by the Florida Greenways Commission in calling for the establishment of a statewide network of conservation lands, open spaces, and trails (Florida Greenways Commission 1994). More recently, the term has been applied to stormwater management practices that use natural systems or mimic natural processes to infiltrate, evapotranspirate, and/or recycle stormwater runoff (U.S. Environmental Protection Agency, n.d.).[3]

These two definitions – a landscape-scale network of natural areas, greenways, and green spaces and local green stormwater management practices – form a continuum across scales, unified by the idea that green infrastructure provides ecosystem services and benefits for people and other species (Rouse and Bunster-Ossa 2013). Components of a connected green infrastructure network can include, among others, natural areas, forests and farmlands, parks, natural waterways and riparian corridors (sometimes referred to as blue infrastructure), the urban tree canopy, and local design features such as green streets, green roofs, bioswales, and rain gardens.

Inventory and Analysis

Various tools and sources of data are available to assess the extent (coverage) and condition of the urban tree canopy, a critical component of green infrastructure.[4] Identifying the existing tree canopy and opportunities to expand its coverage can inform development of policies to maximize the benefits provided by this resource, such as reduced stormwater runoff, improved air quality, carbon sequestration, and amelioration of the urban heat island effect. Information on the urban tree canopy and other green infrastructure components can be overlain with protected land status data to identify gaps and opportunities to establish a connected network.

The Trust for Public Land, which focuses on creating, preserving, and expanding parks and open space, regularly conducts an inventory of parklands in the 100 largest cities in the United States. According to the inventory, the average amount of parkland in these cities is approximately 13 acres per 1,000 people (The Trust for Public Land 2019). Even more important than the amount of parkland is the *accessibility* of parks and open spaces to the residents of communities, large and small. The U.S. Conference of Mayors has adopted a resolution setting a goal for all Americans to live within a ten-minute walk to a park or green space (U.S. Conference of Mayors 2017). Local governments evaluating the adequacy of their park and open space resources can use this and other sources as a basis for determining needs.[5]

Table 6.8 Green Infrastructure

Policy Directions

Protect, develop, and manage a network of green open spaces and resources, such as natural habitat areas, parks, greenways, and the urban tree canopy.

Utilize green stormwater management practices that reduce or retain stormwater runoff on the site.

Ensure equitable access to green infrastructure resources, particularly for underserved populations.

Applications

Use regulations and incentives (such as conservation development and transfer of development rights), public investments, and partnerships (for example, with nonprofit land conservation organizations) to create a connected green infrastructure network.

Develop design standards for the use of green stormwater management standards as an alternative to conventional gray engineering approaches.

Develop a program to increase tree canopy coverage, especially in areas where tree cover may be deficient.

> **Example: Lancaster County, Pennsylvania**
>
> *Greenscapes*, the Green Infrastructure Element of the *Lancaster County Comprehensive Plan*, defines a vision, goals and objectives, strategies, and tools to preserve, conserve, restore, and enhance natural resources through a countywide green infrastructure system. *Greenscapes* emphasizes the need for cross-sectoral collaboration by government, institutions, nonprofits, civic groups, private landowners, developers, and businesses to create the green infrastructure system. It provides a toolbox of implementation tools that can be used by these different groups, divided into four broad categories: policy and planning, regulation, capital investment, and outreach and partnerships.

Natural Hazards and Resilience

Local communities are subject to a range of natural hazards. Natural hazards include both *shocks* (extreme weather events such as hurricanes and other disasters such as wildfires and earthquakes) and *stresses* (prolonged or chronic conditions such as drought, the urban heat island effect, and poor air quality) (Arup n.d.). As noted, the frequency and severity of many hazards are being exacerbated by climate change. Risks will vary based on location and geography, but all communities are vulnerable to different types of natural hazards.

In a planning context, the term resilience is commonly used to refer to recovery following natural disasters or human-caused disruptive events. While disaster preparedness and recovery have traditionally been the realm of emergency management and hazard mitigation professionals, the comprehensive plan provides the opportunity to set the direction for a more integrated approach to increasing disaster resilience. This approach encompasses both hazard mitigation (actions taken to avoid or minimize risk to life and property from hazard events) and planning for a rapid and complete recovery after a disaster strikes.[6] It should be combined with broader efforts to reduce social vulnerabilities, address inequities, and strengthen community resilience (for example, by addressing the social determinants of health – the conditions where people live, work, learn, and play – which affect a wide range of health risks and outcomes).

Inventory and Analysis

Natural hazards and at-risk areas of the community should be identified and mapped as part of the inventory and analysis. Various sources of information can be used to map areas vulnerable to shocks (for example, flooding, wildfire, earthquakes, and landslides) and stresses (for example, high temperatures and poor air quality). The *Flood Insurance Rate Maps* (FIRM) are the standard source of spatial information on flooding (Federal Emergency Management Agency 2020). However, these maps show estimated flood risk at the time detailed engineering studies were conducted and may be outdated. Moreover, they do not account for new development that can alter flood conditions within watersheds or for projected climate change effects such as sea-level rise and increased storm frequency and severity. These limitations should be clearly stated in the inventory and analysis and, where possible, supplemental information sources used to identify at-risk areas. For example, sea-level rise in coastal areas can be projected using the *Sea Level Rise Viewer* (Digital Coast n.d.).

Table 6.9 Natural Hazards

Policy Directions

Restrict or limit new development in floodplains, coastal shorelines, areas at risk of wildfire, geologically unstable areas, and other areas prone to natural hazards.

Reduce risk from natural hazards through mitigation, prioritizing vulnerable communities.

Plan for post-disaster recovery, including restoration of essential services, reconstruction, economic recovery, and human wellness.

Applications

Identify areas susceptible to flooding, wildfires, earthquakes, landslides, and other natural hazards in the inventory and analysis.

Develop regulations, incentives, and other approaches to limit development in areas that are susceptible to natural hazards.

Prepare a pre-disaster plan for post-disaster recovery that addresses emergency response, recovery, and long-term actions to increase resilience to future disasters.

Example: Manitou Springs, Colorado

Plan Manitou is the integrated comprehensive plan and hazard mitigation plan for the City of Manitou Springs, a community of approximately 5,000 residents at the base of Pikes Peak. The city has a history of natural disasters, including wildfires and flash floods. *Plan Manitou* was funded through a Resilience Planning Grant from the U.S. Department of Housing and Urban Development, with assistance of the Colorado Department of Local Affairs. The integrated plan is designed to guide future growth; support economic, environmental, and social sustainability; promote health and food access; preserve historic and cultural assets; and foster tourism. A prominent feature of the plan is its Reinvestment and Resiliency Framework. This section incorporates risk management and hazards mitigation, along with other environmental factors, in scenario planning and decision-making for the city's subareas (Compact of Colorado Communities 2018).

Natural hazard mapping can be overlain with social vulnerability maps to identify at-risk populations and with maps of sensitive environmental resources to identify priorities for conservation. The goal is to minimize human harm and property damage through planning and implementation.

Summary

Land, water, biological communities (flora and fauna), air, and climate form the life support system for human habitation. Natural systems are inextricably linked with built environment systems and are essential to support healthy, sustainable communities. Ensuring that the contributions of natural resources to human well-being are explicitly recognized and valued – the Harmony with Nature principle – is best realized through a holistic approach that addresses the natural environment systems as an integrated ecosystem, with the overall goal of maintaining and restoring ecosystem services and benefits for people and other living species.

Landforms, topography, and soils shape the physical setting of a community and its suitability for different land uses. Water supports natural ecosystems and human needs for drinking water, irrigation, consumption by industrial and other land uses, and wastewater and stormwater management. Similar to the ecosystem approach, the One Water planning framework addresses these needs holistically: through coordinated planning and water resource management to sustain the health of the hydrologic systems on which human well-being depends. Particularly in urban areas, air quality has diminished because of harmful emissions from stationary and mobile sources. Impacts on poor and minority communities have been disproportionate. The comprehensive plan should prioritize actions to address these inequities by reducing pollution emissions and mitigating their effects.

Naturally occurring plant and animal communities have been extensively altered by human disturbance and the introduction of invasive and other nonnative species. In its broadest definition, green infrastructure is a strategically planned, community-wide network – consisting of preserved and restored natural habitat areas, parks, open spaces, the urban tree canopy, and other green spaces and resources – that is designed to restore natural functions and maximize ecosystem services and benefits. Environmentally sensitive areas containing land, water, and/or biological resources that are easily disturbed by human activity should be protected and can provide the foundation for the green infrastructure network.

Climate change caused by increasing levels of carbon dioxide in the atmosphere impacts both natural and human ecosystems. These impacts include more frequent and severe natural hazards, including shocks (such as hurricanes and wildfires) and stresses (such as drought and the urban heat island effect). The comprehensive plan should incorporate strategies to mitigate and adapt to climate change and natural hazards to reduce social vulnerabilities, address inequities, and build broader community resilience. Planning with a climate lens across natural, built, social, and economic systems is required to address the implications of climate change for communities.

Notes

1 See Chapter 1, Table 1.1 and Appendix A (extracted from Godschalk and Rouse 2015).
2 A number of the policy directions and applications are derived from the Comprehensive Plan Standards (Godschalk and Rouse 2015).
3 Green stormwater management practices are also referred to as low-impact development.
4 For example, i-Tree is a suite of assessment tools developed by the U.S. Forest Service that can be used to quantify the benefits provided by community forests and trees at multiple scales (U.S. Department of Agriculture n.d.).
5 For example, see Barth (2016).
6 Note the difference between the definitions of hazard mitigation (actions taken to avoid or minimize risk to life and property from hazard events) and climate change mitigation (efforts to reduce or prevent emissions of greenhouse gases).

References

American Lung Association (2019). *State of the Air Report*. Accessed at https://www.stateoftheair.org/

Arup, supported by the Rockefeller Foundation (n.d.). City Resilience Index. Accessed at https://www.cityresilienceindex.org/#/

Barth, David. (2016). *Alternatives for Determining Parks and Recreation Level of Service*. PAS Memo. Chicago, IL: American Planning Association.

Cesanek, William, Vicki Elmer, and Jennifer Graef (2017). *Planners and Water*, Planning Advisory Service Report 588. Chicago, IL: American Planning Association.

Clean Water Act [33 U.S.C. §1251 et seq.] (1972, amended 1977, 1987). United States Code, Office of the Law Revision Council of the U.S. House of Representatives.

Compact of Colorado Communities (2018). *Manitou Springs: Hazards Planning Pays Off*. Accessed at https://www.compactofcoloradocommunities.org/

Digital Coast (n.d.). *Sea Level Rise Viewer*. U.S. Department of Commerce, National Oceanic and Atmospheric Administration, Office for Coastal Zone Management. Accessed at https://coast.noaa.gov/digitalcoast/tools/slr.html

Eugene, Oregon (n.d.). *Native and Invasive Plant Policies*. Accessed at https://www.eugene-or.gov/648/Native-and-Invasive-Plant-Policies

European Environmental Agency (2018). *Land Systems at European Level – Analytical Assessment Framework*. Accessed at https://www.eea.europa.eu/themes/landuse/land-systems

Federal Emergency Management Agency (2020). *The Flood Insurance Rate Maps*. Accessed at https://www.fema.gov/flood-maps

Flood Disaster Protection Act. [42 U.S.C. § 5121 et. seq.] (1973, amended 1982, 2004). United States Code, Office of the Law Revision Council of the U.S. House of Representatives.

Florida Greenways Commission (1994). *Creating a Statewide Greenway System: Report to the Governor*. Tallahassee, FL: Florida Greenways Commission.

Infield, Elizabeth Hamin, Yaser Abunnasr, and Robert Ryan, eds. (2018). *Planning for Climate Change: A Reader in Green Infrastructure and Sustainable Design for Resilient Cities*. Philadelphia, PA: Routledge Press.

Infrastructure Canada (2019). *Climate Lens – General Guidance*. Ottawa, ON, Canada: Canadian Parliament and the national Minister of Infrastructure and Communities.

Lincoln Institute of Land Policy (2019). *Land Lines: Colorado River Basin Issue*, 31:1 (January). Boston, MA: Lincoln Institute of Land Policy.

Mikati, Ihab, Adam Benson, Thomas Lugen, Jason Sacks, and Jennifer Richmond-Bryant (2018). *Disparities in Distribution of Particulate Matter Emission Sources by Race and Poverty Status. American Journal of Public Health (AJPH)*, 108:4. Washington, DC: American Public Health Association. pp. 480–485.

Rouse, David C. and Ignacio F. Bunster-Ossa (2013). *Green Infrastructure: A Landscape Approach*, Planning Advisory Service Report 571. Chicago, IL: American Planning Association.

The Trust for Public Land (2019). *ParkScore.* Denver, CO: The Trust for Public Land.

U.S. Chamber of Commerce (2010). *Consequences of Non-Attainment.* Issue Brief. Accessed at https://www.uschamber.com/consequences-non-attainment

U.S. Conference of Mayors (2017). *Resolution, 85th Annual Meeting* (Miami Beach, FL). Washington, DC: U.S. Conference of Mayors.

U.S. Department of Agriculture, U.S. Forest Service (n.d.). i-Tree Tools. Accessed at https://www.itreetools.org/

U.S. Environmental Protection Agency (n.d.). *Green Infrastructure Glossary.* Accessed at https://www.epa.gov/green-infrastructure/what-green-infrastructure

U.S. Fish and Wildlife Service (2020). *National Wetlands Inventory.* Washington, DC: U.S. Department of the Interior.

U.S. Geological Survey (2016). *National Land Cover Database.* Washington, DC: U.S. Department of the Interior.

U.S. Global Change Research Program (2018). Volume II. Accessed at https://nca2018.globalchange.gov/

U.S. Water Alliance (2016). *One Water Roadmap: The Sustainable Management of Life's Most Essential Resource.* Accessed at http://uswateralliance.org/sites/uswateralliance.org/files/publications/Roadmap%20FINAL.pdf

Wapner, Paul (2010). *Living Through the End of Nature: The Future of American Environmentalism.* Cambridge, MA: The MIT Press.

Chapter 7

Built Environment Systems

Land Use, Development, and Community Character

As with the natural environment (with which it is inextricably connected), the *built environment* is a complex, dynamic system comprising subsystems, such as land use, mobility networks, and utility infrastructure. This chapter addresses several major aspects of the built environment: land use and development patterns, community character, and green development. Chapter 8 addresses mobility and infrastructure systems.

Communities across the United States are in various stages of development, from those that are growing, to those that are relatively stable but susceptible to change, and to those that are experiencing population loss. Rural communities have distinct needs and challenges compared with urban and suburban communities. Built environment systems should reflect each community's unique context and sense of place. Planning frameworks can be tailored for rural places, towns, counties, and small, mid-sized, and large cities to ensure that they are complete communities in their own right. Working with principles of equitable development, choice, human scale, and the wise and efficient use of resources, planning for the built environment can improve quality of life and health for all members of a community.

DOI: 10.4324/9781003024170-9

Sustainability, Resilience, Equity

A sustainable built environment promotes the efficient use of resources, reduces greenhouse gas emissions, is in harmony with natural ecosystems, and advances human well-being. Climate has impacted human settlements throughout history. In the 21st century, it has become evident that buildings, transportation systems, and other components of the built environment contribute to climate change through greenhouse gas emissions. Green development practices reduce these contributions and other negative effects of the built environment on natural resources and systems.

A resilient built environment minimizes risks from natural and human-made disasters that can harm people, property, and essential facilities and services. Resilient planning for the built environment mitigates hazards (for example, by avoiding development in the floodplain) and adapts to the effects of a changing climate. When disasters strike, a resilient community is prepared to respond in ways that ensure people have places to shelter and that essential infrastructure and services are maintained. Resilience also provides a foundation for communities to rebuild in more sustainable and enduring ways following a disaster.

An equitable built environment is one in which resources are equitably distributed throughout the community, providing opportunities for those who are disadvantaged or have suffered from discrimination. Planning for an equitable built environment requires addressing the legacy of exclusionary land use and development practices that restrict opportunities for those of lesser means. An equitable approach to planning the built environment enables a community to ensure full opportunity and access for all people regardless of race, ethnicity, religion, age, gender, or disability.

Complete Communities: A Systems Approach for the Built Environment

In Chapter 6, a framework for addressing the natural environment is presented as an ecosystems approach. Chapters 7 and 8 advance the overarching theme of *complete communities* as framework for planning the built environment.

A complete community is one in which all community members have their basic needs met. Complete communities offer housing for people at all stages of life; a mix of land uses, businesses, and jobs opportunities; easy access to different mobility choices; schools, parks, civic spaces and other forms of social infrastructure; and access to services needed for daily life, such as community facilities, health care, and places to shop for groceries and goods. Complete communities are vibrant, walkable, less reliant on automobiles, and resource efficient, resulting in opportunities for active living, reduction in stress, and a smaller carbon footprint. In short, a complete communities framework enables all types of locales to become vibrant, healthy, and sustainable places in which to live, work, and play (Figure 7.1).

Figure 7.1 Complete Communities Framework

Complete Communities Example: Houston, Texas

The purpose of Houston's Complete Communities Initiative is to transform neighborhoods into healthy and resilient places with inclusive services and amenities. To advance equity and fairness, the initiative focuses on deficiencies in facilities and services in Houston's most "under-resourced" neighborhoods. The program is organized through the mayor's office as a collaborative effort that includes community members and representatives from various city departments.

Ten neighborhoods have been the primary focus of the initiative. For each neighborhood, a data book is developed, as well as an action plan. The action plan lays out a strategy for community engagement, economic opportunity, education, health, safety, housing, parks, mobility, infrastructure, neighborhood character, and community amenities. An investment fund has been established to finance improvements in the focus neighborhoods (Houston n.d.)

Land Use and Development Patterns

Land use can be defined as the organization and spatial arrangement of the environment by people to support human activities and populations. Development patterns (the placement of buildings, facilities, and infrastructure across the landscape) are the physical expression of land use.

The comprehensive plan has traditionally focused on the use of land and how it is developed. Land-use planning should consider which lands should be protected, which lands offer sustainable resource use, which lands present hazards, and which lands are best suited to support human settlement and activities. A complete communities framework provides the basis for an integrated and multifaceted approach to replace the past emphasis on segregating different uses. In rural areas, this means supporting the rural economy, character, and lifestyles. In urban areas, this means providing a mix of uses and services, supported by physical, social, and natural infrastructure to meet community members' needs. Sustainability, resilience, and equity are increased by compact development patterns, infill, and redevelopment as alternatives to the 20th-century paradigm of growing outward through sprawling, low-density development.

Inventory and Analysis

There are a number of approaches and tools that can be used to assess land use and development in the comprehensive plan inventory and analysis. *A developable lands analysis* can be used to assess the amount and condition of vacant and underutilized land that is suitable for development.[1] This analysis can be used in conjunction with past development trends and future population and employment forecasts to understand factors related to land supply and demand.

Analyses can be conducted for various land-use types and relationships, such as resource lands, industrial lands, and land-use mixes and densities. A *resource lands analysis* identifies lands with important natural habitat and environmentally sensitive resources; working forests and farmland; prime agricultural soils; and mineral resources. The analysis should factor in the contributions to the regional economy, local and regional food production, and ecological benefits. Information on hazards, nuisances and health risks, and opportunities for future remediation of sites should be included for resource extraction lands.

An *industrial lands analysis* can be used to inventory and analyze factors related to supply and demand for industrial and manufacturing uses. These factors include industry types (sectors and subsectors) and how they are changing over time; the amount and location of available land for those sectors; supporting infrastructure; and zoning and environmental regulations.[2] Infrastructure information includes utilities (water and wastewater, energy, and telecommunications) and multimodal accessibility (including vehicular, rail, and air service).

The land-use inventory and analysis should address not only the amounts of different land uses, but also the mix of and relationships between land uses, as a basis for understanding and guiding urban form and development patterns. Factors to consider include the distribution of different land uses; the pattern of buildings and structures; the connectivity and condition of streets, sidewalks, and paths; and the location and extent of surface parking.

Actual and allowed densities vary within and across communities. Evaluating densities in the comprehensive plan is important to determine facility and service needs, provide for efficient infrastructure delivery, and understand demand for alternative mobility modes. Transit-supportive densities, for example, can be measured by number of dwelling units and/or jobs per acre.

A *susceptibility to change analysis* is useful to identify infill and redevelopment potential (and possible effects such as gentrification and displacement) in predominantly developed communities. This analysis identifies areas that may be subject to conversion to other land uses, disinvestment, or reinvestment due to changing market conditions. Examples include large vacant or underutilized properties (including surface parking lots), obsolescent commercial uses, neighborhoods experiencing decline and disinvestment, and neighborhoods with investment activity that could displace existing residents.

Resource Lands

Resource lands include working landscapes for agriculture, forestry, and resource extraction. They also include lands with sensitive and valuable natural resources, such as riparian areas, shorelines and wetlands, floodplains, steep slopes, and habitat areas (see Chapter 6). Resource lands are important to the economy, community character, and provide important ecosystem services.

Table 7.1 Resource Lands

Policy Directions
Preserve and maintain resource lands for economic opportunity and the ecosystem services and community benefits they provide.
Limit incompatible uses that may affect working resource lands and environmentally sensitive areas.

Applications
Develop conversation easement, purchase of development rights, and other programs to conserve and maintain working resource lands.
Implement regulatory tools and incentives such as conservation overlay districts, transfer of development rights, and conservation development to preserve resource lands.
Revise zoning and other regulations to allow uses such as urban agriculture and minimize potential incompatibilities and conflicts with adjacent land uses.

Example: Thurston County, Washington

The comprehensive plan for Thurston County (which includes Olympia, Washington's state capitol) includes a Natural Resource Lands element that addresses the county's four main natural resource industries: agriculture, aquaculture, forestry, and mineral resources. (Environmentally sensitive resources are addressed in a separate plan element.) The element notes the importance of natural resource lands to the local and regional economy, as well as the aesthetic, recreational, and environmental benefits they provide to the public. For each natural resource industry, the plan identifies an overall vision, describes the planning context and existing programs, and establishes a detailed framework of goals, objectives, and policies to guide decision-making.

Land-use planning has traditionally treated resource lands as separate from the built environment or (in the example of farmland in a growing metropolitan region) as "holding areas" for future development. While predominantly found in rural areas, resource lands can occur in urban environments. Examples include urban farms and community gardens, remnant forest patches, and undeveloped riparian corridors. A more holistic approach would consider how resource lands can be sustained and connected across rural, suburban, and urban contexts to maintain productive uses, preserve sensitive resources, and provide valuable ecosystem services and benefits. Local food production, for example, strengthens the economy while providing access to fresh and healthy food for community members.

Mixed Land-Use Patterns

The spectrum of developed land uses includes detached, attached, and multifamily residential housing; commercial and office; manufacturing and industrial; and public and institutional uses such as community facilities, educational campuses, and utilities. In the 21st century, there has been growing recognition that rigid separation of these uses in future land-use plans and implementing zoning regulations has resulted in communities becoming more segregated and fragmented rather than complete places. Contemporary planning practice is responding by placing a greater emphasis on the relationships and synergies between different uses and the mobility networks that connect them.

Mixed land-use patterns are characterized by residential and nonresidential located in close proximity to one another. Mixing land uses and providing housing in close proximity to destinations (for example, shops, schools, community facilities, and workplaces) can increase walking and biking and reduce automobile use. Planning for mixed use involves blending compatible land uses, whether in a single building, a complex of buildings, or in a compact neighborhood or district.

Mixed-use development can be horizontal (that is, locating different uses next to each other), or vertical (that is, locating different uses in the same structure, typically residential or office above retail). Mixed land-use patterns should incorporate safe, convenient, accessible, and attractive design features (for example, sidewalks, street furniture, bicycle facilities, and street trees) to promote walking and biking (Godschalk and Rouse 2015).

Table 7.2 Mixed Land-Use Patterns

Policy Directions

Encourage mixed land-use patterns that integrate residential and compatible nonresidential uses.

Incorporate design features into mixed land-use patterns to promote walking and biking.

Applications

Identify existing and potential mixed-use areas in the comprehensive plan inventory and analysis.

Revise zoning and development regulations to facilitate the mixing of residential and compatible nonresidential uses.

Coordinate land use and mobility planning and investments to support walkable, bikeable mixed land-use patterns.

Strategically locate civic and public facilities, such as service centers, schools, and libraries, to provide a more complete, community-serving land-use mix.

Example: Miami-Dade County, Florida

The Land Use Element of the *Comprehensive Development Master Plan* for Miami-Dade County (a consolidated government) calls for an increase in urban infill development to develop mixed-use, multi-modal, sustainable communities. Mixed-use development is identified as a more efficient use of infrastructure and facilities to support alternative mobility modes. Development in mixed-use areas should fit the existing scale and intensity, both vertically and horizontally. Design standards are used to ensure compatibility, with an emphasis on pedestrian-oriented street connectivity.

The plan identifies three types of places as appropriate for mixed-use development: (1) urban centers (regional, metropolitan, and community), (2) mixed-use corridors, and (3) transit corridors (within a half-mile radius). Densities and intensities for each type are defined by floor area ratios and unit counts. The city-county compiles a list of mixed-use projects approved each year, including transit-supportive projects and those in designated centers.

Compact Development

Compact development refers to development that uses land efficiently through creative design of residential, commercial, or mixed uses at the site, neighborhood, or district scales. Compact development often approximates the density and intensity of development that was typical of American communities in the first half of the 20th century (Ohio Balanced Growth Program 2015). Benefits of compact, mixed-use development include increased walking and transit use; reduced energy consumption, pollution, and greenhouse gas emissions; more efficient and cost-effective provision of public infrastructure and facilities such as libraries and recreation centers; and conservation of open space and environmental resources. In addition, compact places with more people and activities can enhance safety, security, and well-being.

Planning for compact places must address the local setting, character, and community needs. Development densities and intensities will vary according to context; for example, what is appropriate for a central city district differs from what is appropriate for a town center or neighborhood.[3] *Transit communities* (also referred to as *transit-oriented development*) are a form of compact, mixed-use development adjacent to transit stations or stops. The mix of uses in a transit community typically includes residences, employment, retail and services, and entertainment. Residents benefit from convenient access to a transit system that connects to destinations throughout the region. Increased transit use can reduce vehicle-miles traveled, associated air pollution and greenhouse gas emissions, and the need to own personal vehicles. Reduced automobile ownership can decrease the need for parking and other automobile-oriented infrastructure.

Table 7.3 Compact Development

Policy Directions
Encourage compact, mixed-use development patterns with densities and intensities appropriate to the community context.
Focus compact development in areas that provide multimodal mobility options.
Provide densities that promote efficient and cost-effective delivery of infrastructure and services, including sufficient population to support regular transit service.

Applications
Revise zoning and development standards to support mixed land-use patterns that are walkable and bikeable and easily served by transit.
Target mobility, infrastructure, and other public investments to support compact development patterns and centers and to leverage desired private investments in these areas.
Promote equitable transit-oriented development that enables all community members to benefit from dense, mixed-use, and pedestrian-oriented land-use patterns near transit hubs.

Large cities and urban regions have a range of compact place types. These can include traditional urban downtowns, secondary employment and mixed-use hubs, and smaller compact places (such as town and neighborhood centers). These places share a common emphasis on mixed uses and multimodal accessibility, including walking and access to transit.

Example: Aurora, Colorado

Aurora Places, the comprehensive plan for Aurora, Colorado, organizes development patterns around a typology of place types rather than traditional land-use categories. Several place types provide focuses for compact, mixed-use development of different types, scales, and densities. Examples include *Urban Districts*, which are citywide centers of employment, culture, and activity; *Industry Hubs*, which are centers of mixed commercial, industrial, and employment uses; and *City Corridors*, which support main street commercial activities and mixed-residential housing. Mobility options and connections vary according to the purpose, uses, and intensity of each place type, consisting of different mixes of transit, bicycle, walking, and vehicular access.

Manufacturing and Industrial Uses

Manufacturing and industrial uses provide employment opportunities and other economic benefits, tax revenues, and services for community members. Planning for these uses traditionally emphasized separation from residential and other uses due to external impacts such as noise, air and water pollution, and freight traffic. Land-use incompatibility is a continuing issue that can be addressed through mitigation measures such as physical separation of incompatible uses, performance standards, and buffer requirements. The evolving nature of 21st-century industrial activities provides opportunities for greater integration of uses and for flexible development forms that can be adapted to meet market changes. Contemporary uses and trends include light manufacturing (production of finished goods from partially processed materials); precision manufacturing; processing of locally grown foods and manufacture of local products; and increasing demand for warehousing and distribution sites driven by e-commerce.

Manufacturing and industrial districts accommodate uses such as business operations, product development, fabrication, and processing, and warehousing and distribution. In some instances, similar businesses intentionally cluster in these districts to take advantage of operational and market synergies. (Other site selection factors include size, infrastructure availability, and transportation access, among others.) An *eco-industrial park* is a cluster of businesses that collaborate to improve economic and environmental performance through practices that share and reuse resources and reduce waste.

Some communities in the United States are experiencing loss of traditional industries and a corresponding reduction in demand for sites dedicated to industrial activities. Others are experiencing increased pressure for conversion of industrially zoned land to other uses, thus threatening to displace existing manufacturing and industrial uses. The comprehensive plan can establish a long-range policy framework and strategy to meet needs for manufacturing and industrial uses, either integrated into mixed-use settings or in designated districts.

Table 7.4 Manufacturing and Industrial Uses

Policy Directions
Develop a strategy to maintain economically productive and viable manufacturing and industrial uses.
Plan for emerging and new manufacturing and industrial uses.
Applications
Conduct a developable lands analysis to determine the amount and capacity of land available for manufacturing and industrial uses.
Designate manufacturing and industrial districts and implement land-use policies and regulations to minimize the conversion of industrially zoned lands to other uses.
Encourage the use of green, resource-efficient, and eco-industrial business practices.

Example: Seattle, Washington

Seattle has two formally designated *manufacturing industrial centers*: Ballard Interbay and Duwamish. These centers were identified through a regional planning process managed by the Puget Sound Regional Council. The intent of formal designation of is to maintain productive economic activities and employment opportunities, to limit encroachment from other uses, and to provide lands for future manufacturing and industrial uses. The *Seattle 2035 Comprehensive Plan* notes that the number of jobs in the two centers has declined but still account for 16 percent of all jobs in the city. The plan establishes a strategy to accommodate a projected 115,000 additional jobs over the 20-year-plan horizon in urban centers, urban villages, and the manu-facturing/industrial centers, which provide site features and services required by some types of businesses and jobs. The plan prioritizes these areas for multi-modal transportation investments.

Infill and Redevelopment

Contiguous development patterns (that is, where new development occurs adjacent to existing development) allow for more efficient use of land and cost-effective provision of public infrastructure, facilities, and services compared with greenfield development at the urban fringe. *Infill and redevelopment* of vacant or underutilized land in existing developed areas can take advantage of already existing infrastructure and services, providing a more fiscally sustainable alternative to costly, environmentally damaging sprawl.[4] Infill also helps create compact, walkable development patterns that support transit use and reduce the need for private automobiles.

Infill development and redevelopment of obsolescent uses can play an important role in a strategy commonly referred to as *retrofitting suburbs*. The 20th-century growth paradigm of separated residential subdivisions, commercial strips, and office parks at the urban edge is changing as suburban locales seek to become more complete communities. Job centers have become more common throughout metropolitan regions, resulting in shifting commuter patterns. At the same time, demographic change in suburban communities is impacting lifestyle preferences, housing needs, and demand for complementary land uses.

In the 21st century, suburban communities are reimagining their mixes of land uses, mobility and accessibility connections, and built form, community character, and sense of place. Strategic use of infill and redevelopment can help create more compact, connected development patterns that better serve the needs of residents. Examples include redeveloping oversized surface parking lots, redesigning commercial strip corridors, incorporating green infrastructure networks, and providing alternatives to automobile use. These approaches and more can be used to transform suburban areas into more complete, full-service communities (Williamson and Dunham-Jones 2021).

Table 7.5 Infill and Redevelopment

Policy Directions

Direct development to vacant and underutilized lands in existing developed areas where infrastructure, facilities, and services are available or can be efficiently provided.

Guide development away from greenfield sites at the urban fringe, which are more expensive to serve with infrastructure and services.

Applications

Conduct developable land and susceptibility to change analyses to identify new development opportunities, prioritizing infill and redevelopment of vacant and underutilized parcels.

Revise development codes and regulations to enable infill and redevelopment, including but not limited to design standards and parking requirements.

Upgrade and maintain existing infrastructure and facilities to support infill and redevelopment.

Example: Fairfax County, Virginia

Fairfax County is a rapidly growing county located in the Washington, DC metropolitan area. The Countywide Policy Element of the *Fairfax County Comprehensive Plan* encourages mixed-use centers, infill, and redevelopment that provide community-supporting retail and service uses. The plan provides guidance for new development to respect the existing community context and to achieve an overall harmonious development pattern.

Tysons Corner, which has a major concentration of retail and office uses, is designated in the countywide plan as an urban development area and a priority for infill and redevelopment. Adopted by amendment to the comprehensive plan, the *Tysons Corner Urban Center Plan* establishes a vision to transform Tysons from a suburban office park and activity center into an active, people-focused, "24/7" urban center. Examples of suburban retrofit strategies include buildings with active street-level uses; streets with traffic calming, sidewalk furniture, and other amenities for pedestrians; and pocket parks designed as community gathering places.

Rural Land Uses

Rural areas have distinctive resources, economies, and characteristics of place that are reflected in land uses such as working farms and forests, natural habitat areas, and small towns and villages. Jurisdictional authority for rural land use varies across the country. The most common model is for unincorporated areas that lack urban infrastructure and services to fall under the jurisdiction of county government. In some states, particularly in the Northeast, towns or townships are responsible for land-use planning and development regulation. Pennsylvania is a hybrid model in which county planning commissions develop county-wide comprehensive plans and provide planning support for local jurisdictions.

Regardless of the jurisdictional context, it is important for the comprehensive plan to address the value rural areas have for nearby cities and towns, and vice versa. Rural land uses should be maintained to support rural character and the rural economy, which benefit the character and economy of the region as a whole. Infill and redevelopment should be prioritized for new development, followed by contiguous development that is planned as a transition to surrounding rural uses. The annexation of rural areas by incorporated municipalities and their conversion to urban uses should occur only in limited circumstances to accommodate defined needs.

Compact development patterns are important considerations in planning for the rural towns and villages that function as centers of rural areas. The character of these places is tied to a distinctive scale that relates to compactness, building form, and the mix of uses. The hub of a town or village center may be only several blocks long or focused on a single intersection. Notwithstanding its size, fostering a critical mass of activity and reinforcing a sense of place in a rural center while maintaining surrounding rural uses can provide economic, environmental, and social benefits. For example, an active and vibrant rural center can provide a hub for transit service that connects to larger towns and cities.

The *rural–urban interface* refers to areas on the fringe of urban development. In some regions, typically where zoning and other planning tools have been coordinated with the provision of urban infrastructure, facilities, and services, there is a distinct demarcation between rural lands and character and urban lands and character. In other instances, there may be a transitional area where outwardly expanding urban development intermixes with rural lands.

Urban growth areas, urban growth boundaries, or *urban service areas* can be used to limit the encroachment of urban land uses onto rural and resource lands. Urban growth areas can be established by counties, cities, rural towns, or regional planning agencies. In addition to protecting rural lands and sustaining the rural economy, they benefit utility providers and taxpayers by facilitating more efficient and cost-effective service delivery.

Table 7.6 Rural Land Uses

Policy Directions
Maintain functional integrity, productivity, and ecosystem services provided by rural land uses.
Minimize the expansion of urban land uses into rural areas.
Preclude urban levels of service in rural areas.

Applications
Develop and implement strategies to maintain and strengthen the economic viability of agriculture and other base components of the rural economy.
Establish urban growth areas, growth boundaries, or service areas to limit expansion of urban uses into rural areas.
Coordinate land-use planning, zoning, infrastructure, utility, and service provision, and annexation policy to support designated urban service and rural resource areas.

Example: Sacramento County, California

The Land Use Element of the *Sacramento County General Plan* includes a section entitled Rural Growth Management and Design. The goal of this section is to maintain "a viable rural and recreational economy in all non-metropolitan areas outside of the Urban Service Boundary." Objectives and policies address rural towns, agricultural lands, and agricultural-residential lands. For rural towns, the objective is to accommodate limited urban growth consistent with infrastructure capacity, natural constraints, and the economic base. The objective for agricultural lands is to ensure the continuation of agricultural production and to preserve open space. For agricultural-residential lands, the objective is to accommodate limited expansion consistent with protecting prime agricultural lands, open space, and groundwater supply and quality. Policies include limiting the expansion of sewer and water treatment and delivery systems and encouraging infill development.

Community Character

Community character refers to the qualities that define a community's identity and sense of place, including its physical design, history and culture, and social dimensions of place. Community character is not fixed in time but continues to evolve and change from one generation to the next. The comprehensive plan provides a vehicle for articulating what defines community character and identity; for identifying the physical, historic, cultural, and social elements of place; and for establishing goals, policies, and strategies to maintain and strengthen community character in the future.

This section addresses key aspects of community character, including community design, cultural and historic resources, and civic spaces, public places, and the arts. Community design refers to the physical organization of the built environment. Cultural and historic resources, civic places, public places, and the arts are vital components of community character that find expression in the built environment.

Inventory and Analysis

A variety of tools and resources are available to assess community character and form in the inventory and analysis. The rural-to-urban transect can be used to characterize community-wide form based on the gradation between natural and human made elements in the physical environment (Bohl and Plater-Zyberk 2006). A related approach is to map and assess major community design elements, such as neighborhoods, corridors, and districts. These elements can be classified based on physical form characteristics or other distinguishing features, for example: traditional and suburban neighborhoods; automobile-oriented commercial corridors; walkable, mixed-use commercial districts; and major open spaces and riparian corridors.

For cultural and historic resource analysis, the *Standards and Guidelines for Archeology and Historic Preservation* are a comprehensive source of information on significant structures, sites, districts, and landscapes (National Park Service 2020c). Federal designation programs include the *National Historic Landmark Program* and the *National Register of Historic Places* (National Park Service 2020a; 2020b). States and localities also maintain registers of historic places. These designations can offer tax credits for eligible property owners while providing a degree of regulatory protection and stability for historic resources.

Arts and cultural inventories are a tool that can be used to understand another essential component of community character. The purpose of an arts and cultural inventory is to identify, map, and assess a community's artistic and cultural resources and creative assets (Soule, Hodgson, and Beavers 2011). The inventory should be conducted in collaboration with members of the arts and cultural community, such as artists and representatives of arts, cultural, and educational institutions.

Community Design

Community design (also called urban design) refers to the organization of and relationships between the physical elements of place at scales beyond the individual building. These scales range from local settings to neighborhoods, districts, city (or other community), and region. Local settings include blocks, streets, open spaces, and other places in which people directly experience their environs. Neighborhoods and districts consist of physical networks of buildings, blocks, streets, open spaces, and land uses, including anchors such as community gathering places and institutional campuses. At the citywide and regional scales, land use, development patterns, and other components of the physical environment are shaped by built and natural infrastructure systems such as highways, utilities, and hydrology.

Planning (intentionally or not) affects community design by establishing (1) policies for the spatial distribution of land uses and infrastructure systems at the community-wide and regional scales and (2) policies and standards that shape physical character and form at the district, neighborhood, and local scales. Spatial planning across all of these scales has been heavily influenced by the Euclidean approach of separating uses and regulating development density and intensity. In the 21st century, an alternative approach has emerged that focuses on community form and relationships between elements of the built environment (for example, buildings, streets, and parking) rather than uses. Examples of this approach include form-based codes, traditional neighborhood development, and the Smart Code.

Table 7.7 Community Design

Policy Directions
Use an integrated framework for community design across the community-wide, district/neighborhood, local, and site scales.
Ensure that the framework addresses social equity and opportunity for all community members.

Applications
Evaluate the impacts of existing development regulations and standards on community form, design, and sense of place.
Based on the evaluation, revise development regulations and standards to promote improved community form and design across scales.
Establish design standards appropriate to the community context and character.

Example: Long Beach, California

The Urban Design Element of the *Long Beach General Plan* begins with the role of urban design in realizing the vision of "a city that thrives." The introduction identifies a series of "bold moves" to move the vision forward; examples include fostering compact and connected development, healing the urban fabric, and improving relationships among buildings, streets, public spaces, and people. The core of the element provides strategies and policies for five *livable environments*: (1) *Great Places*, (2) *Urban Fabric*, (3) *Place Types*, (4) *Public Spaces*, and (5) *Edges, Thoroughfares, and Corridors*. The concluding chapter provides direction for implementing, administering, and maintaining the element and its provisions.

The comprehensive plan can establish a policy framework for improved community design that supports the plan vision and goals. Implementing strategies should address the impacts of conventional planning practices (for example, use, setback, and parking requirements) on community form. Integrating the different systems that shape community form, such as land use, mobility, and infrastructure, is key to creating complete communities. It is imperative that the framework address the role of community design in advancing social equity and expanding (rather than restricting) inclusion and opportunity for all community members.

Cultural and Historic Resources

Cultural resources are tangible remains of past human activities, such as buildings, structures, archaeological sites, earthworks, and landscapes. Historic resources are buildings, sites, districts, landscapes, and other cultural resources that have been determined to be significant to the history or culture of a local community, state, or nation.

Cultural and historic resources are vitally important to community character, identity, and sense of place. They contribute to the local economy through tourism and other economic activities. Conservation and reuse of historic structures provide environmental benefits by reducing the need to construct new buildings that consume land and resource.

The comprehensive plan should include or reference an inventory of cultural or historic resources within the community, including resources listed on the National Register of Historic Places or designated through other federal, state, or local programs. It is important to note that not all significant sites and structures have an official designation. Resources can be determined to be eligible for listing in the National Register if they meet the Register's evaluation criteria (which include a requirement that they be at least 50 years old).

The comprehensive plan should also include policies and strategies to protect, conserve, and adaptively reuse cultural and historic resources for compatible purposes. These policies and strategies should address not only resources that have or are eligible for formal designation, but also sites, districts, and other resources that contribute to the community's unique character and heritage.[5]

Table 7.8 Cultural and Historic Resources

Policy Directions
Protect, conserve, and adaptively reuse cultural and historical resources as an integral part of the community fabric.
Leverage cultural and historic resources to provide economic, environmental, and social benefits.

Applications
Develop an inventory of cultural and historic resources, including designated properties, properties eligible for designation, and other resources important to local heritage, character, and identity.
Implement incentives and regulatory mechanisms to preserve cultural and historic resources and to protect historic buildings from alteration and demolition.

Example: Raleigh, North Carolina

The Raleigh 2030 Comprehensive Plan includes a Historic Preservation Element whose purpose is "to sustain and promote the identity of Raleigh as a city with great historic communities and assets." The element begins by summarizing Raleigh's history, describing the city's historic preservation programs, and identifying growth-related issues that are eroding its physical heritage. The element includes maps of national and locally designated landmarks, districts, and places. Historic preservation policies address (1) Raleigh's historic identity; (2) planning, zoning, and neighborhood conservation; (3) housing and building codes, rehabilitation, and adaptive use; (4) coordination and outreach to increase awareness and support for historic preservation efforts; and (5) funding and incentives for historic preservation. Implementation actions include conducting surveys and inventories of historic resources; encouraging repair, rehabilitation, and adaptive reuse of historic structures; and mechanisms such as historic easements, tax and loan incentives, and transfer of development rights.

Civic Spaces, Public Places, and the Arts

Civic spaces are locations in which community members can gather and people can interact in a social setting. Public places host events, performances, exhibitions, and other civic activities. Town squares, pedestrian promenades, and community parks

are examples of civic spaces. Example of public places include museums, performance venues, concert halls, sports facilities, and city or town halls. Civic spaces and
public places are an important component of social infrastructure. They can express
shared identity, local heritage, and sense of place. The design of civic spaces and
public places should reflect these special qualities.

Like civic spaces and public spaces, the visual and performing arts are important
to community character, identity, and sense of place. They can improve the aesthetic
quality of spaces and places, contribute to the local economy, celebrate local culture,
and engage community members in ways that strengthen social connections, foster
creative expression, and improve health and well-being.

Creative placemaking is an approach to strategically shaping the physical and
social character of a neighborhood, town, city, or region around art and cultural

Table 7.9 Civic Spaces, Public Places, and the Arts

Policy Directions
Provide and maintain quality civic spaces and public places for community use and benefit.
Strengthen arts and culture as an important component of community identity and the local economy.

Applications
Establish design standards for public buildings, facilities, and spaces.
Implement programs (for example, percent for art) to incorporate art into public and private places and buildings.
Engage community members and partners from the public, private, and nonprofit sectors in creative placemaking initiatives.

Example: Cheney, Washington

In recognition of the critical importance of the arts to community character
and quality of life, Cheney's *Comprehensive Plan 2017–2037* includes an
element titled Culture and the Arts. This element provides an overview of the
city's arts and cultural assets, including museums, theaters, and performance
venues; historic structures and districts; and arts and cultural groups, such
as music ensembles, ethnic community centers, and art and theater groups.
Goals and policies address the importance of arts and culture to Cheney's
community character, economy, and quality of life, as well as the importance of broader goals such as supporting Cheney's historic and agricultural
heritage, sustaining the downtown, and maintaining healthy neighborhoods
to a thriving arts and cultural environment. The element recommends establishment of an arts commission to lead the development of arts and cultural
programs for the enrichment of community members.

activities. Among other outcomes, it can animate public and private spaces, rejuvenate structures and streetscapes, improve public safety, and generate economic activity, jobs, and income (Markusen and Gadwa 2010).

Green Development

Green development encompasses a range of practices that are energy and resource efficient, reduce waste and pollution, and improve health and productivity. Various rating systems and certification programs for buildings, sites, districts, and cities can provide guidance for incorporating green development into comprehensive plan policies and implementation. Green development practices include, among others, increased energy efficiency and use of renewable sources; water conservation and recycling; retention and treatment of stormwater on site; natural habitat preservation and use of native plant species; use of sustainably sourced and recycled materials; reduced waste; and improved human health and well-being through building orientation and design.

One of the first programs to establish green building standards was *Leadership in Energy and Design (LEED)* (U.S Green Building Council 2020). Other green building standards include the *International Green Construction Code* (International Code Council 2018), *National Green Building Standard* (National Association of Home Builders 2020), *Green Globes for New Construction* (Green Building Initiative 2019), *International Living Building Challenge* (International Living Future Institute 2021), and the *WELL Building Standard* (International WELL Building Institute 2018).

Table 7.10 Green Development

Policy Directions
Use green building and development principles and practices to achieve outcomes such as energy and resource efficiency, waste reduction and pollution prevention, and improved health and productivity.
Applications
Develop an integrated green development strategy and action plan.
Establish green building and development standards for significant public investment projects, including buildings, facilities, infrastructure, and site development.
Implement green development standards through code requirements, regulatory incentives, and assistance programs (for example, weatherization grants to homeowners).
Site and orient buildings to maximize health benefits for occupants, including optimal access to light and fresh air, minimal exposure to noise and pollution, and safety and protection from hazards.

Green development approaches can be applied to all uses, including residential, commercial, mixed use, and industrial/manufacturing.[6] Green development standards extend beyond buildings to the site, district, and community scales. Examples include the *SITES v2 Rating System for Sustainable Land Design and Construction* (American Society of Landscapes Fund et al. 2014), *Ecodistricts Protocol* (Ecodistricts 2018), and *LEED for Cities and Communities* (U.S. Green Building Council 2020).

Example: Vancouver, British Columbia

Initially developed in 2009–2011, the *Greenest City Action Plan* establishes goal areas and measurable targets to guide Vancouver toward becoming the greenest city in the world by 2020 (Vancouver 2012). The goal areas include climate and renewables, green buildings, green transportation, zero waste, access to nature, clean water, local food, clean air, green economy, lighter footprint, and green operations. Examples of 2020 targets set by the initial plan include:

■ Reduce community-based greenhouse gas emissions by 33 percent from 2007 levels (climate and renewables).
■ Make over 50 percent of trips by foot, bicycle, and public transit (green transportation).
■ Reduce average distance driven per resident by 20 percent from 2007 levels (green transportation).

Vancouver continues to implement, monitor progress, and update the action plan on an ongoing basis. The 2019–2020 update reported that the green transportation targets had been met (54 percent of trips made by foot, bicycling, or public transit; 37 percent reduction in average distance driven by residents since the 2007 baseline) but the climate and renewables target had not (9 percent reduction in 2019 compared with the baseline) (Vancouver 2020).

Summary

A complete community is one in which all community members have their basic needs met. These needs include decent and affordable housing at all stages of life; access to jobs and quality facilities, services, and social infrastructure; multimodal mobility options; and more. Sustainable, resilient, and equitable land-use and development patterns, along with the elements that build community character, are essential to creating complete communities.

Outcomes of past land-use and development practices include separation and fragmentation of uses, automobile dependency, uncontrolled expansion of urban uses into rural areas, environmental and fiscal impacts, and social inequity as reflected in unequal access to resources. A more sustainable approach promotes integration of land uses with other built and natural systems, compact, mixed-use development patterns, and infill and redevelopment rather than greenfield development at the urban fringe.

Community character refers to the qualities that define a community's identity and sense of place. An important component of community character, *community design* refers to the organization of and relationships between physical elements of the built and natural environment. The comprehensive plan can establish an integrated policy framework to improve community design and urban form across the community-wide, district, local, and site scales through regulations, incentives, and investments. The comprehensive plan should also include policies and strategies to protect, conserve, and adaptively reuse cultural and historic resources. Civic spaces, public places, and the arts are types of social infrastructure that build shared identity and sense of place. Creative placemaking can be used to engage community members, artists, and partners in initiatives to improve the physical and social qualities of places.

Green development encompasses a variety of sustainability practices that are energy and resource efficient, reduce waste and pollution, and improve health and productivity. Various rating and certification systems can inform development of comprehensive plan policies and standards to increase sustainability.

Notes

1 A simple process can be used to determine the availability and capacity of developable lands. First, identify the total area of vacant and underutilized lands and their capacity of based on zoning regulations and plan designations. Next, subtract land areas that are not developable, such as environmentally sensitive lands. Last identify and subtract land areas needed for future public facilities and infrastructure. The result is the total area and capacity of lands available for development.

2 A primary resource for industry types is the *North American Industry Classification System* (NAICS) (U.S. Census Bureau 2017).

3 Density refers to the number of units (for example, people, dwellings, or building square footage) in a given land area. Intensity refers to the amount of building on a given site, measured by factors such as floor area ratio, building site coverage, and building block coverage (Forsyth 2003).

4 One report found that sprawl increases per capita land consumption by up to 80 percent and automobile use by up to 60 percent, creating social costs of over $1 trillion a year (Misra 2015).

5 A *neighborhood conservation overlay district* is a tool that can be used to protect the character of an area that may not be eligible for formal designation.

6 The resource-efficient economy, circular economy, and eco-industrial parks are examples of green development approaches to industrial and manufacturing uses.

References

American Society of Landscape Architects Fund, The Lady Bird Johnson Wildflower Center at The University of Texas at Austin, and the United States Botanic Garden (2014). *SITES v2 Rating System for Sustainable Land Design and Development.* Washington, DC: Green Business Certification Inc.

Bohl, Charles and Elizabeth Plater-Zyberk (2006). "Building Community across the Rural-to-Urban Transect," San Francisco, CA: *Places Journal*, 18:1, pp. 5–17.

EcoDistricts (2018). *The EcoDistricts Protocol* (Version 3.1). Portland, OR: EcoDistricts.

Forsyth, Ann (2003). *Measuring Density: Working Definitions for Residential Density and Building Intensity.* Minneapolis, MN: Design Center for American Urban Landscape, University of Minnesota.

Godschalk, David and David Rouse (2015). *Sustaining Places: Best Practices for Comprehensive Plans*, Planning Advisory Service Report 578. Chicago, IL: American Planning Association.

Green Building Initiative (2019). *Green Globes for New Construction.* Portland, OR: Green Building Initiative.

Houston, Texas (n.d.). Houston Complete Communities Initiative. Accessed at https://www.houstontx.gov/completecommunities/

International Code Council (2018). *The International Green Construction Code.* Country Club Hills, IL: International Code Council, Inc.

International Living Future Institute (2021). *Living Building Challenge* (4.0 Basics). Seattle, WA: International Living Future Institute.

International WELL Building Institute (2018). *WELL Building Standard v2.* New York, NY: International WELL Building Institute.

Markusen, Ann and Anne Gadwin (2010). *Creative Placemaking.* Washington, DC: National Endowment for the Arts.

Misra, Tanvi (2015). *How Much Sprawl Costs America.* New York, NY: Bloomberg CityLab. Accessed at https://www.bloomberg.com/news/articles/2015-03-24/a-new-report-says-sprawl-costs-america-1-trillion-a-year.

National Association of Home Builders, with International Code Council (2020). *National Green Building Standards* (ICC-700). Washington, DC: National Association of Home Builders.

National Park Service (2020a). *National Historic Landmarks Program.* Washington, DC: U.S. Department of the Interior.

National Park Service (2020b). *National Register of Historic Places.* Washington, DC: U.S. Department of the Interior.

National Park Service (2020c). *The Secretary of the Interior's Standards and Guidelines for Archeology and Historic Preservation.* Washington, DC: U.S. Department of the Interior.

Ohio Balanced Growth Program (2015). "Compact Development" (Chapter 3) in *Best Local Land Use Practices* Columbus, OH: State of Ohio.

Soule, Jeffrey, Kimberly Hodgson, and Kelly Beavers (2011). *How Arts and Cultural Strategies Create, Reinforce, and Enhance Sense of Place.* Arts and Culture Briefing Paper 3. Chicago, IL: American Planning Association.

U.S. Census Bureau (2017). *North American Industry Classification System* (NAICS). Washington, DC: U.S. Department of Commerce.

U.S. Green Building Council (2020). *LEED v4.1 for New Buildings and Spaces; LEED v4.1 for Cities and Communities: Existing*. Leadership in Energy and Design (LEED). Washington, DC: U.S. Green Business Certification Inc.

Vancouver (2012). *Greenest City 2020 Action Plan*. Vancouver, BC: City of Vancouver.

Vancouver (2020). *Greenest City 2020 Action Plan – Implementation Update*. Vancouver, BC: City of Vancouver.

Williamson, June and Ellen Dunham-Jones (2021). *Case Studies in Retrofitting Suburbia: Urban Design Strategies for Urgent Challenges*. Hoboken, NJ: John Wiley & Sons, Inc.

Chapter 8

Built Environment Systems

Mobility and Infrastructure

This chapter continues the discussion of built environment systems begun in Chapter 7, focusing on multimodal mobility (the ways in which people move about the community) and utility infrastructure and services (including water, sewer, solid waste, and energy). The chapter concludes with a discussion of telecommunications (broadband) infrastructure, which has become a vitally important 21st-century utility.

Together with the land-use and development patterns that they interact with, support, and shape, mobility and infrastructure systems are essential components of a livable built environment and a complete community. In a complete community, all community members can access destinations for daily needs such as work, school, recreation, shopping, and services. Often taken for granted except when interrupted during natural disasters or other emergencies, reliable, safe, and affordable utility services are required for a community to function. As discussed in Chapter 7, mobility and infrastructure systems influence community form and character at the community-wide, district, local, and site scales.

Sustainability, Resilience, Equity

Mobility and infrastructure systems profoundly affect the sustainability of the built environment. They are major sources of greenhouse gas emissions that contribute to global climate change and of pollutants that impact air and water quality and human health. As primary drivers of growth and expansion at the

---

DOI: 10.4324/9781003024170-10

urban fringe, they negatively affect rural lands and natural resources, as well as the fiscal sustainability of local governments. Fiscal impacts are reflected in aging infrastructure systems with deferred maintenance needs. Sustainable mobility and infrastructure systems reduce greenhouse gas emissions and improve energy efficiency; provide multimodal travel options; are coordinated with land-use patterns to support compact development, infill, and redevelopment; and prioritize maintenance of existing infrastructure and facilities over new construction.

Resilient mobility and infrastructure systems are planned and constructed to minimize risks and disruptions caused by natural and human-made disasters. Resilient practices include, among others, locating essential facilities and infrastructure outside of hazard areas; using construction methods that increase resistance to damage caused by hazards; and incorporating redundancies or backups in case essential services fail. An emergency response and recovery plan should be in place to quickly restore facilities, infrastructure, and services after a disaster strikes.

Equitable mobility and infrastructure systems provide reliable, safe, and affordable access to facilities and services for all community members, regardless of age, economic status, gender, race, ethnicity, or disability. Too often, socioeconomic inequality is reflected in disparities such as substandard, aging infrastructure, poor drinking water quality, and lack of access to high-speed internet service in underserved communities and neighborhoods. Addressing these disparities requires identifying deficiencies and gaps and redirecting mobility and infrastructure investments to correct them. Convenient, safe, and affordable alternatives to automobile use, including regular transit service, should be provided for all community members.

Mobility and Accessibility

Transportation planning in the 20th century was directed toward building roads, highways, and other facilities to efficiently move vehicles and goods. As private automobile usage increased in the post-World War II era, much of the focus was on "solving" vehicle congestion by constructing new roadways, providing additional lanes on existing roadways, and widening streets and thoroughfares to meet traffic engineering specifications. Too often these "solutions" resulted in increased automobile use and recurrence of congestion. Other negative impacts included worsening air quality from transportation-related pollutants, contamination of water resources by runoff from streets and parking lots, increased exposure to noise, and more traffic fatalities.

Nearly half of the nation's population lives in areas that do not meet federal air quality standards. Transportation-related pollution from automobiles and trucks can be responsible for as much as half of the nitrogen oxide and carbon monoxide in the local air. Transportation-related pollution (for example, from fuel, particle matter, and salt runoff) also damages water and waterways. In addition, traffic noise is harmful to physical, emotional, and mental health.

In contemporary planning practice, the focus has shifted to facilitating *mobility and accessibility* to destinations for people. All communities – urban and rural, small and large – rely on the availability of mobility choices that are convenient and safe for community members. A robust mobility system offers multiple, interconnected travel options (modes) for users, including motorists, pedestrians, bicyclists, transit riders, and users of new mobility services (for example, rideshare and e-scooters), as well as accommodating freight and goods movement and delivery (Figure 8.1). Accessibility refers to the ease with which people of all ages, socioeconomic status, and abilities can access destinations. The goal of the mobility system is to provide multimodal accessibility for all people, including those who are unable to drive, lack the economic means to own a motor vehicle, or otherwise choose not to use an automobile.

Planning for multimodal accessibility is closely tied to land-use and development patterns. The spatial distribution of land uses at the district, community, and regional scales impact trip generation, travel behavior, and how easy or difficult it is to access destinations. For example, mixed land-use patterns can provide more mobility options than ones with separated uses. At the local scale, mobility and accessibility are impacted by design characteristics such as density, building orientation, location of parking, streetscape design, and proximity to transit.

The 21st-century comprehensive plan provides a systematic framework for integrating land use and mobility planning. It sets the policy direction for achieving multiple goals related to multimodal accessibility, such as expanding mobility choices, improving health, increasing safety, and reducing vehicle miles traveled and greenhouse gas emissions. It is a powerful tool that can accelerate replacement of the 20th-century transportation-planning approach by a new paradigm – one that is based on mobility and accessibility in order to achieve more sustainable, resilient, and equitable outcomes for people and communities.

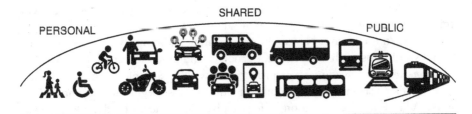

Figure 8.1 Mobility Modes

Inventory and Analysis

An inventory and analysis of multimodal mobility begins with an assessment of existing travel modes and facilities, including roadways, bus and rail transit, pedestrian and bicycle facilities, aviation, and rail, ports, and other freight and goods facilities. For roadways, the standard approach uses a hierarchical road classification system (highways, arterials, collectors, and local streets) and level-of-service standards ranging from A (free-flowing) to F (gridlock) to assess traffic flow. This focus on efficient movement of vehicles to the exclusion of other considerations is a primary reason for the destructive effects of 20th-century transportation planning on communities, landscapes, and the environment.

While private automobiles remain the predominant means of transportation in the United States,[1] the paradigm has shifted toward meeting mobility needs via all modes of travel, including vehicles, public transit, walking, and bicycling. This shift is reflected in the development of multimodal level-of-service standards to measure performance for all users of the mobility system.[2] An effective mobility system provides convenient connections between modes, for example: walking, biking, and driving connections to transit stations, or connections between local and regional transit and intercity rail and air service. The inventory and analysis should assess the completeness of the mobility system and connectivity between different modes.

Transit is an integral part of a multimodal mobility system. In 2019 (prior to the COVID-19 pandemic), there were about 34 million transit boardings each workday in the United States (or approximately 10 billion transit trips a year). Yet nationwide, about 45 percent of the population does not have access to public transit. Communities and regions with transit service reduce the nation's carbon emissions by 37 million metric tons annually (American Public Transportation Association 2019). The inventory and analysis should address transit service, including existing service routes, frequency of and gaps in service, and the needs of transit-dependent riders. This analysis should be coordinated with the regional or local transit agency in cases where the local jurisdiction is not itself the provider.

A key issue for transit service is safe connectivity to and from stations and stops, commonly referred to as *first-and-last-mile connections*. Obstacles and gaps in connectivity to the transit network should be identified, along with opportunities to address them. A transit *walkshed* is typically defined as one-half mile around a station or stop via the local street system. Bicyclists will travel longer distances to access transit, dependent on the availability of safe routes and facilities to accommodate bicycles when they arrive. New mobility is creating additional ways to get to transit stations and stops, such as rideshare, e-scooters, and other micromobility options.

Non-motorized mobility refers primarily to walking and bicycling. Nearly every trip, whether via transit, automobile, or other means, begins and/or ends with a walk. Addressing the condition, safety, and completeness of sidewalk, pathway, and trail networks facilitates walking to access destinations and for recreation, with corresponding health benefits from physical activity.

Bicycling is more than a recreational activity; it serves as a way to get to and from work and other destinations, providing an alternative to driving alone.[3] Similar to the assessment of pedestrian networks, the inventory and analysis should address the condition, safety, and connectivity of dedicated and shared bicycle facilities, such as protected bike lanes, sharrows, and multi-use trails.

Various audit and checklist tools are available to measure the performance of nonmotorized modes (National Highway Traffic Safety Administration n.d.; WalkScore n.d.). These tools can help identify missing links in sidewalk and bicycle networks and the connectivity of routes to schools, transit, parks, and other destinations. Such routes should be safe, free of hazards and barriers, and accessible to all community members.

Freight and goods movement is essential to a healthy economy and to fulfill the needs of community members and businesses. Freight includes cargo, parts and components, and products that are imported, exported, or transferred by ships, rail, trucks, and air. Goods are delivered locally via truck or van. New technologies such as automation and e-commerce are changing methods and patterns of goods shipment and delivery. Local impacts include increasing demand for warehouse and distribution uses; curb access and loading zones for goods delivery to stores and businesses; and delivery vehicles (including drones) on local streets. The inventory and analysis should address major patterns of freight and goods movement through the community, as well as issues such as heavy truck traffic on local streets and congestion from delivery vehicles in commercial and residential areas.

The condition of mobility facilities should also be addressed in the inventory and analysis, including age, service life, and level of maintenance. Too often, required maintenance is deferred due to budget constraints, leading to deterioration, reduced level of service, and eventual need for costly rehabilitation or replacement (Chang et al. 2017).

Mobility System Management

The goal of *mobility system management* is to provide for the mobility needs of all users in an efficient, cost-effective manner that minimizes the need to expand existing or provide new facilities. Strategies and solutions are multimodal, intermodal, and cross-jurisdictional in nature, transcending modal, political, and organizational boundaries to manage system demand and capacity.

Strategies to reduce or eliminate private automobile trips are referred to as *transportation demand management*. They include providing alternatives such as ridesharing, transit use, walking, bicycling, and telework. Changes in behavior can also reduce trips; examples include combining trips, flexible work schedules, and telework. Walkable, transit-supportive, and mixed-use development patterns, along with parking management, also contribute to demand management.

A variety of programs and strategies can improve the capacity and performance of existing mobility facilities without costly investments. Examples include synchronizing traffic signals, instituting variable speed limits, prioritizing buses at intersections, providing real time information on travel conditions, and reconfiguring facilities (for example, improving pedestrian and bicycle crossings).

Maintenance and preservation are critical aspects of system management. Mobility facilities are expensive to build and operate and require ongoing maintenance and repair. Roadways, railbeds, sidewalks, and trails are in regular need of resurfacing and restoration. Signage, traffic signals, lighting, stormwater management facilities, and the like also require upkeep. Deferred maintenance can significantly impact users and the environment, resulting in reduced levels of service, delays, safety hazards, and risk of catastrophic failure.

The comprehensive plan can establish a decision-making framework for prioritizing maintenance and preservation of existing mobility assets over investments in costly new facilities. The framework should address the need for asset management and maintenance during the life cycles of existing facilities (see discussion of utility infrastructure below).

Rural Mobility

Mobility needs and issues in rural towns and areas are different from those in urban and suburban communities. Rural communities have more agricultural and other resource lands, lower densities, and a smaller population base. Rural mobility facilities (for example, small-town main streets and scenic roadway corridors) should have standards that reflect the scale and character of their rural context (a concept referred to as *context-sensitive design*). The mobility system plays an important role in supporting the viability of the rural economy. Conflicts can arise between automobiles and vehicles and equipment used for agriculture, forestry and lumber production, or other rural economic uses.

Many rural residents lack access to automobiles or other reliable mobility options. Transit can be a challenge in rural areas, which lack the densities typically needed to support service. However, there are a number of examples of rural transit agencies that provide fixed-route, flex-route, and demand responsive service for community members (Phillips and Marcus 2019). Rural transit service can be developed to connect rural town centers to one another, to urban communities and cities, and to regional and intercity service.

New Mobility

The emergence of transportation network companies such as Uber and Lyft, micromobility options such as e-scooters, and other technology-enabled mobility services has had a disruptive effect on transit and other existing travel modes. *New mobility* refers to a suite of public and private transportation services – mostly available on-demand without requiring an advance reservation – made possible by mobile technology and real-time location data. A related concept developed in

Europe, *Mobility as a Service* (MaaS), is the integration of different travel options into a single mobility service accessible on demand (Dalton 2018). New mobility services include, among others, ride hailing and sharing, micromobility options such as e-bicycles and e-scooters, car and bike sharing, and various forms of fixed and flexible route transit. These services need to be available through an integrated platform to qualify as MaaS.

Table 8.1 Mobility and Accessibility

Policy Directions
Develop an accessible and safe multimodal mobility system that provides choices for all users and accommodates the efficient movement of goods.
Integrate land use and mobility planning and prioritize mobility investments to support adopted land use and development patterns.
Prioritize maintenance and preservation of existing mobility assets over construction of new facilities.
Address rural mobility needs in a manner that maintains the rural economy and character.

Applications
Replace roadway level-of-service standards based on traffic flow with an integrated set of performance measures for all modes and users.
Support alternatives to driving alone, such as transit, bicycling, walking, and rideshare. Work with the regional transit agency to ensure that reliable, affordable, and accessible transit service is available to all community members.
Implement transportation demand and mobility system management strategies to reduce single-occupancy automobile trips and improve system capacity and performance.
Develop strategies to complete missing links and gaps in the mobility system. These include first-and-last-mile connections to transit, safe routes to schools, parks, and other destinations, access to and within mixed-use centers, and other community and neighborhood connections.
Establish context-sensitive design standards for rural mobility facilities.

Example: Alachua County, Florida

The comprehensive plan Alachua County, which includes the City of Gainesville, includes a Transportation Mobility Element whose goal is to "provide a safe, convenient, and efficient multimodal transportation system for all users, including automobile, transit, bicycle and pedestrian mobility." The plan integrates land use and mobility planning, calling for compact, mixed-use and integrated development patterns that promote walking, biking, and transit use. Desired outcomes include reduced vehicle miles traveled and greenhouse gas emissions, as well as improved connectivity between residential areas and employment centers.

There is evidence that on-demand new mobility services can reduce transit ridership and walking trips. Passenger pickup and drop-off on urban streets creates congestion and competition for limited curb space. On the positive side, convenient new mobility services offer the potential to reduce private automobile ownership and use. A widespread shift in travel behavior from single-occupancy vehicle trips to shared rides in fleets of electric vehicles operated by mobility providers would significantly reduce vehicle miles traveled, greenhouse gas emissions, parking demand, and other negative effects of automobile use.

Cities across the nation are developing plans addressing the impacts of new mobility and related technological trends to supplement or replace traditional long-range transportation plans. Austin's *Smart Mobility Road Map*, for example, addresses emerging technologies in five key areas: (1) shared-use mobility, (2) electric vehicles, (3) autonomous vehicles, (4) data and technology, and (5) land use and

Table 8.2 New Mobility

Policy Directions
Address the potential effects of new mobility technologies and develop policies to maximize positive and minimize negative impacts.
Ensure that all community members, including transit-dependent populations and persons lacking digital access, have equitable and affordable access to mobility services.

Applications
Provide for the needs of electric vehicles, including vehicular charging stations, in the design and construction of buildings, street systems, and parking facilities.
Develop policies, regulations, and standards, fee structures and pricing mechanisms, fiscal strategies, and public–private partnerships to address the costs and benefits of new mobility services.
Plan for the long-term impacts of autonomous vehicles on the built environment and land use.

Example: Cambridge, Massachusetts

Envision Cambridge, the comprehensive plan for Cambridge, Massachusetts, incorporates a strategic focus on evolving mobility technology as one of eight key trends for the city's future. It includes a Mobility Plan with the goal of providing all community members with a variety of safe, affordable, convenient, and sustainable mobility choices. A key strategy is to "establish new regulatory frameworks to prepare for technology-driven disruptions in mobility systems," such as autonomous vehicles and motorized micromobility devices. Actions include developing policies to address equity, safety, and ensure the use of shared and electric vehicles; developing flexible curb regulations and pricing mechanisms to manage uses such as transit lanes, bike and e-scooter parking, and shared-ride or autonomous vehicle loading.

mobility. The *Road Map* uses the lenses of equity and affordability to evaluate the potential impacts of these technologies on the city. Findings and recommendations were incorporated into the *Austin Strategic Mobility Plan* (Austin 2017, 2018).

While full deployment will likely be measured in decades rather than years, autonomous vehicles are an emerging technology that have the potential to transform travel behavior and mobility systems. Of particular concern for the comprehensive plan are the projected secondary impacts of autonomous vehicles on the built environment and development patterns. These may include, among others, narrower and more efficient rights-of-way; reduced overall parking demand; greatly increased demand for drop-off areas and reduced demand for onsite parking; opportunities to redevelop parking areas and rights-of-way for other uses; and momentum for dispersed development in rural areas (Crute et al. 2018).

Mobility by Design

Previous sections of this chapter address the mobility system and its relationship to land use and development at the community-wide scale. This section focuses on the design and integration of mobility facilities into the community fabric at the local scale. Originally developed in the 20th century, engineering design standards for roadways, streets, and other mobility facilities prioritize safe and efficient movement of vehicles regardless of the local context. In the 21st century, transportation planning agencies at all levels of government have become more flexible in adapting these standards to address the local context and character.

The concept of designing mobility facilities in harmony with the local community is referred to as *context sensitive design* or *context sensitive solutions*. Originally developed in the 1990s, context-sensitive design seeks to preserve and enhance community character while balancing economic, social, and environmental goals with the operational needs of a roadway or other facility. Context-sensitive solutions can be applied along main streets and thoroughfares, in urban neighborhoods and suburban communities, and in rural areas and centers (Moore and Wright 2017). In urban settings, context-sensitive design balances vehicular flow, pedestrian movement, and adjacent land-use activity, through measures such as on-street parking, sidewalk and streetscape improvements, and safe pedestrian crossings. In rural areas, context-sensitive design factors in rural and small-town character, adjacent land uses and resources (for example, rural centers, farmland, and forests), and ecological functions (for example, natural habitat areas and wildlife corridors).

Contemporary mobility design applications include complete streets, green streets, and living streets. While these applications are described separately below, they can be integrated to provide solutions that fit the local context.

Complete streets are designed to accommodate the safety and convenience of all users, including motorists, pedestrians, bicyclists, and transit users. Complete streets accommodate different mixes of modes and functions, promoting social interaction, economic activity, and more vibrant, livable communities. Key complete street features include medians, curb extensions, and roundabouts; wide sidewalks and well-demarcated crosswalks; and bicycle lanes and transit facilities. There is no one-size-fits-all approach to complete streets; communities may want to consider developing a typology of different concepts to fit various local contexts (Smart Growth America 2012).

The concept of *green streets* was developed as an approach to stormwater management that incorporates vegetation, pervious surfaces, and other features that capture, absorb, and filter stormwater rather than discharging it directly into the storm sewer system. Green streets are important components of a green infrastructure network that provides environmental, economic, and health co-benefits. The green street concept has been expanded to include pedestrian-oriented features such as wide sidewalks, street furniture, and traffic-calming measures. Street trees and the urban tree canopy are important elements that reduce stormwater runoff and provide other benefits, such as improved air quality and amelioration of the urban heat island effect (Figure 8.2).

A *living street* provides a place for people to gather, interact, and participate in community activities and events. The Living Streets Alliance defines living streets as: "public spaces that connect people to places and to each other" (Living Streets Alliance 2019). Existing streets and roadways can be transformed into living streets by temporarily or permanently closing them to traffic. A similar concept is the *shared street*, which is open to low-speed motor vehicles but gives priority to pedestrians and bicyclists. Shared streets typically lack curbs and sidewalks, meaning that the road surface can be used by pedestrians, bicyclists, and for recreational and community activities.

The COVID-19 pandemic, during which many communities closed street segments and parking spaces to accommodate outdoor dining, has generated momentum for further application of living and shared street concepts. The comprehensive plan can set the direction to rethink the design of streets, parking, and other mobility facilities to implement context-sensitive, complete, green, living, and shared solutions.

Figure 8.2 Complete Streets as Green Streets

Source: National Association of City Transportation Officials.

Table 8.3 Mobility by Design

Policy Directions
Employ context-sensitive design solutions to road improvement and other mobility projects to ensure compatibility with local character, minimize negative impacts, and enhance community vitality and livability.
Employ new approaches to designing and retrofitting streets and other components of the mobility system that integrate context-sensitive, complete, green, living, and shared street solutions.

Applications
Work with transportation planning agencies to develop and implement context-sensitive design standards for mobility projects.
Develop integrated complete and green street standards to guide retrofit and improvement projects.
Identify opportunities to apply living and shared street solutions to increase social and commercial activity.

Example: Boston, Massachusetts

The vision of Boston's Complete Streets initiative is to create streets that are "multimodal, green, and smart." The intent is to put transit-users, bicyclists, and pedestrians on "equal footing" with motorists, and to ensure that streets are "safe and shared comfortably" by all users and ages. Based on public engagement, the initiative emphasizes community greening, mitigating climate impacts, and promoting health and wellness. Priorities include transit service, accessible surfaces, and low-impact development (or green street) treatments. Standards for street design and reconstruction projects address street types, sidewalks, roadways, intersections, and "smart curbsides" (Boston 2013).

Managing Parking

The 20th century witnessed the proliferation of cheap and convenient parking to serve increasing numbers of privately owned automobiles and trips taken by car. The result is that large swaths of American communities are dedicated to surface lots, garages, and streets – in some instances exceeding 50 percent of a downtown area. It has been estimated that the United States has approximately 2 billion parking spaces for 250 million cars, or about eight per car (not counting the space required for vehicular access and circulation). This oversupply of parking creates enormous external costs for people and society, such as increased traffic congestion, air pollution, and greenhouse gas emissions; higher housing costs; disruption of community design and walkability; environmental and economic damage; and inequity for those who cannot afford to own a car (Shoup 2018).

Minimum off-street parking requirements that have little or no relationship to actual demand are a major contributor to excess parking supply. Technological trends such as telework, e-commerce, and the coming advent of autonomous vehicles are making parking standards developed for 20th-century commuting and shopping patterns even more obsolete. For residential, commercial, and mixed-use buildings, excessive parking requirements add to development costs that are passed on to homeowners, tenants, and customers. One study found that parking spaces required for shopping centers in Los Angeles increase construction costs by 67 percent if located in an aboveground structure and by 97 percent if underground (Shoup 2014). While less expensive to construct, surface parking lots occupy extensive areas that often sit empty and could be used for much more productive purposes.

Managing parking begins by inventorying the existing parking supply (off-street and on-street, privately and publicly owned, structured and surface parking) in districts of concern, how well it is utilized, and how much it costs. Satellite imagery and field sampling are used to identify occupancy and turnover rates. Existing parking requirements and design standards (for example, size of parking spaces) should be evaluated for their effects on development costs and the built environment. Occupancy rates can be compared with requirements to determine the validity of minimum parking standards for different uses based on demand.

Approaches to managing parking fall into two main categories: regulatory standards and demand management (including pricing mechanisms). Many communities are eliminating minimum parking requirements, replacing minimum with maximum requirements, or reducing or eliminating parking requirements in locations served by transit (Shoup 2018). Examples of demand management strategies include shared or joint use parking to take advantage of synergies between different land uses, eliminating long-term parking subsidies such as "early bird" and preferential employee pricing, and providing real-time parking information. On-street parking can be priced to balance demand and supply so that one or two spaces are typically open on each block, with the revenues applied to improving public services on the metered streets (Shoup 2018). A parking management district or transportation management association can be established to implement and monitor the effectiveness of an integrated parking management strategy.

In addition to addressing parking supply and demand management, the comprehensive plan should address the impacts of parking on the physical character of the built environment. Context-sensitive design standards can be developed to better integrate parking into the fabric of urban, suburban, and rural communities. Common practices include locating parking to the rear of buildings; breaking up surface parking lots with planting areas and pedestrian walkways; and locating retail uses on the ground floor of parking structures. In addition, *green parking standards* can be developed to incorporate shade trees, plantings, and green stormwater management features into parking facilities.

Table 8.4 Managing Parking

Policy Directions

Use integrated parking management strategies for commercial and mixed-use districts.

Account for the short- and long-term impacts on parking demand of technological trends such as e-commerce, teleworking, and autonomous vehicles. Address redevelopment of excess parking for interim and long-term uses.

Applications

Eliminate minimum off-street parking standards and enact maximum standards.

Implement parking demand management strategies such as shared use, elimination of subsidies for long-term parking, and pricing mechanisms that balance demand and supply.

Establish a parking management district or transportation management association to implement the parking management strategy.

Develop context-sensitive and green design standards for parking facilities.

Example: Olympia, Washington

The Transportation Element of the *Olympia Comprehensive Plan* prioritizes complete streets and pedestrian, bicycle, and transit mobility. The goal for parking is to reduce the number of employees who commute alone by car (a paradigm shift from the conventional practice of providing parking to meet demand). The plan calls for discouraging drive-alone commutes by managing the cost and supply of parking while giving priority to business patrons. Policies include reducing the supply of inexpensive parking for employees, eliminating parking requirements along bus corridors, and consolidating driveways and allowing on-street parking on collector streets. The plan also addresses the role of parking as a safety buffer between travel lanes and sidewalks, bicycle parking, and a commercial parking tax as a potential new funding source.

Utility Infrastructure

Utility infrastructure systems are essential for a community to function but are often taken for granted by the public – other than when service is interrupted. Essential utility systems include water (potable water, stormwater, and sanitary sewer), solid waste, and energy. In the 21st century, broadband infrastructure has emerged as the fifth "essential utility."

Utilities are managed by a mix of governmental and quasigovernmental agencies, authorities, and private companies, many of which are not under the direct purview of the local jurisdiction. The comprehensive plan can establish a coordinated framework for how utility services can best be provided to meet community needs while supporting broader community goals.

Sustainable Utility Infrastructure

It is not necessary to compile detailed data on utility systems for the comprehensive plan. Important information for planning purposes includes:

- Service areas (current and planned expansions) in relation to land-use and development patterns.
- Current and future capacity in relation to current and projected future demand.
- Age and condition of existing facilities.
- Planned capital improvements that will significantly affect any of the above.

The analysis should identify key issues to be addressed in the comprehensive plan. Different utilities form a complex "system of systems" that support, interact with, or impact each other and other community systems, such as land use, mobility, and environmental resources. The following text highlights selected issues for the sustainable provision of utility infrastructure and approaches to addressing them.

Issue: Uncoordinated management of utility infrastructure. Utility systems are typically managed by separate agencies who collectively construct, operate, and maintain a complex network of overhead and underground lines and pipes, structures, and other facilities. Particularly in older urban areas where underground utilities have been installed over decades, the result is a patchwork quilt of lines and pipes that are difficult to maintain, repair, and replace.

An alternative approach is the *utility corridor,* an underground passageway that allows lines and pipes from different systems (for example, water mains, sewer pipes, electrical and cable lines, and even steam lines for district heating) to be grouped together. This approach eliminates conflicts between lines, increases accessibility, minimizes trenching, reduces maintenance, repair, and upgrade costs, and accommodates installation of newer systems, such as fiber optic cable (Province of Alberta 2004).

In another example of the benefits of coordination, the One Water approach can be used to integrate management of drinking water, stormwater, and wastewater treatment (which are often handled by separate agencies) over the full water cycle, from source to use to return to the water ecosystem. This approach capitalizes on linkages and synergies between different water cycle stages, resulting in more efficient, sustainable, and cost-effective use of water resources.

Issue: Deferred maintenance. As is the case with mobility infrastructure, aging infrastructure with deferred maintenance needs is a major issue for the sustainability of utility systems. For example, an estimated 250,000–300,000 water main breaks occur each year, drinking water systems lose approximately $2.1 trillion gallons per year, and the investment gap to meet total water infrastructure capital needs stood at around $81 billion in 2019 (American Society of Civil Engineers 2020).

To address deferred maintenance, maintenance and repair of existing infrastructure should be prioritized over utility expansions and extensions that will add to the costs of system maintenance over time. *Asset management* focuses on facility maintenance, rehabilitation, and replacement with the goal of extending the service life and improving the quality of existing infrastructure. This approach can be used to assess costs and allocate resources for construction, operation, maintenance, and eventual replacement over the full life cycle of a facility.

Issue: Land use and environmental impacts. While utility systems provide essential functions and services for the community, they require the construction and operation of facilities that may have significant impacts on the environment and surrounding land uses. Examples include power plants and energy substations; solid waste transfer and disposal sites and incinerators; wastewater treatment facilities; and regional detention facilities. Associated impacts can include noise, odors, and glare; emissions and pollutants that affect air and water quality; and visual, health, and safety concerns. Older facilities with the greatest impacts are often located in poor and underserved communities, which is an environmental justice issue.

To address this issue, the comprehensive plan should identify the locations of existing utility facilities with significant land use or environmental impacts and include policies to ameliorate those impacts. Siting and performance criteria should be established to minimize the impacts of new facilities. Finally, utility providers should explore opportunities to reduce impacts through sustainable design, construction, and operations (next issue).

Issue: Sustainability. Utility facilities and operations can significantly impact community sustainability. Water utilities, for example, provide water to meet community demand that may exceed the capacity of the sources from which it is drawn. Solid waste handling and disposal are a byproduct of resource extraction and material consumption, resulting in harmful effects to human health. Power generation plants produce greenhouse gas emissions from fossil fuel consumptions.

Local utilities across the nation are implementing sustainable practices to mitigate these impacts. Water conservation, reclamation, and reuse, for example, can significantly reduce consumption and contribute to the long-term sustainability of ground and surface water supplies. Solid waste authorities can implement community waste reduction, recycling, and composting programs. While local governments generally have no direct control over power generators, they can implement energy conservation programs and encourage use of renewable sources.

Issue: Coordinating land use and utility infrastructure. Utility systems – particularly public water and sewer service – are major drivers of urban development. In existing developed areas, adequate utility infrastructure is necessary to support infill, redevelopment, and compact development patterns. Extension of utility service into rural areas can facilitate encroachment of urban land uses on rural resource lands.

To address these issues, utility service areas should be coordinated with urban growth areas, boundaries, or service areas (see Chapter 7). Inside these areas or boundaries, utility infrastructure should be available with sufficient capacity to support the urban uses, densities, and intensities permitted by zoning and development regulations. Outside these areas, land-use policy and regulations should allow rural, low-density uses and public utility service should be extended only in a limited, defined circumstance. Alternative facilities are required to provide water supply and sewage disposal for rural uses, such as on-site wells, on-site septic systems, and community water and wastewater treatment systems for towns and villages. Ongoing operations and maintenance are required to ensure proper functioning, maintain water quality, and minimize environmental impacts caused by these facilities.

Adequate facilities provision (also referred to as *concurrency*) is another tool used to coordinate land use and utility infrastructure. The purpose of concurrency is to ensure the timely provision of infrastructure and services for new development. Florida, Montana, and Washington provide direction and assistance for addressing

Table 8.5 Sustainable Utility Infrastructure

Policy Directions

Coordinate management of different utility systems to provide more efficient, cost-effective service and leverage environmental, economic, and social co-benefits.

Prioritize maintenance and repair of existing utility infrastructure over investment in new facilities.

Avoid and minimize the impacts of new and existing facilities on the environment and adjacent land uses, prioritizing effects on poor and underserved neighborhoods.

Employ sustainable design, construction, and operational principles and practices for utility infrastructure systems.

Coordinate utility service with land-use policy and regulations to support desired development patterns.

Applications

Use utility corridors or other strategies to coordinate installation, maintenance, repair, and replacement of different types of utility infrastructure.

Use an integrated One Water approach to manage drinking water, stormwater, and wastewater treatment more effectively.

Apply an asset management approach to maintain existing infrastructure in good condition and extend its service life.

Remediate the impacts of existing facilities, such as power plants, waste disposal sites, and wastewater treatment facilities, that are adversely impacting surrounding land uses and environmental systems.

Establish siting criteria and performance standards to avoid or minimize the land use and environmental impacts of new utility facilities.

Implement water conservation, reclamation, and reuse practices to maintain the long-term sustainability of water supply sources.

Implement solid waste reduction, recycling, and composting programs.

Develop strategies for energy conservation and use of renewable energy sources.

Align public water and service areas with urban growth areas and strictly limit utility extensions into adjacent rural areas.

Enact provisions to ensure that adequate infrastructure and services are available to serve new development.

concurrency in local comprehensive planning. Washington state, for example, defines concurrency as ensuring that needed "improvements or strategies are in place at the time of development, or that a financial commitment is in place to complete the improvements" during the current capital improvement program cycle (State of Washington 1990).

Examples: Eagle (Idaho) and Lancaster County (Pennsylvania)

Eagle and Lancaster County are examples of the application of sustainable utility practices in two very different contexts. Eagle is a growing suburb of Boise, Idaho. The Utilities, Facilities, and Services Element of *The City of Eagle Comprehensive Plan* emphasizes coordination between the city and other utility and service providers to best plan for and anticipate needs. Goals, objectives, and strategies address coordinated planning and management of water, stormwater, wastewater, solid waste, power, and telecommunications facilities. Strategies call for coordinated placement of utilities in public rights-of-way, including joint-use corridors; context-sensitive facility siting; and discouraging overlapping service areas and/or illogical service boundaries.

Blueprints, the Water Resources Element of the *Lancaster County Comprehensive Plan,* promotes "watershed-based, integrated water resources management to protect, conserve, and improve water resources" in the county. Major issues addressed by the plan include stormwater impacts on water quality and flooding; coordination of water and sewer infrastructure with growth and development patterns; and impacts of the county's extensive agricultural lands on stream quality. *Blueprints* calls for coordination between water and sewer service providers and municipalities to (1) align utility service areas with urban growth boundaries and (2) deliver essential services to both urban and rural settlements in a cost-effective manner. The plan provides a tool that can be used to evaluate wastewater management alternatives to large public systems in rural centers and Identified Needs Areas.

Broadband Infrastructure

As the COVID-19 pandemic clearly demonstrated, access to reliable, high-speed access to the Internet service has become essential to daily life, work, education, and the economy. High-speed access is made possible by broadband, which transmits wide bandwidth data via various types of technology, including fiber optics, wireless, cable, DSL, and satellite. While broadband access is provided by private companies, local governments can use smart city applications to provide more effective services for residents and businesses, improve the efficiency and sustainability of municipal operations, and engage community members in civic processes.

Disparities in internet access between advantaged and disadvantaged communities – referred to as the digital divide – is a major issue for broadband infrastructure. According to the Federal Communications Commission, 97 percent of urban residents have access to high-speed service, a number that falls to 65 percent in rural areas and 60 percent on Tribal lands (Federal Communications Commission n.d.). Where service is available, less affluent residents may lack the means to take advantage of it.

Other issues include the (1) coordinating broadband infrastructure components such as fiber-optic cables, wireless transmission facilities, and sensors (the so-called "Internet of Things") with other utility infrastructure systems and (2) integrating broadband infrastructure into the physical fabric of the community. Similar to *New* or *Smart Mobility Plans*, some communities are developing *Smart City Plans* to address issues and take advantage of opportunities related to broadband technology.

Table 8.6 Broadband Infrastructure

Policy Directions
Address broadband infrastructure as an essential community utility in the comprehensive plan.
Coordinate the installation and maintenance of broadband infrastructure with other community utilities.

Applications
Develop policies and strategies to leverage the potential of broadband and smart city technology to help realize community goals and achieve sustainable, resilient, and equitable outcomes.
Partner with technology companies to provide all community members with reliable, affordable high-speed access to the Internet.
Establish design standards to integrate broadband infrastructure components into the built environment.

Example: Chula Vista, California

Chula Vista's *Smart City Action Plan* identifies goals, objectives, initiatives, and performance measures for the use of broadband and smart city technology to "grow the economy, engage the community, improve government efficiency, and enhance quality of life." The goals are organized around a vision of Chula Vista as a connected, responsive, transparent, and innovative city. Objectives include, among others:

- Build a comprehensive municipal network connecting city sensors and facilities (Connected City).
- Ensure universal internet and technology access for all communities (Connected City).
- Foster vibrant community engagement (Responsive City).
- Use data and analytics to improve city services and broaden public access to information about city performance (Transparent City).
- Advance environmental sustainability goals (Innovative City).

Selected examples of initiatives identified in the plan include working with internet service providers to offer affordable service to residents at all income levels; updating street design standards to include fiber-optic conduit; and incorporating smart city commitments into the next General Plan update.

Summary

Mobility and utility infrastructure systems are essential components of a livable built environment and complete community. In the 20th century, transportation planning focused on the efficient movement of vehicles and goods. In the 21st century, the focus has shifted to providing multimodal access to destinations for people. Travel modes include walking, biking, transit, vehicles, and new mobility services. Efficient movement of freight and goods remains an important mobility system function that has been impacted by the increase in e-commerce deliveries to local residences. New mobility services such as ride share, bike share, and other micromobility options are disrupting transit and other established travel modes. New mobility is creating opportunities and challenges to meeting mobility needs, including those of under-served and disadvantaged populations, as well as the potential to increase sustainability if a widespread shift to shared rides in electric vehicles were to occur.

Coordination of mobility, utility infrastructure, and land-use planning is important to realize desired land use and development patterns at the community-wide scale. In more local settings, context-sensitive solutions can be used to design infrastructure and facilities that fit with community character and scale.

Roadway classification standards based on efficient traffic flow and minimum off-street parking requirements derived from outmoded 20th-century standards have had destructive effects on the physical fabric of communities across the nation. They are becoming even more obsolete as a result of technological change in the 21st century. Minimum parking standards should be eliminated and replaced by management strategies that balance supply with actual demand. Excess parking areas offer opportunities for conversion to productive interim and long-term uses.

Broadband infrastructure has become the fifth essential utility of the 21st century, required for daily life, work, education, and economic activity. As with other utility and mobility systems, comprehensive plan policies, strategies, and actions can shape the use of broadband infrastructure and smart city technology to realize community goals and achieve sustainable, resilient, and equitable outcomes.

Notes

1 In 2018, the American Community Survey estimated that 76.3 percent of Americans drove alone to work, virtually unchanged since 2014.
2 The *Highway Capacity Manual*, the main reference guide for evaluating roadway system performance, now incorporates performance measures and techniques

for multimodal mobility analysis, including walking, biking, public transit, and automobiles (Transportation Research Board 2010).

3 Data from the National Household Travel Survey shows that about 1 percent of all trips in the United States between 2009 and 2017 were taken by bicycle. The share of these trips for work increased from 12.7 percent to 20.2 percent during this period (The League of American Bicyclists 2020).

References

Alberta, Province of (2004). *Purpose of Transportation/Utility Corridors.* Edmonton, AB: Alberta Government.

American Public Transportation Association (2019). *Public Transportation Facts.* Washington, DC: American Public Transportation Association.

American Society of Civil Engineers (2020). *The Economic Benefits of Investing in Water Infrastructure.* Reston, VA: American Society of Civil Engineers, Value of Water Campaign.

Austin, Texas (2017). *Smart Mobility Roadmap: Austin's Approach to Shared, Electric, and Autonomous Vehicle Technologies.* City of Austin, TX.

Austin, Texas (2018). *Austin Strategic Mobility Plan.* City of Austin, TX.

Boston, Massachusetts (2013). *Boston Complete Streets Design Guidelines.* City of Boston, MA.

Chang, Carlos, Soheil Nazarian, Marketa Vavrova, Margot Yapp, Linda Pierce, William Robert, and Roger Smith (2017). *Consequences of Delayed Maintenance of Highway Assets.* National Cooperative Highway Research Program. Transportation Research Board. Washington, DC: National Academies of Sciences, Engineering, Medicine.

Chula Vista, California (2017). *Smart City Strategic Action Plan.*

Crute, Jeremy, William Riggs, Timothy Chapin, and Lindsay Stevens. (2018). *Planning for Autonomous Mobility*, Planning Advisory Service Report 592. Chicago, IL: American Planning Association.

Dalton, Jeremy (2018). *What is "New Mobility Anyway?"* Portland, OR: MethodCity Planning LLC.

Federal Communications Commission (n.d.). Bridging the Digital Divide for All Americans. Accessed at https://www.fcc.gov/about-fcc/fcc-initiatives/bridging-digital-divide-all-americans

Living Streets Alliance (2019). *Complete Streets Tucson.* Tucson, AZ. Accessed at https://www.livingstreetsalliance.org/complete-streets

Moore, Paul and Stephanie Wright (2017). *Implementing Context-Sensitive Design on Multimodal Corridors: A Practitioner's Handbook.* Institute of Transportation Engineers and Congress for New Urbanism, with support by the Federal Highway Administration and Nelson/Nygaard.

National Highway Traffic Safety Administration (n.d.). *Walkability Checklist.* Washington, DC: U.S. Department of Transportation.

Phillips, Robin and Cara Marcus (2019). "Progressive Rural Transit Services Offer Lessons in Mobility, Access for All." *Metro Magazine.* Torrance, CA: Bobit Business Media.

Shoup, Donald (2014). "The High Cost of Minimum Parking Requirements," Chapter 5 in Mulley, Corinne and Stephen Ison (eds.), *Parking: Issues and Policies.* Bingley: Emerald Group Publishing, pp. 87–113.

Shoup, Donald (2018). *Parking and the City.* Philadelphia, PA: Routledge (Planners Press).

Smart Growth America, with National Complete Streets Coalition (2012). *Complete Streets Local Policy Workbook*. Washington, DC: Smart Growth America.

The League of American Bicyclists (2020). Trends in Rates of Biking and Walking for Commuting. Accessed at https://data.bikeleague.org/show-your-data/national-data/rates-of-biking-and-walking/

Transportation Research Board (2010). *Highway Capacity Manual 2010*. Washington, DC: National Academies of Sciences, Engineering, Medicine.

Walk Score (n.d.). *Walk Score Methodology*. Accessed at https://www.walkscore.com/methodology.shtml#:~:text=Walk%20Score%20measures%20the%20walkability%20of%20any%20address%20using%20a, within%20a%205%20minute%20walk%20

Washington, State of (1990, subsequently amended). "Comprehensive Planning – Mandatory Elements" (see subsection on concurrency), in *Growth Management—Planning by Selected Counties and Cities*. Chapter 36.70A.070(6)(b) (concurrency). Olympia, WA: Revised Code of Washington.

Chapter 9

Social Systems

The Merriam-Webster definition of a social system is "the patterned network of relationships constituting a coherent whole that exist between individuals, groups, and institutions." For comprehensive planning purposes, these relationships can be characterized as the interactions of community members with each other, social institutions, and with the community systems addressed in Part II of this book. These interactions are manifested in topics, issue areas, and outcomes that the comprehensive plan can and should address. Examples include social infrastructure, housing, and community health.

The 20th-century comprehensive plan focused on land use and physical development. Social systems and networks were a secondary focus or considered the realm of other professions, such as social services and public health. As understanding of the vital role these systems and networks play in shaping communities and meeting the needs of community members has increased, comprehensive planning practice has expanded to address social as well as physical dimensions of place.

This chapter addresses the role of social systems in the comprehensive plan. It begins by establishing the overarching theme of planning with an equity lens. Weaving equity and fairness throughout the comprehensive plan is necessary to achieve a complete and sustainable community. It then addresses several key planning topics that reflect social systems and relationships: neighborhoods, environmental justice, social infrastructure, housing, and gentrification. Housing is an example of a social system that cuts across and interacts with other community systems, such as land use, mobility, and the economy.

DOI: 10.4324/9781003024170-11

Sustainability, Resilience, and Equity

Environment, economy, and equity are considered the three pillars of sustainability. Too often, the role of equity in sustainability has been overlooked. A survey of local jurisdictions found that only 21.8 percent of approximately 1,800 adopted sustainability plans addressed social equity, compared with 67.6 percent that addressed economic development and 69.1 percent that addressed energy conservation (International City-County Management Association 2016). A sustainable community is an equitable one in which all community members have equal rights, share equitably in societal benefits, and have equal access to decision-making processes.

Social equity is foundational to resilience: the ability of individuals, communities, and systems to recover from and adapt to misfortune and change. Resilience is reduced by socioeconomic inequality and disparities in resources, education, and health outcomes between different segments of the community. It has been repeatedly demonstrated that poor and disadvantaged populations are most vulnerable to the impacts of natural and human-caused disasters. A healthy environment free of toxins and pollutants – with safe, affordable, and decent housing – and strong social infrastructure and support systems all contribute to reducing vulnerability and increasing the capacity of communities to recover quickly and successfully from disasters.

Planning with an Equity Lens

The American Planning Association's *Planning for Equity Policy Guide* calls for an equity in all policies approach, or using an *equity lens* to view, frame, and consider the policies and practices of planning (American Planning Association 2019). The Comprehensive Plan Standards for Sustaining Places identify interwoven equity (fairness and equity in providing for the needs of all community members and groups) as one of six required comprehensive plan principles (Godschalk and Rouse 2015).

The major purpose of planning with an equity lens is to ensure fairness for all people, particularly disadvantaged populations. Poor, underserved, and minority groups are disproportionately impacted by decisions that result in land, water, and air pollution; resource disparities and disinvestment in existing communities; poor health outcomes; and more. By integrating equity considerations into the planning process and implementation, planners and decision-makers can proactively consider costs and benefits for all community members and groups.

An equity lens should be applied throughout the comprehensive planning process, anchored by authentic participation that engages all community members and groups. In the first major phase of the process (Where Are We Now and Where Are We Headed?), using an equity lens provides a more complete understanding of the community's past, current conditions and issues, and challenges and opportunities for the future. In the second phase of the process (Where Do We Want to Go?), the equity lens ensures that the vision and goals for the future express the values, needs, and aspirations of all community members. In the third phase of the process (How Do We Get There?), the lens can be used to consider who will be impacted by or benefit from proposed scenarios, strategies, policies, and actions. Following plan adoption, the lens should be used during implementation to monitor whether goals, objectives, and performance measures related to equity are being met.[1]

Inventory and Analysis

Planning with an equity lens begins by developing an understanding of demographic characteristics and trends in the inventory and analysis. Factors to consider in this analysis include total population, population characteristics (such as age, gender, race, ethnicity, immigration status, education, and income), the distribution of population numbers and characteristics across the community, and how these conditions have changed over time.[2] Deficiencies and needs can be explored through needs assessments, level of service analyses for community-serving systems (for example, parks and recreation) and by mapping and overlaying demographic information on spatial data layers.

It is also important to understand patterns of racism and injustice through historical research, demographic analysis, and by engaging diverse voices in the planning process. Different communities have different racial and ethnic groups that have been subjected to prejudice and discrimination over time. Discrimination based on factors such as religious affiliation, age, gender, sexual orientation, or income is also part of the history of unfairness in the United States.[3]

Neighborhoods

A neighborhood is a social construct, a place of social interaction among neighbors, and a basic geographic scale at which to engage community members in the planning process, decision-making, and implementation. A neighborhood is a complex, dynamic system in which subsystems, such as land use, mobility networks, and natural resources, interact and connect to the larger community. Social inequality is manifested by stark disparities between different neighborhoods, often located in relatively close proximity.

Applying an equity lens means prioritizing the needs of at-risk, distressed, and disadvantaged neighborhoods. At-risk and distressed neighborhoods are experiencing conditions such as declining property values, high foreclosure rates, population loss, or physical deterioration. Residents of disadvantaged neighborhoods have reduced access to capital and other resources caused by factors such as poverty, unemployment, and low levels of educational attainment. Policies and actions to address these conditions include, among others, providing access to quality public facilities and services, improving older or substandard infrastructure, increasing economic opportunity through workforce training and development, and investing in local parks and green infrastructure to improve environmental quality.

An equity lens can be used to ensure that capital improvements and other public expenditures are distributed fairly to meet the needs of all neighborhoods. It is useful to include community members in decision-making on public investments, which results in greater transparency and accountability. Outcomes can include increased equity, awareness, and monitoring of who benefits from public investments and programs.

Table 9.1 Planning with an Equity Lens

Policy Directions

Address equity and fairness in all planning policies, practices, and decisions.

Engage all segments of the community in the planning process and implementation, especially disadvantaged populations that have traditionally been excluded from decision-making processes.

Applications

Identify the needs of underserved community members and groups and work with partners to address gaps, including access to jobs, quality facilities and services, decent housing, education and training, and a healthy environment.

Work with the residents of at-risk, distressed, and disadvantaged neighborhoods to improve physical, social, and environmental conditions and increase economic opportunity.

Apply an equity lens to the capital improvements program and other public investments to remedy past disparities and disinvestment in underserved neighborhoods.

Example: Seattle, Washington:

Race and Social Equity is a core value driving the *Seattle 2035 Comprehensive Plan*. The introduction to the plan notes that in Seattle, like the rest of the nation, "people have been denied equal access to education, jobs, homes, and neighborhoods because of their race, class, disabilities, or other real or perceived differences." Goals and policies addressing race and social equity are incorporated throughout the elements of the plan. Examples include providing fair and equal access to housing; ensuring that environmental benefits are equitably distributed and that environmental burdens are minimized and equitably shared by all; encouraging coordinated service delivery of food, housing, health care, and other basic necessities for people and families in need; and providing for inclusive and equitable community involvement. Plan monitoring includes indicators to measure the city's progress in becoming a more equitable place.

Environmental Justice

Environmental justice is defined as the fair treatment and meaningful involvement of all people regardless of race, color, national origin, or income with respect to the development, implementation, and enforcement of environmental laws, regulations, and policies (U.S. Environmental Protection Agency n.d.b). *Fair treatment* means that no groups bear a disproportionate share of adverse environmental consequences resulting from governmental policies and decisions, or from industrial, commercial, or other *locally unwanted land uses* whose negative externalities impact nearby communities. *Meaningful involvement* means that all people have an opportunity to participate in and shape decisions about activities that may affect their environment and health.

All too often, the prevalent practice has been to locate incinerators, landfills, and industrial activities in low-income neighborhoods and communities of color. The goals of environmental justice are to provide all communities and community members with (1) the same degree of protection from environmental and health hazards and (2) equal access to decision-making processes. Planning for environmental justice involves remediating damage that has been done to underserved and disadvantaged communities, considering potential negative impacts in siting new facilities and uses, and implementing projects, programs, and initiatives that result in tangible benefits for communities that have experienced such impacts.[4]

Environmental justice concerns also apply to vulnerability to the effects of natural disasters and climate change. People and communities are differentially exposed to natural hazards and disproportionately affected by climate-related health risks such as the urban heat island effect. Populations experiencing greater health risks include children, older adults, low-income communities, and communities of color (U.S. Global Change Research Program 2018).

Table 9.2 Environmental Justice

Policy Directions

Protect underserved and vulnerable communities and populations from environmental harm, environmental health hazards, and the negative impacts of climate change.

Provide meaningful opportunities for all community members to participate in decisions that may affect their environment or health.

Applications

Repair damage and rectify impacts in communities that have experienced harm from environmentally damaging activities and uses.

Ensure that new projects located in communities that have experienced environmental injustice provide benefits for community members, and that any potential negative impacts are avoided or mitigated.

Identify and develop strategies to address risks to vulnerable populations from natural hazards and climate change.

Example: Inglewood, California

In 2016, California passed legislation requiring local jurisdictions with disadvantaged communities to incorporate environmental justice policies into their general plans, either in a separate element or through integration into other elements of the plan. *Disadvantaged communities* are defined as "low-income areas that are disproportionately affected by environmental pollution and other hazards that can lead to negative health effects, exposure, or environmental degradation" (California Governor's Office of Planning and Research 2020).

The City of Inglewood adopted a new Environmental Justice Element in its general plan pursuant to this requirement. *CalEnviroScreen 3.0*, a tool developed by the California Office of Environmental Health Hazard Assessment, was used to identify disadvantaged communities within the city. Environmental justice goals and policies address six major topics: meaningful public engagement, land use and the environment, mobility and active living, access to healthy food, healthy and affordable housing, and public facilities. The land use and environment goal is to reduce exposure to environmental pollution through sound planning and public decision-making. Policies address general environmental health, residential uses and other sensitive receptors, and industrial and commercial facilities.

Social Infrastructure

Social infrastructure refers to the physical places and organizations that shape the way people interact, such as civic buildings, libraries, parks, and schools (Klinenberg 2018). Examples of different types of social infrastructure are shown in Table 9.3. *Social capital* (the network of relationships, values, and norms that foster trust and willingness to help others) depends upon the presence of social infrastructure. Robust social infrastructure makes a community healthier and more resilient to shocks and stresses.[5]

Because it transcends traditional planning topics such as physical facilities operated by a local government, social infrastructure is a relatively new system to address in the comprehensive plan. Social infrastructure overlaps and intersects with other community systems, such as civic buildings, streets, and green infrastructure, which collectively comprise what is referred to as the *public realm*. Important dimensions of social infrastructure include its role in bringing people together through social and cultural relationships, shared identity, and sense of place, as well as the connections it provides to education, economic opportunity, and community resources. Providing venues, programs, and opportunities for performances, arts and crafts, and the exchange of ideas contributes to health, personal growth, and community well-being. Social infrastructure can help ensure that local heritage and culture are celebrated and passed down from generation to generation.

Table 9.3 Social Infrastructure Examples

Type	Examples
Civic	Arts and cultural facilities
	Government buildings
	Museums
	Performance venues
Community	Community centers
	Libraries
	Parks and recreational facilities
	Public places and gathering spaces
Healthcare	Clinics
	Hospitals
	Medical offices
Educational	Colleges and universities
	Schools
	Training centers

Educational facilities, such as public schools, vocational centers, and institutions of higher education, are a key component of social infrastructure. While these facilities and programs typically operate independently of local governments, they are vitally important to community well-being and offer opportunities for partnerships to realize comprehensive plan goals and policies.

Table 9.4 Social Infrastructure

Policy Directions
Provide accessible places, programs, and opportunities that strengthen social infrastructure and the social capital it supports.
Support cultural heritage, the arts, and creative placemaking as key components of social infrastructure.
Work with public schools and educational institutions to ensure that community members have access to quality education and training opportunities.

Applications
Leverage social infrastructure to reinforce social networks and increase the capacity of community members, businesses, and organizations.
Locate and design schools, libraries, and other social infrastructure to enhance community identity, sense of place, and to provide places for people to gather and connect.
Connect social infrastructure through a well-designed, accessible public realm that provides opportunities for walking, biking, and transit use.

> **Example: Colorado Springs, Colorado**
>
> The vision for *PlanCOS*, the comprehensive plan for Colorado Springs, Colorado, embraces arts, culture, and education as essential to community identity and the lives of community members. The plan identifies six cultural "typologies" as the focus for efforts to support and grow "places and spaces… that are most important to the value and expression of our history, arts, culture, education, and tourism." Examples include Defining Institutions, such as the University of Colorado-Colorado Springs and the Pikes Peak Center for Performing Arts; and Community Assets, such as public libraries, primary and secondary schools, and community centers. In addition, Creative Districts and Corridors "create supportive environments for creative organizations, artists, and enthusiasts to live, work, and share ideas."

Housing for All

Housing is an important social system and topic to address in the comprehensive plan. *Decent, safe, and affordable housing* should be available to all community members. Decent housing means that every home should be in a state of good repair, free of toxic materials, and advance the well-being of residents. How buildings are sited and oriented can impact health and wellness through factors such as access to sunlight, fresh air, accessibility, and mobility. Safe housing provides a place of refuge and security from natural disasters and other threats. Affordable housing refers to the availability of reasonably priced housing, particularly for individuals and households with earnings below the medium income. Retaining existing housing sock is key to an affordable supply of housing.

Housing needs and demands vary across demographic groups and the local housing supply must respond to that diversity. In the 21st century, housing needs and demands are rapidly evolving due to changing demographics in communities and regions across the country. Examples include changes in household composition, such as increasing numbers of single-person and single-parent households, as well as a growing population of seniors, many of whom live alone or in multi-generational households. In addition, communities are becoming more ethnically diverse and home to new immigrants. These factors are important to consider when addressing current and future housing demand and supply.

Inventory and Analysis

Housing needs are affected by a variety of dynamic factors related to supply, shifting demographics, market conditions, and demand. For example, a community with an existing stock of predominantly single-family housing, an aging population, and declining household sizes may well face a mismatch between housing supply and demand. A housing needs assessment can be conducted as part of the inventory and analysis to determine how well the current and projected future supply of housing matches the needs of and affordability for all population groups and income levels. Information needed to conduct this assessment includes:

- Current housing characteristics, including total supply, types (configuration, sizes, price points), tenure (rental versus ownership), age, and condition.
- Rental and home sale prices compared with income levels (to measure housing affordability).
- Projections of future population and housing supply.
- Special housing needs (for example, seniors, persons with disabilities, persons experiencing homelessness).
- Opportunities and constraints to future housing provision (for example, land supply, regulatory barriers, energy demands).

The axiom has long been used that no more than 30 percent of annual income should be spent on housing (including rent or mortgage, utilities, taxes, and insurance). An analysis of housing affordability should also consider transportation and other household costs.

Fair, Decent, and Affordable Housing

The Fair Housing Act of 1968 prohibits discrimination in the sale, rental, and financing of homes based on race, color, national origin, religion, familial status, and disability. Ensuring fair, decent, and affordable housing for all is a continuing challenge in the 21st century. Many communities continue to be impacted by the historic legacy of redlining and other discriminatory practices. Extreme racial disparities in homeownership and wealth persist. The comprehensive plan can play an important role in promoting equal access to safe, decent, and affordable housing, along with increased opportunity for people of color to access good jobs, healthy food, quality schools, and other resources needed for success (National Low Income Housing Coalition 2018).

Many communities are experiencing escalating housing costs and increasing numbers of residents who find it difficult to buy homes or rent apartments at prevailing market rates. In addition to low-income and poor residents, the effects are being felt by middle-income workers (typically classified as those earning between 60 and 120 percent of the area median income).

Homelessness is another important issue to address in the comprehensive plan. Having a safe and secure home is a basic human need. For a complexity of reasons, such as economic insecurity, physical or mental health status, and family situation, people in communities across the United States can experience homelessness.[6] Approximately 60,000 families with children are homeless on any given night (National Alliance to End Homelessness 2018).

A range of strategies can be included in the comprehensive plan to address homelessness and affordable housing needs. Examples include partnering with housing and social service agencies to provide housing solutions and support services for persons experiencing homelessness; establishing community land banks dedicated to affordable housing; creating housing trust funds and other funding sources for affordable housing; and enacting regulatory reforms and incentives to encourage affordable housing construction.

Table 9.5 Fair, Decent, and Affordable Housing

Policy Directions

Ensure the provision of safe, decent, and affordable housing for all people, regardless of race, ethnicity, disability, gender, family status, belief, age, or special needs.

Preserve and maintain existing affordable housing stock.

Provide affordable workforce housing that is accessible to jobs.

Provide emergency shelter, transitional housing, and permanent supportive housing solutions for persons experiencing homelessness.

Applications

Develop universal design principles and standards to ensure housing accessibility and safety for all populations.

Work with housing agencies, regional planning bodies, the private sector, and other partners to implement initiatives and programs to increase the supply of affordable and workforce housing.

Adopt regulatory requirements and incentives for affordable housing set-asides, as allowed by state enabling legislation.

Identify funding sources to preserve existing and construct new affordable housing.

Create assistance programs and provide outreach that bring together housing resources, advocates, and members of the community experiencing homelessness.

Example: Raleigh, North Carolina

The Housing Element of the Raleigh 2030 Comprehensive Plan is organized around four themes: Quality and Diversity of Housing; Affordable Housing; Addressing Homelessness and Special Needs; and Fair Housing, Universal Design, and Aging in Place. The element begins with an analysis of the city's housing market, with a focus on affordable housing challenges. The analysis includes an assessment of regional impediments to fair housing choice. Quality and Diversity of Housing policy examples include promoting mixed-income neighborhoods and the geographic dispersal of affordable units throughout the city; encouraging energy efficiency; and providing housing diversity. Affordable Housing policy examples include establishing a permanent funding source; expanding housing assistance programs; and encouraging affordable workforce housing options, such as accessory dwelling units and cottage courts. Policies to address homelessness emphasize prevention, assistance, and supportive services.

Housing diversity

Changing demographics are creating the need for a more diverse housing supply. The 20th-century paradigm of single-family, owner-occupied homes as the prevalent housing type is in decline. According to the U.S. Census Bureau, the percentage of two-parent households fell from 85 percent of the total in 1960 to 65 percent in 2020. This trend is projected to continue as the population ages, becomes more diverse, and family structures change. Some researchers conclude that we are already at a tipping point and that, by 2030, there will be significant excess in the supply of single-family homes. In addition, the demand for distinct housing types at different stages of life is being supplanted by demand for flexible home designs that can accommodate all life cycle needs, including seniors who prefer to age in place. These changes are important to consider in developing comprehensive plan strategies and policies to meet future housing needs (Hinshaw 2007).

The standard paradigm that local governments have used to plan for housing is also changing. Shifting demographics and lifestyle preferences indicate the need to add new forms of housing to traditional housing types such as single-family detached, attached, and multifamily units. Alternatives include *secondary or accessory dwelling units* located on the same lot as an existing house; microunits (forms of apartments or condominiums with much smaller square footage); and patio homes, cottage homes, or other housing types sited on very small lots.

Table 9.6 Housing Diversity

Policy Directions
Provide a range of housing types of different sizes, configurations, tenures, and price points located in buildings of different sizes, configurations, age, and ownership structures.
Ensure that housing choices accommodate varying lifestyle and affordability needs and make it possible for households of different sizes and income levels to live in close proximity.
Provide for intergenerational housing.
Application
Conduct an analysis of housing conditions, supply, and demand to identify gaps in meeting community housing needs.
Implement housing initiatives and programs to fill gaps in the community's housing stock.
Update regulations and codes to allow a broader range of housing types, encourage green and healthy construction methods such as LEED for buildings, and incorporate universal design and other features that allow people to age in place.
Monitor housing policies, programs, and initiatives for progress in closing gaps in housing need, supply, and demand.

Cohousing communities include individual homes with shared facilities, such as a common dining area, shared recreational facilities, and common gardens. Other emerging housing types include prefabricated modular homes, tiny houses, shipping container homes, and pop-up houses. The latter typically require minimal or no foundation support, which allows them to be flexibly sited in various locations (including as secondary units).

While emerging forms of housing can help meet changing market demand, they may not be permitted by existing regulations, building codes, and financing mechanisms designed for traditional housing types. The comprehensive plan can set the direction to address changing demographics, market demands, and needs through an integrated and inclusive strategy for housing diversity.

Example: Tigard, Oregon

The goal of the Housing Element of the *Tigard Comprehensive Plan* is to "provide opportunities to develop a variety of housing types that meet the needs, preferences, and financial capabilities of Tigard's present and future residents." The plan acknowledges that "a one-size-fits-all" approach does not work when it comes to meeting housing needs. Housing policies include enacting land-use policies, codes, and standards to encourage a variety of housing types; supporting housing affordability, special-needs housing, ownership opportunities, and housing rehabilitation; and providing for high- and medium-density housing in town centers, regional centers, and along transit corridors. The plan supports the development of a range of housing types, such as shared housing, accessory dwelling units, smaller homes, adult foster homes, and other assisted living arrangements "that allow the elderly to remain in the community as their needs change."

Gentrification

Gentrification and the potential displacement of existing residents is a housing-related concern, particularly in urban communities with strengthening housing markets. Gentrification refers to a process of middle-class or affluent residents moving into a poor neighborhood to renovate and rebuild homes and commercial properties. The result can be increases in rents, property taxes, or mortgages that are unaffordable for long-time residents or businesses. In addition to the social, economic, and cultural aspects of community change, displaced individuals and groups can suffer loss of livelihoods, family and community connections, and negative health impacts.

A related concept, *environmental gentrification*, refers to investments in parks or other environmental improvements that attract new, wealthier residents and increase property values. For example, a study of the 606 (Bloomingdale) Trail, a 2.7-mile linear park and active transportation corridor in Chicago, found that housing prices along a portion of the trail rose 48 percent between 2013 (when construction began) and 2016 (Smith et al. 2016).

Evidence regarding the actual effects of gentrification on original neighborhood residents is mixed. For example, a study of neighborhood change between 2000 and 2014 in the 100 largest metro areas concluded that (1) gentrification modestly increased out-migration (although those who moved out were not observed to be measurably worse off), (2) many remaining adult residents benefited from declining exposure to poverty and increasing housing values, and (3) children benefited from greater educational and economic opportunity (Brummet and Reed 2019). Regardless, the comprehensive plan can define policies and strategies to minimize potential negative impacts of gentrification and provide positive benefits for existing residents.

Table 9.7 Gentrification

Policy Directions
Work with existing residents to identify and meet local needs and priorities such as housing, jobs, and smaller scale green infrastructure investments.
Ensure that projects and investments in low-income and minority neighborhoods serve local residents and do not contribute to community change or displacement.
Applications
Implement policies and programs to retain existing housing and residents, including actions to rehabilitate and restore homes to a state of good repair.
Implement policies and programs to maintain continued housing affordability and the ability of residents to remain in their homes.
Ensure that new housing, infrastructure, park, or other investments benefit existing residents.
Implement job training, workforce development, and other programs to increase economic opportunities for existing residents.

Summary

A community is, first and foremost, a social system comprising people, groups, and institutions who interact with each other and with other community systems. Healthy connections and relationships between social, natural, built environment, and economic systems are necessary for a community to be complete, sustainable, and equitable.

The primary social issues of the 21st century are social inequity, economic inequality, and the legacy of centuries of racism and discrimination. Planning with an equity lens (also referred to as interwoven equity) means framing, developing, and evaluating all comprehensive plan goals, policies, and actions for fairness and their impact in meeting the needs of all people. All segments of the community, including disadvantaged community members who have traditionally been excluded from decision-making processes, should be engaged in the comprehensive planning process and implementation.

Applying an equity lens means ensuring environmental justice and equal protection from environmental harm, health hazards, and the negative effects of climate change. It also means working with the residents of at-risk, distressed, and disadvantaged neighborhoods to improve physical, social, and environmental conditions and increase economic opportunity. This process should prioritize the needs of existing residents and minimize potential negative impacts from gentrification.

Social infrastructure refers to the physical places and organizations that shape the way people interact, such as schools, libraries, arts and cultural facilities, and community gathering places. These places and interactions build social capital that is an important component of a healthy and resilient community.

Finally, decent, safe, and affordable housing for all is key to ensuring a sustainable and equitable community. The comprehensive plan should include policies and strategies to meet the housing needs of all community members, as well as to provide diverse housing options to accommodate changing demographic groups and lifestyle preferences.

Notes

1 While intended for use by agencies and organizations, the Equity and Empowerment Lens developed by Multnomah County, Oregon is a good example of an equity lens that could be adapted for planning (Balajee et al. 2012).
2 Demographic change over time can be assessed using the *American Community Survey* and decennial census data. (U.S. Census Bureau 2019, 2020).
3 The profound, interrelated impacts of these factors on community members are expressed in the concept of *intersectionality*. The Merriam-Webster definition of intersectionality is "the complex, cumulative way in which the effects of multiple forms of discrimination (such as racism, sexism, and classism) combine, overlap, or intersect, especially in the experiences of marginalized individuals or groups."
4 The U.S. Environmental Protection Agency has developed an Environmental Justice Screening and Mapping Tool (ESCREEN) that can help communities identify and address potential environmental justice areas and issues. This tool combines 11 environmental indicators, 6 demographic indicators, and 11 indexes that combine environmental and demographic information (U.S. Environmental Protection Agency n.d.a).
5 For example, analysis of the July 1995 heat wave in Chicago (during which 739 more people died than the norm) revealed that the number of deaths was far higher in a neighborhood with weak social infrastructure than in an otherwise comparable neighborhood with strong social infrastructure (Klinenberg 2018).
6 HUD's annual *Homeless Populations and Subpopulations Report* tabulated 567,715 persons across the U.S. who were homeless during the last ten days of January 2019, including 186,695 who were unsheltered (U.S. Department of Housing and Urban Development 2019).

References

American Planning Association (2019). *Planning for Equity Policy Guide.* Chicago, IL: American Planning Association.

Balajee, Sonali S., et al. (2012). *Equity and Empowerment Lens (Racial Justice Focus).* Portland, OR: Multnomah County Accessed at https://multco-web7-psh-files-usw2.s3-us-west-2.amazonaws.com/s3fs-public/E%26E%20Lens%20Final-090613.pdf

Brummet, Quentin and Davin Reed (2019). *The Effects of Gentrification on the Well-Being and Opportunity of Original Resident Adults and Children.* Philadelphia, PA: Federal Reserve Bank of Philadelphia.

California Governor's Office of Planning and Research (2020). *State of California General Plan Guidelines, Chapter 4: Required Elements.* Sacramento, CA: Governor's Office of Planning and Research.

Godschalk, David and David Rouse (2015). *Sustaining Places: Best Practices for Comprehensive Plans,* Planning Advisory Service Report 578. Chicago, IL: American Planning Association.

Hinshaw, Mark (2007). *True Urbanism: Living in and Near the Center.* Chicago, IL: American Planning Association.

International City-County Management Association (ICMA) (2016). *Summary Report: Local Government Sustainability Practices.* Washington, DC: ICMA.

Klinenberg, Eric (2018). *Palaces for the People: How Social Infrastructure Can Help Fight Inequality, Polarization, and the Decline of Civic Life.* New York, NY: Broadway Books.

National Alliance to End Homelessness (2018). Family Homelessness in the United States: A State-by-State Snapshot. Accessed at https://endhomelessness.org/resource/family-homelessness-in-the-united-states-state-by-state-snapshot/

National Low Income Housing Coalition (2018). Fair Housing Act Overview and Challenges. Accessed at https://nlihc.org/resource/fair-housing-act-overview-and-challenges

Smith, Geoff, Sarah Duda, Jin Man Lee, and Michael Thompson (2016). *Measuring the Impacts of the 606: Understanding How a Large Public Investment Impacted the Surrounding Housing Market.* Chicago, IL: Institute for Housing Studies at DePaul University.

U.S. Census Bureau (2019). *2015 to 2019 American Community Survey.* Washington, DC: U.S. Department of Commerce.

U.S. Census Bureau (2020). *Census of Population and Housing.* Washington, DC: U.S. Department of Commerce.

U.S. Department of Housing and Urban Development (2019). *2019 CoC Homeless Populations and Subpopulations Report – All States, Territories, Puerto Rico, and DC.* Washington, DC: U.S. Department of Housing and Urban Development.

U.S. Environmental Protection Agency (n.d.a). EJSCREEN: Environmental Justice Screening and Mapping Tool. Accessed at https://www.epa.gov/ejscreen

U.S. Environmental Protection Agency (n.d.b). Learn About Environmental Justice. Accessed at https://www.epa.gov/environmentaljustice/learn-about-environmental-justice

U.S. Global Change Research Program (USGCRP) (2018). *Fourth National Climate Assessment. Volume II: Impacts, Risks, and Adaptation in the United States.* Washington, DC: USGCRP.

Chapter 10

Economic Systems

While natural systems comprise the community's life support system, the economy can be characterized as the community's lifeblood, without which residents could not meet their material needs. The economy is a system of producing and trading goods and services using a medium of exchange, which in the modern world is the financial system (although other means exist, including barter and its contemporary extension, the sharing economy). Because we live in an era in which residents purchase goods and services from around the globe, what economists call the *economic base* is needed to generate jobs and money for the local community and region.

In the 21st century, planning for economic systems has evolved from the older model of continuously pursuing more growth (and the boom-and-bust cycles that inevitably result) to address broader considerations such as economic resilience, economic opportunity, and resource efficiency. This chapter is organized around these three interrelated themes. Topics addressed include asset-based economic development, disaster preparedness and economic recovery, land and infrastructure needs, resource efficiency, and fiscal sustainability.

Sustainability, Resilience, and Equity

A sustainable economy is one in which finite resources are stewarded and conserved for future generations. Stewardship includes limiting negative externalities such as environmental pollution, consumption of nonrenewable resources, and greenhouse gas emissions that contribute to climate change. Emerging economic models, such as the green, circular, and sharing economies, can lead to more environmentally sustainable outcomes. Economic

---

DOI: 10.4324/9781003024170-12

sustainability also involves stabilizing employment and income from boom-and-bust cycles, as well as strategies to promote investment in existing communities.

A resilient economy has the ability to avoid, withstand, and recover quickly from the effects of major shocks or disruptions to its economic base, such as a natural disaster or severe economic downturn (U.S. Economic Development Administration n.d.). Characteristics of a resilient economy include a diverse employment base, reliance on local assets to meet many of its needs, a workforce with the training and skills to shift between jobs or industries, and a robust disaster planning system encompassing hazard mitigation, pre-disaster preparedness, and post-disaster economic recovery. Economic resiliency builds on local assets and opportunities and provides for the reliable delivery of services and goods to the community.

An equitable economy is one in which all community members benefit from living wages, decent and affordable housing, access to employment and jobs training, and lessening of economic stress on individuals and families. It ensures that groups that have suffered discrimination for reasons such as gender, race, and ethnic origin can access resources such as education, training, and government services and receive fair treatment in the labor market.

Economic opportunity has a strong connection to public health and personal well-being. Job security and living wages allow individuals to receive reliable health care and experience reduced physical, mental, and emotional stress. Moreover, economic initiatives and programs can be used to bridge disparities and establish equity for all community members.

Inventory and Analysis

A traditional approach to community economic planning begins with an *economic base analysis*. This analysis identifies key industries that generate jobs by exporting goods or services (for example, manufacturing, professional services, and health care) or otherwise bringing revenue into the community (for example, tourism). The analysis addresses elements of the community that affect the economic base, including the local workforce, the availability of land and buildings, mobility and utility infrastructure, and tax and regulatory conditions. Other factors to consider include school quality, availability of workforce development programs, housing availability and affordability, recreational opportunities, and the health of the environment. Additionally, access to high-speed internet service has become vitally important to allow companies and workers to participate in a global economy (Nuñez 2017). Natural, historic, cultural, social, institutional, and other community assets are increasingly important to consider in the 21st-century economy as companies and skilled workers make location decisions based on quality of life.

A *market analysis* is another tool to help establish an economic baseline for the comprehensive plan. A market analysis should factor in local supply and demand, sale and lease prices, potential revenues, and implications for fiscal sustainability. When conducting the analysis, it should be noted that housing or other projections based on past trends will not necessarily continue in the future, as market conditions can change.

An *economic sector analysis* is a third method commonly used to understand a local or regional economy. This analysis identifies key sectors (for example, health care, manufacturing, or information technology), major employers within those sectors, and workforce characteristics (distribution by age and occupation, education, income levels, and unemployment). The *North American Industry Classification System* (NAICS) is the standard used for this purpose (U.S. Bureau of Labor Statistics 2020a).

Economic Resilience

Communities aspire to have a resilient economy with a healthy economic base that offers job opportunities for all community members at a living wage. Achieving this goal is challenging, given national and global trends beyond the control of communities and local factors such as historic legacy and characteristics of people and place.

In the second half of the 20th century, the market economy supported a sizable middle class. Recent trends have created a growing divide between the rich and the poor and a decline in the share of wealth held by middle-income households (Horowitz, Igielnik and Kockhar 2020). These trends include globalization; technological advancements such as the Internet and automation; and the transition from a manufacturing to a service economy in which access to knowledge and information is key to success.

Two major systemic shocks – the Great Recession of 2008 and the COVID-19 pandemic of 2020 – highlight the need for new approaches to meeting the economic challenges of the 21st century. The recession was the result of a failure of the financial system that resulted in millions of Americans losing their homes, jobs, and savings. It was followed by an uneven recovery that accentuated the divide between the nation's least and most advantaged communities, families, and individuals (Fikri, Lettieri, and Steller 2018). During the COVID-19 pandemic, the unemployment rate spiked to levels not seen since the Great Depression. Relatively low-paying job sectors such as restaurants and bars, travel and transportation, and personal services were most severely impacted, again highlighting structural inequities in the economic system (Dey and Loewenstein 2020).

The increasing frequency and severity of natural disasters are another major cause of economic disruption. Over a 40-year period beginning in 1980, the United States experienced approximately 250 weather and climate disasters, each with estimated costs of $1 billion or more; the cumulative costs of these events exceeded $1.6 trillion (Smith 2019).[1] In the early 21st century, the annual average number of billion-dollar disasters was more than double the long-term average. A study of the impacts on wealth inequality of natural disasters since the turn of the century found that white households and those with more education gain wealth after disasters, while minority households and renters lose wealth (Howell and Elliott 2019). Given these trends, the challenge for the 21st-century comprehensive plan is to define a new vision for and approach to achieving a prosperous economy that offers opportunity for all while yielding sustainable, resilient, and equitable outcomes.

Asset-Based Economic Development

Asset-based economic development builds on natural, social, cultural, and other resources that already exist in the community or local region. It is a bottom-up approach, as opposed to the traditional approach of identifying perceived gaps and deficiencies in the local economy and attracting new investment or industries from elsewhere to fill those gaps. Asset-based economic development takes advantage of local culture and history, available facilities and services, local talent and skills, natural surroundings, and regional resources (Read 2011).

Asset-based economic development can be used by any community, from small towns and rural regions to medium-sized and large cities, to create a more resilient economy. Advocates of this approach assert that it fosters sustainable long-term growth, greater returns on local investment, improved job creation and retention, increases in per capital income, enhancements in the local tax base, and strengthened regional networks. As an example, communities can capitalize on historic, cultural, agricultural, and/or natural resources to attract visitors who will spend money on local products and services (University of Delaware n.d.).

Disaster Preparedness and Economic Recovery

Planning to minimize economic disruption and promote economic recovery in the aftermath of a disaster – whether natural or human-caused – should be conducted before disaster strikes. Extreme weather and other disruptive events are often measured in monetary terms by the direct physical damage they cause to buildings, properties, and infrastructure. Disasters have secondary and tertiary impacts as well, such as business closures and loss of revenue, service disruptions (for example, power outages, access to essential supplies, and childcare), and interruptions in supply chains, deliveries, and the distribution of goods and services. Business owners are impacted, as are their employees, suppliers, other places that produce and sell goods, and so on.

A disaster preparedness and economic recovery plan allows communities to restore economic activities and services more quickly and efficiently after a disaster strikes. Such a plan should identify strategies and actions to both prepare for and respond to the disaster. Examples of *disaster preparedness* include:

- Ensuring redundancy in telecommunications and broadband networks to protect commerce and public safety in the event of a disaster.
- Identifying and addressing essential systems that are at risk of failure during a disaster (for example, aging infrastructure).
- Promoting understanding by local businesses of vulnerabilities as a basis for pre-disaster preparedness and post-disaster continuity.
- Employing safe development practices.

Examples of *disaster response* include:

- Defining key roles, responsibilities, and key actions to take after a disaster strikes.
- Having a communications process in place that can be used in the event of a disaster.
- Establishing a capability to rapidly contact key officials to communicate business sector needs and coordinate impact assessment efforts (U.S. Department of Commerce n.d.).

Table 10.1 Economic Resilience

Policy Directions
Capitalize on community and regional assets to increase economic resiliency and create economic opportunities.
Mitigate risks and facilitate restoration of economic activities and services in the event of a disaster.

Applications
Identify cultural, historic, and environmental assets, facilities and services, talents and skills, and other local and regional resources as the basis for an asset-based economic development approach.
Develop a pre-disaster preparedness and post-disaster recovery plan that defines roles, responsibilities, communications, and key actions to prepare for and respond to disasters.
Work with community members and businesses to understand where vulnerabilities and risks are likely.
Identify essential systems that are at risk of failure during a disaster. Develop actions to upgrade these systems and strategies for quick recovery in the event that a disaster occurs.
Define roles, responsibilities, communications, and key actions to prepare for and respond to disasters.

Example: Madelia, Minnesota

Located in southern Minnesota, Madelia is a small city with approximately 2,300 residents. The city's *Economic Resiliency Plan* has a primary goal of diversifying the economy beyond its current reliance on manufacturing, health care, and retail. The plan includes a focus on economic disturbances that result from natural or human-caused disasters. The catalyst for the plan was a fire that destroyed several buildings and businesses in the downtown, which impacted nearly 20 percent of the city's service sector jobs (Madelia 2018).

The city employed a robust community engagement process to develop the plan. The plan includes an extensive analysis of the existing city and regional economy, as well as an analysis of community strengths, weaknesses, opportunities, and threats. The plan recommendations call for the city to capitalize on its assets to create a more diverse, resilient economy. Strategies include supporting arts and cultural activities, strengthening the tourism and hospitality industry, and addressing climate change impacts such as flooding and drought.

Economic Opportunity

Economic opportunity refers to the ability of all community members to access secure jobs at living wages. Numerous barriers exist to economic opportunity, such as high levels of income inequality, unequal access to educational opportunities, residential segregation by race and income, and disproportionate levels of investment (for example, in rural and urban places, or affluent and poor neighborhoods). Addressing these barriers requires a holistic approach that leverages change across community systems, with the goal of creating conditions in which all community members can realize their human potential. For example, a healthy natural environment provides important physical and mental health benefits. Built environment systems, such as walkable neighborhoods with decent housing and multimodal mobility options, similarly promote health and provide access to jobs. Social systems that help prepare individuals to participate in the workforce include, among others, early childhood development, education, and social infrastructure and services. In short, all community systems must work together to support economic opportunity for all members of the community.

Increasing economic opportunity requires broad-based, cross-sectoral partnerships between different levels of government, public schools, community colleges and vocational schools, other educational institutions, major employers and businesses, and civic and philanthropic organizations. These groups should be engaged in the comprehensive planning process together with community members from all walks of life, especially those experiencing economic challenges. Increasing economic opportunity also requires collaboration with practitioners with knowledge of job and market conditions; regional and global economic trends; equity considerations; financing, tax, and lending practices; and more.

In contrast to 20th-century economic development practices (which focused on attracting businesses to a community through means such as tax incentives), economic opportunity focuses on developing the potential of the people who already live in the community. Therefore, *workforce development* is key to increasing economic opportunity. This need is particularly important given the impacts of information and communications technology and trends such as automation on traditional job sectors. In addition to equipping community members with the skills needed to succeed in the 21st-century economy, workforce development programs benefit local employers and businesses by developing an educated and trained pool of potential employees.

Table 10.2 Economic Opportunity

Policy Directions

Address economic opportunity in tandem with other comprehensive plan goals and policies, such as those addressing the natural environment, land use, mobility, equity, housing, health, and community facilities and services.

Increase economic opportunity by creating complete communities that provide a full range of services, businesses, and jobs.

Applications

Develop programs and strategies to retain existing jobs and create new employment opportunities, working with major employers, businesses, education providers, civic organizations, and institutions.

Apply an equity lens to ensure that economic opportunities are available to disadvantaged and minority populations.

Work with public schools, academic institutions, and training centers, to ensure that members of the community have access to relevant workforce education and skills.

Example: Durham, North Carolina

The Economic Development Element in Durham's comprehensive plan includes a goal to "increase citizen access to high quality jobs and reduce poverty while increasing Durham's tax base." A supporting objective calls for collaboration with educational institutions to ensure that the city's workforce is well-educated and prepared for jobs in the local economy. Specific policies address vocational education and customized training, the training needs of local employers, and bilingual education and training. The plan designates Durham's Workforce Development Board for the Office of Economic and Workforce Development with the responsibility of working with partners to implement these policies. The mission of the Board is to "facilitate, plan, and coordinate workforce development resources to maximize the efforts of government, business, and education."

Land and Infrastructure Needs

Economic opportunity and the community's tax base depend on the availability of adequate land and infrastructure to support economic activity and jobs. This means ensuring that physical capacity and supporting systems (for example, roads and utilities) are sufficient to accommodate commercial, industrial, and mixed-use development and redevelopment to meet changing market demands. The comprehensive plan provides the opportunity to plan for the appropriate amount of land and structures that are located, sized, and constructed to support the production of goods and services based on current and projected economic conditions.

Land and infrastructure needs are relevant to growing places experiencing increased economic demand, as well as to places experiencing population decline and the potential need to "right-size" facilities and infrastructure for fiscal sustainability.[2] In some circumstances, communities may need to realign or even decommission out-of-date physical infrastructure. Communities in transition have the opportunity to develop more sustainable and resilient infrastructure, including energy systems that are less reliant on fossil fuels.

The comprehensive plan also provides a mechanism to address the mobility and accessibility needs of employers, employees, and customers. Employment clusters, office centers, and compact, mixed-use development patterns provide opportunities to design convenient and reliable mobility connections. Mobility systems to support economic activity and opportunity for community members should offer a variety of travel modes, including transit, rideshare, bicycling, and walking. Easy accessibility is especially important for residents who may not own or use automobiles.

Table 10.3 Land and Infrastructure Needs

Policy Directions
Provide sufficient land and supporting infrastructure to accommodate economic activity and jobs.
Ensure that adequate funding is available to develop, operate, and maintain essential facilities and infrastructure.
Provide a range of mobility options for community members to access employment centers.

Applications
Conduct a buildable lands analysis to determine the community's physical capacity to meet current and projected future economic needs.
Plan for ongoing maintenance, operations, and life-cycle costs of essential facilities and infrastructure in the capital improvement program, including deferred maintenance of existing infrastructure.
Partner with technology providers to develop and maintain affordable broadband infrastructure for businesses and community members.

> **Example: Clay County, Florida**
>
> Florida legislation provides the statutory authority for local governments to include an optional Economic Development Element in their comprehensive plans. The Economic Development Element of the *Clay County Comprehensive Plan* establishes two major goals: (1) "achieve and maintain a diversified and growing economy...that assures maximum employment opportunities while maintaining the quality of life and quality of the environment" and (2) "... develop a highly skilled and globally competitive workforce to meet the needs of employers in Clay County." Policies address the provision of sufficient land to support economic activity and employment; the adequacy of supporting infrastructure, including traditional utilities (such as water and sewer) and information and communications technology; and the attraction of a younger, more diverse, and entrepreneurial workforce.

Resource-Efficient Economy

Resource efficiency means using Earth's limited resources in a sustainable manner while minimizing environmental impacts (European Commission n.d.). A resource-efficient economy uses renewable resources, recycles materials, and reduces waste, thus providing environmental, social, and health benefits while creating business and job opportunities. For example, renewable energy jobs are among the fastest-growing occupations in the United States.[3] In another example, local food production, processing, and distribution provide local employment benefits, reduce energy usage and other associated with importing food, and increase access to healthy foods for community members.

Economic concepts that relate to and overlap with the resource-efficient economy include the green, circular, and sharing economies. These concepts offer alternatives to the dominant 20th-century economic model, which persists today. This model consumes finite resources, encourages waste, exacerbates inequality, and generates negative externalities (for example, air and water pollution) that impact environmental and human health.

Green Economy

The *green economy* is commonly defined as low carbon, resource efficient, and socially inclusive. An inclusive green economy improves human well-being and builds social equity while reducing environmental risks and scarcities (UNEP n.d.).

Green businesses and jobs are the foundation of the green economy. Green businesses use sustainable models and practices to provide environmentally sound products and services. Green jobs contribute to conserving natural resources and creating a healthy environment while providing inclusive, living wage employment opportunities. Green jobs occur across employment sectors, including manufacturing and goods production, research and development, professional and personal services, and sustainable management and administration. Renewable energy and green building are important green business sectors. Green businesses and jobs can employ circular economy practices in which waste is reused.

Circular Economy

A *circular economy* aspires to eliminate waste and reduce the continual consumption of new resources. Reuse of resources and materials is emphasized, along with repair and refurbishing of equipment and products. Repurposing waste results in less pollution, including a reduction in greenhouse gas emissions. The circular economy contrasts with the so-called linear economy of extraction, production, consumption, and waste – and the health and environmental impacts that result (Figure 10.1).

The circular economic model is an example of the systems approach cited throughout this book. It is frequently used by corporations and businesses, including food, construction, and mobility industries. Drawing on numerous sources, the non-profit group Circle Economy identifies eight elements that define the circular economy:

Core Elements

1. Prioritize regenerative resources.
2. Stretch the lifetime.
3. Use waste as a resource.

Enabling Elements

4. Rethink the business model.
5. Team up to create joint value.
6. Design for the future.
7. Incorporate digital technology.
8. Strengthen and advance knowledge.

(Circle Economy n.d.)

Local governments are on the front lines for addressing energy use, waste, and pollutants that contribute to environmental degradation and climate change.[4] They hold core responsibilities in key sectors for the circular economy, including mobility and solid waste. They influence goods and service production, delivery, consumption, and disposal through municipal operations, infrastructure investments, policies, and regulations. Given these roles, local governments can advance the circular economy by acting as a role model for businesses and community members, facilitating connections and dialogue, and directing policies, regulations, and investments to support the transition from a linear economy (Organization for Economic Cooperation and Development 2020).

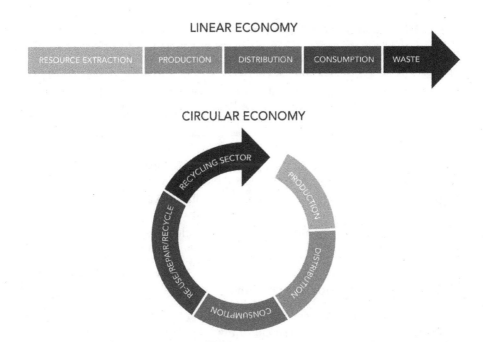

Figure 10.1 Linear versus Circular Economy

Source: Metro Vancouver.

Sharing Economy

As defined in the 1980s, the *sharing economy* referred to a model of shared production, exchange, and consumption of goods or services by individuals or organizations (Meier 2015). The practice has grown to include borrowing or renting goods and services, typically using an online platform to make transactions. The principles of a sharing economy support the overall purpose and intent of the resource-efficient economy described above. For example, convenient carshare and rideshare services reduce the need to own a private automobile.

How the sharing economy will continue to evolve remains to be seen. On the one hand, it provides benefits such as maximizing the use of existing resources and reducing waste through shared consumption. It also can create new jobs, increase economic activity, and spur creative solutions to societal problems. On the other hand, questions include whether the sharing economy consistently improves resource-efficiency, how reliable it is, and whether it is fair and equitable for all community members (Meier 2015). Similar to the circular economy, local governments have an important role to play in advancing the positive benefits of the sharing economy through policy, regulations, and investments.

Table 10.4 Resource-Efficient Economy

Policy Directions
Promote green businesses and jobs.
Promote the reduction and elimination of waste, greenhouse gas emissions, and pollutants, and the reuse of resources and materials, by local businesses.

Applications
Provide incentives and financial support to green businesses.
Adopt green practices in municipal operations (for example, recycling and reduction of waste streams; energy-efficient buildings and vehicular fleets).
Engage community members and businesses in dialogue and action to advance sustainable, resilient, and equitable economic outcomes.
Implement policy and regulatory frameworks to reduce negative impacts and maximize the positive benefits provided by the sharing economy.

Example: Fort Walton Beach, Florida

The Economic Development Element of the *Fort Walton Beach Comprehensive Plan* identifies environmental sustainability as key to ensuring competitiveness in the 21st-century economy. The plan calls for the city to promote itself as a "green local government" that encourages clean energy, environmental protection, and environmentally friendly business and industry. Supporting policies include, among others, promoting alternatives to driving alone, developing greenways along major arterials, and encouraging water conservation and reuse. The plan calls for developing a target list and potential sites for renewable energy industries, such as wind and solar.

Fiscal Sustainability

Adequate financing and funding of local governmental facilities, services, and operations is required for economic vitality and the well-being of community members. Fiscal sustainability involves balancing revenues and expenditures to provide necessary and desired facilities, services, and amenities. It is incumbent on local governments to identify a responsible and equitable mix of revenue sources to support both operating and capital expenditures. Stable funding for operations and maintenance over the entire lifecycle of public facilities and infrastructure is a key component of fiscal sustainability.

Revenue sources for operating expenditures include local taxes (primarily property taxes, sales tax, and/or income tax), allocations from other levels of government (referred to as intergovernmental transfers), and user fees and charges. Major capital expenditures are normally funded by bonds, including general obligation bonds (repaid from general revenues raised by the jurisdiction) and revenue bonds (repaid from revenues generated by the expenditure, for example water or sewer bills). Other funding sources include impact fees on new development, subarea financing systems (for example, business improvement districts), tax increment financing, and governmental and philanthropic grants (Ingram and Yu-Huang Hong 2009).

Working with partner organizations and agencies, the local government also plays a role in supporting the fiscal sustainability of community members and businesses. Ensuring that individuals and households have the resources available to ensure economic stability is in the best interest of society as a whole. Supporting living wage jobs, affordable housing, and the reduction of economic burden and stress yields economic and health benefits that can contribute to the fiscal health of local governments. Communities can also benefit from providing new or existing businesses with start-up assistance (for example, incubator space), financial support (for example, loans and incentives), technical training, access to high-speed Internet service, and other types of support. Outcomes can include stabilization and growth of the local employment base and increased local tax revenues.

Business improvement districts are formed by businesses that agree to pay an additional tax or levy to fund projects or programs (for example, capital improvements, increased security, or maintenance) in a defined geographic area. The purpose is to make the district more attractive to customers and other potential businesses. However, many communities have districts where existing businesses may not have the means to support an improvement district. Such districts offer the opportunity for targeted support to increase economic vitality and encourage the types of investment that occurs in other business districts, thus contributing to equity and fiscal sustainability.

Fiscally Sustainable Growth

It is well documented that outward expansion of existing development (commonly referred to as urbanization or sprawl) is costly, stretches the capacity of jurisdictions to provide public facilities, infrastructure, and services, and has negative environmental impacts. The effects of growing outward are experienced by small towns and rural places, mid-sized communities, and large cities alike.

Depending on variables such as local tax structures and the type of development, cost–benefit analyses demonstrate that the public costs of growth beyond the existing urban edge generally exceed revenues generated. These costs include initial construction and ongoing maintenance of supporting infrastructure (such as roads, water, and sewer) and other public facilities and services required to service new development (such as schools, safety, and fire protection). The resulting deficits strain the fiscal sustainability of local governments and increase the tax burdens placed on community members and businesses. Conversely, established downtowns, neighborhoods, and commercial areas served by existing infrastructure are more financially productive as measured by return on public investment (or a simpler metric, value per acre) than newer, low-density residential and commercial development (Marohn 2019). The conclusion is that promoting infill and redevelopment in existing developed areas is more fiscally sustainable than extending infrastructure and services to subsidize growth outside of those areas.

Financing Redevelopment

Communities pursuing infill and redevelopment opportunities have a rich array of fiscal tools available to leverage reinvestment and revitalization for fiscal sustainability. Taxation tools include tax abatements and credits, special taxing districts, and tax increment financing. Developer impact fees can provide funding for public

Table 10.5 Fiscal Sustainability

Policy Directions

Ensure that funding and revenue streams are adequate to finance quality public infrastructure, facilities, services, and operations and maintenance.

Prioritize infill and redevelopment in developed areas served by existing infrastructure over utility extensions and other subsidies for new growth beyond the edge of urban development.

Applications

Monitor revenue streams and identify opportunities for new sources of funding to supporting needed public facilities and services.

Implement policies, regulations, fiscal tools, and incentives to encourage investment in existing developed areas and discourage growth in areas that are fiscally challenging to serve.

Example: Palo Alto, California

The *City of Palo Alto Comprehensive Plan 2030* includes a Business and Economics Element that addresses the fiscal health of the city. The plan states that "continued fiscal health is crucial to providing the range and quality of infrastructure, services, amenities and maintenance that residents expect" and identifies a balanced ratio of revenues to expenses as the key indicator. An analysis of revenues and expenses over the seven years prior to adoption of the plan reveal that revenues consistently outpaced expenditures during that time period. The plan includes a fiscal responsibility goal calling for careful management of revenues and expenditures to maintain fiscal health.

As part of comprehensive plan development, the city retained a consultant to conduct a fiscal analysis of six alternative scenarios for Palo Alto's future growth (Economics & Planning Systems, Inc. 2017). The analysis concluded that all six scenarios would generate net revenues for the City of Palo Alto general fund, confirming the city's ability to continue to provide and operate facilities and services for present and future residents, businesses, and employees.

infrastructure, facilities, and services. Bonds, grants, and loan programs can be used to finance redevelopment activities such as brownfield remediation and reuse. Special improvement districts can be established to fund infrastructure improvements, cultural facilities, and social amenities. Other redevelopment tools include revolving loan programs and land banks (Chen and Ebdon 2014).

Summary

The predominant economic development model of the 20th century focused on pursuing growth, often by attracting new businesses to move into the community using tax subsidies or other incentives. A more holistic, robust economic model has emerged in the 21st century, with its foundation in sustainability, resiliency, and equity. Key themes include economic resilience, economic opportunity, and a resource-efficient economy.

Economic resilience refers to the ability of local and regional economy to maintain a healthy economic base with job opportunities for all community members, no matter what shocks and stresses it experiences. Such resilience is difficult to achieve in the 21st century, given the economic effects of events such as the Great Recession and COVID-19 pandemic and trends such as globalization and accelerating technological change. Asset-based economic development, which relies on local assets and reduces dependency on outside resources, is one approach communities can use to build economic resilience. Given the increasing frequency and severity of natural disasters in the 21st century, it is important for communities to prepare for and have a plan in place to recover quickly from the economic disruptions caused by a disaster.

Economic opportunity refers to the ability of all community members to access secure jobs at living wages. Like economic resilience, economic opportunity is difficult to achieve given barriers such as socioeconomic inequality, unequal access to quality education, health care, and other services, and residential segregation by race and income. Increasing economic opportunity requires broad, cross-sectoral partnerships to effectuate change across multiple community systems, such as education, mobility, housing, and social infrastructure and services. Workforce development – equipping community members with the training and skills needed to succeed in the 21st-century economy – is key to increasing economic opportunity.

A resource-efficient economy uses renewable resources, materials, and recycles waste, thus providing environmental, social, and health benefits while creating business and job opportunities. Related concepts include the green economy, circular economy, and sharing economy. These emerging concepts offer alternatives to the dominant economic model of the 20th century, which consumes finite resources, encourages waste, exacerbates inequality, and negatively impacts environmental and human health.

Notes

1 Smith (2019) states that according to NOAA, "the number and cost of disasters are increasing over time due to a combination of increased exposure, vulnerability, and the fact that climate change is increasing the frequency of some types of extremes that lead to billion-dollar disasters."

2 The Imagine Flint Master Plan is an example of a comprehensive plan that proposes right-sizing of water and sewer infrastructure. The plan states that "the city should coordinate gradual implementation of green spaces and lower density neighborhoods with (the) utilities department in order to reduce fixed infrastructure costs and 'right size' water and sewer piping" (Morckel 2020).

3 The Bureau of Labor Statistics projects that wind turbine service technicians and solar photovoltaic installers will be the fastest and third-fastest growing occupations from 2019 to 2029, with growth rates of 61 percent and 51 percent, respectively (U.S. Bureau of Labor Statistics 2020b).

4 Cities represent almost two-thirds of global energy demand and produce up to 80 percent of greenhouse gas emissions and 50 percent of global waste (Organization for Economic Development and Cooperation 2019).

References

Chen, Can and Carol Ebdon (2014). *Financing Tools for Urban Redevelopment*. Omaha, NE: Omaha by Design.

Circle Economy (n.d.). Key Elements of the Circular Economy. Accessed at https://www. circle-economy.com/circular-economy/key-elements

Dey, Matthew and Mark Loewenstein (2020). "How Many Workers Are Employed in Sectors Directly Affected by COVID-19 Shutdowns, Where Do They Work, and How Much Do They Earn?" *Monthly Labor Review* (April). Washington, DC: U.S. Bureau of Labor Statistics.

Economics & Planning Systems, Inc. (2017). *Fiscal Analysis of the City of Palo Alto Comprehensive Plan*. Palo Alto, CA: City of Palo Alto.

European Commission (n.d.). Resource Efficiency. Accessed at https://ec.europa.eu/ environment/resource_efficiency/

Fikri, Kenan, John Lettieri and Sarah Steller (2018). *Escape Velocity: How Elite Communities Are Pulling Away in the 21st Century Race for Jobs, Businesses, and Human Capital*. Washington, DC: Economic Innovation Group.

Horowitz, Juliana, Ruth Igielnik, and Rakesh Kockhar (2020). Trends in Income and Wealth Inequality. Pew Research Center. Accessed at https://www.pewresearch.org/ social-trends/2020/01/09/trends-in-income-and-wealth-inequality/

Howell, Junia and James Elliott (2019). "Damages Done: The Longitudinal Impacts of Natural Hazards on Wealth Inequality in the United States" *Social Problems*, 66:3 (August). Oxford, England: Oxford University Press, pp. 448–467.

Ingram, Gregory K. and Yu-Huang Hong, ed. (2009). *Municipal Revenues and Land Policies: Proceedings of the 2009 Land Policy Conference*. Cambridge, MA: Lincoln Institute of Land Policy.

Madelia, Minnesota (2018). *Economic Resiliency Plan*. Madelia, MN: City of Madelia.

Marohn, Charles (2019). *Strong Towns: A Bottom-Up Revolution to Rebuild American Prosperity*. Hoboken, NJ: John Wiley & Sons.

Meier, Marco (2015). The Sharing Economy: Ideal Sustainability or Bartering the Future? Accessed at https://www.linkedin.com/pulse/sharing-economy-ideal-sustainability-bartering-future-marco-meier/

Morckel, Victoria (2020). "Flint (MI) Missed an Opportunity to "Right Size" with Its Water Crisis," Chicago, IL: *Journal of the American Planning Association*, 86:3, pp. 304–310.

Núñez, Luis (2017). *Advancing the Economic Development Element in Comprehensive Plans.* PAS Memo. Chicago, IL: American Planning Association.

Organization for Economic Cooperation and Development (2019). *The Circular Economy in Cities and Regions: Brochure.* Paris, France: OECD Publishing.

Organization for Economic Cooperation and Development (2020). *The Circular Economy in Cities and Regions: Synthesis Report.* Paris, France: OECD Publishing.

Read, Anna (2011). *Asset-Based Economic Development and Building Sustainable Rural Communities. Part 1: Industry and Industry Clusters | A briefing paper from the ICMA Center for Sustainable Communities.* Washington, DC: International City/County Management Association.

Smith, Adam (2019). 2018's Billion Dollar Disasters in Context. Accessed at https://www.climate.gov/news-features/blogs/beyond-data/2018s-billion-dollar-disasters-context

United Nations Environment Programme (UNEP) (n.d.). "Green Economy." Accessed at https://www.unep.org/explore-topics/green-economy

University of Delaware, Institute of Public Administration (n.d.). Asset-Based Economic Development (in Complete Communities Toolbox). Accessed at https://www.completecommunitiesde.org/planning/inclusive-and-active/asset/

U.S. Bureau of Labor Statistics (2020a). *North American Industry Classification System.* Washington, DC: U.S. Department of Labor.

U.S. Bureau of Labor Statistics (2020b). *Occupational Outlook Handbook.* Washington, DC: U.S. Department of Labor.

U.S. Department of Commerce, Economic Development Administration (n.d.). Economic Resilience. Accessed at https://www.eda.gov/ceds/content/economic-resilience.htm

Chapter 11

Healthy Community

As personified by landscape architect Frederick Law Olmsted, who served as Executive Secretary of the U.S. Sanitary Commission during the Civil War, the professions of public health, city planning, and landscape architecture share common historical roots. A major catalyst for planning in the early 20th century was interest in public "health, safety, morals, or general welfare" (Village of Euclid vs. Ambler Realty Company 1926; Gorieb vs. Fox 1927). In the aftermath of the Supreme Court decisions that validated the role of planning and zoning in protecting public health, safety, and welfare, local governments focused on controlling nuisances and separating incompatible land uses through regulation. As the profession evolved alongside other governmental functions, its purview broadened and at the same time became more specialized to address topics such as transportation, housing, economic development, and natural resource conservation. Other disciplines similarly became more specialized; for example, public health professionals focused on disease prevention and environmental health while architects and landscape architects focused on the physical design of buildings and landscapes.

All of the above topics and many more are important to individual and community health. The World Health Organization defines health "as a state of complete physical, mental, and social well-being and not merely the absence of disease or infirmity" (World Health Organization 1946). According to the Institute of Medicine, the mission of the public health profession is to "fulfill society's interest in assuring conditions in which people can be healthy" (Institute of Medicine 1988). Recognizing the critical and overlapping roles played by different disciplines in creating these conditions, planning practitioners, the public health community, and allied professionals are reconnecting in the 21st century around a common interest in improving health through planning and design of the built environment and other community systems.

DOI: 10.4324/9781003024170-13

Figure 11.1 Social Determinants of Health
Source: Centers for Disease Control and Prevention.

The concept of *social determinants of health* was developed by the public health profession to characterize how the conditions in which people are born, grow, live, work, and age influence their health (Artiga and Hinton 2018; Figure 11.1). As the official policy guide for the community's future, the comprehensive plan has an important role to play in improving health outcomes such as mortality, morbidity, and life expectancy. Together, the natural, built environment, social, and economic systems addressed in Chapters 6–9 shape individual and community health. Comprehensive plan goals, policies, and actions can set the direction for achieving the overarching goal of becoming a healthy community. The importance of partnering with professionals in other disciplines (for example, public health, education, and social services) is evident in the categories and subcategories shown in Figure 11.1.

This chapter advances a health-in-all-policies approach (another concept developed by the public health profession) as a framework for a systems approach to achieving the goal of a healthy community. It highlights several topics for which the comprehensive plan can define policies and actions to improve community health: physical activity or active living, environmental health, access to healthy foods, and safety and security.

Sustainability, Resilience, and Equity

In the 21st century, health has emerged as an integrating theme for the comprehensive plan that is foundational to improving sustainability, resiliency, and equity. Health touches on all aspects of natural, built environment, social, and economic systems. The connections between health and community systems were vividly illustrated by the disruptions caused by the COVID-19 pandemic. These included tragic loss of life; severe economic impacts and increased income inequality; interruptions to education, business, travel, and entertainment; social isolation; and disproportionate impacts on communities of color, the elderly, and persons with underlying health conditions – all of which affected physical and mental health and wellness.[1] At the same time, many people experienced the health benefits provided by outdoor physical activity, access to parks and natural areas, and contact with nature.

A sustainable environment, economy, and society that conserve resources, maintain healthy natural systems (including clean air, water, and land), and provide for the needs of all community members are essential to a healthy community. Like sustainability, resilience is a key attribute of a healthy community – and vice versa. A healthy population is better prepared to withstand and recover quickly from shocks and stresses such as those caused by natural and human-caused disasters and a changing climate. However, as demonstrated by the COVID-19 pandemic, the impacts of such events are disproportionately felt by poor, minority, and disadvantaged populations.

Equity and environmental justice are critical health issues. Data from across the nation reveal stark differences in life expectancy (20 years or more) between zip codes in the same city (The Robert Wood Johnson Foundation 2020). Health equity depends upon fair and just treatment of all people, including disadvantaged community members. To address health disparities, all people should have access to a healthy natural and built environment, living wage jobs, nutritious foods, affordable housing and health care, social infrastructure and services, and more.

Inventory and Analysis

Compared with conventional planning topics like land use, transportation, and housing, public health is a relatively new issue area for the comprehensive plan.[2] The following information is useful to characterize community health conditions and identify issues of concern for the comprehensive plan:

- Rates and distribution of chronic conditions and diseases (for example, obesity, diabetes, cardiovascular disease, and cancer).
- Sources of air, water, chemical waste, and noise pollution (for example, roadways with high volumes of vehicular traffic, brownfield sites, and power plants).
- Access to healthy food (areas lacking access to grocery stores or other vendors of affordable, nutritious food are commonly referred to as food deserts).
- Disparities in health outcomes between different demographic groups and neighborhoods.
- Crime and safety conditions (including traffic injuries and fatalities).
- Substance abuse, overdoses, and deaths.[3]

County and city health departments can provide data on community health conditions. Health disparities and socially vulnerable populations are revealed by mapping and comparing this data to demographic characteristics from sources such as the U.S. Census.

Health in All Policies

An initial focus of the rediscovery of the relationship between planning and health has been on physical activity. A wealth of information is now available on the correlations between health, the built environment, and opportunities for people to engage in walking and biking (often referred to as *active transportation* or *active living*). Contemporary comprehensive plans commonly integrate physical activity into goals, policies, and actions for mobility networks, community design, and development patterns.

As exemplified by the social determinants of health, there is a growing awareness of the importance to health of community systems beyond the built environment. *Health in All Policies* (HiAP) is a collaborative approach to improving the health of all people by incorporating health considerations into decision-making across sectors and policy areas (Rudolph et al. 2013). For the comprehensive plan, this means addressing health in goals, policies, and actions across all community systems and components of the plan. Community health relates to the health of the natural environment; how the community is designed and constructed; how people access jobs, goods and services, parks, and other destinations; economic opportunity; safety and security; and so on.

The *Health Assessment Lens* is an example of the HiAP approach applied to community planning and design (Health + Design Initiative 2019). Colorado planners

Equity and Justice   Economic Resiliency

Human Well-Being   Healthy Homes and Buildings

Harmony with Nature   Healthy Community

Education and Wellness   Healthy Connections

Figure 11.2 Health Assessment Lens Categories
Source: Colorado Healthy Places Collaborative.

and allied professionals (representing 23 partner associations through the Colorado Healthy Places Collaborative) developed this tool to help engineers, designers, planners, health practitioners, community members, and decision-makers understand health conditions prior to beginning a project or program.

The *Health Assessment Lens* is organized around eight health categories to inform decision-making (Figure 11.2). Each category begins with a summary of key health considerations, followed by a series of questions. The questions are designed to help identify gaps in information, potential impacts, or likely health benefits. The lens is intentionally designed to be applied at the early scoping phase of a plan or project. It also lends itself to evaluation of existing plans and projects in order to better understand health outcomes.[4]

Table 11.1 Health in All Policies

Policy Directions
Employ a health-in-all-policies framework in developing comprehensive plan goals, policies, and actions.
Holistically address all aspects of health and well-being – physical, mental, emotional, and social – in planning, design, and decision-making.
Identify and address gaps in achieving health equity.

Applications
Use a health lens to identify and address local health conditions and priorities in the comprehensive plan, such as opportunities for physical activity, availability of healthy, locally grown food, social connections, and access to health care.
Develop measures to monitor health outcomes in projects, programs, and initiatives to implement the comprehensive plan, emphasizing health equity for all community members.
Develop and apply criteria to the development review and approval process, using principles such as multimodal connectivity, green infrastructure, mixed uses, and access to facilities and services (American Planning Association 2015).

Example: Stockton, California

The *Envision Stockton 2040 General Plan* identifies public health as one of five "specific topics of concern" raised by the community during the planning process. Goals, policies, and actions related to this topic are marked by icons throughout the elements of the plan. Examples include a land use policy and actions to integrate nature into the city, a transportation policy and actions addressing safe routes to work and school, and a safety policy and actions addressing noise exposure. The plan includes a Community Health Element organized around five key goals: healthy people, restored communities, a skilled workforce, affordable housing, and sustainability leadership.

Environmental Health

The health of humans and the health of environmental systems are inextricably linked. Environmental health focuses on relationships between people and their environment; promotes human health and well-being; and fosters healthy and safe communities (American Public Health Association n.d.). Topics related to environmental health to address in the comprehensive plan include, but are not limited to, toxins and pollutants, access to nature, climate, and noise.

Toxins and Pollutants. Exposure to toxins and pollutants in the natural and built environments seriously impacts human health and well-being. Toxic substances and pollutants generated by industrial or other human activities can be present in the air, water, and soil, as well as buildings and facilities in which people live, work, learn, and play. Removing sources of pollution and cleaning up and restoring brownfield sites, impaired waterways, and other damaged resources improves the health of individuals and communities.

Access to Nature. The health benefits of access to nature are well documented. Benefits can include reductions in stress, depression, and anxiety; reduced recovery time after an illness; and other physiological, mental, and social effects (Repke et al. 2018). Regular physical activity in parks and greenspaces helps children develop reasoning abilities and older adults increase and maintain their capacity for cognitive thinking (Kirkby 1989; Colcombe and Kramer 2003). Strategies to take advantage of the health benefits of nature include incorporating trees and other forms of green infrastructure into the built environment and providing parks and open space within easy walking distance of all community members.

Climate. Climate (the prevalent patterns of temperature, precipitation, sun, and winds) and its expression in day-to-day weather fluctuations are a major environmental influence on human health. Micro-climactic conditions (for example, shade and exposure to cooling breezes during the summer and sun exposure and protection from winds during the winter) can be beneficial to human health. Conversely, prevailing wind patterns can exacerbate air pollution impacts on sensitive land uses. While climate change may bring some localized health benefits (for example, fewer winter deaths in temperate climates and increased food production in certain areas), its effects are overwhelmingly negative (World Health Organization 2018). These effects include, among others, increased deaths from cardiovascular and respiratory disease as a result of extreme heat; deaths, injuries, and mental stress caused by increasingly severe natural disasters; and changes in the geographic range and transmission seasons of vector-borne diseases (for example, those transmitted by mosquitos). The health impacts of climate change can be addressed by mitigation measures that reduce greenhouse gas emissions (which requires a global scale response) and by adaptation measures at the local scale, such as increasing tree canopy to ameliorate the urban heat island effect.

Noise. Noise in the built environment is generated by commercial and industrial activities, vehicular and air traffic, and by the activities of daily life (for example, operating home appliances, entertainment, and even conversation). Noise levels are measured on a logarithmic scale using decibels (dB) as the measurement unit. Noise can harm human health when levels exceed approximately 80 dB (noise emitted

Table 11.2 Environmental Health

Policy Directions

Eliminate or (at a minimum) reduce exposure to toxins and pollutants in the natural and built environments.

Clean up contaminated soils and sites prior to reuse or development.

Ensure that all community members have safe, convenient access to parks, open spaces, and natural areas.

Restore polluted waterways to meet or exceed state and federal standards.

Mitigate stationary and mobile sources of air and noise pollution.

Applications

Identify contaminated soils, brownfield sites, impaired water resources, and sources of air and noise pollution in the inventory and analysis.

Plan for the mitigation and redevelopment of brownfields for productive uses.

Establish level of service standards for the provision of parks and green spaces within walking distance of all residents.

Implement climate change mitigation and adaptation measures such as reducing fossil fuel consumption, increasing the urban tree canopy, cool (highly reflective roofs), and nature-based solutions to reduce flooding impacts.

Establish standards to limit the noise impacts of commercial, industrial, and other noise-generating properties on adjacent properties.

Example: Portland, Oregon

Human health and environmental health are two of five guiding principles for Portland's *2035 Comprehensive Plan* (the others are economic prosperity, equity, and resilience). The human health principle addresses the role of Portland's physical environment in avoiding or minimizing negative health impacts and providing opportunities for community members to lead healthy, active lives. A key strategy is to increase access to complete neighborhoods where people of all ages and abilities have safe and convenient access to the goods and services needed in daily life. The environmental health principle calls for weaving nature into the city and fostering a healthy environment that sustains people, neighborhoods, and fish and wildlife. Strategies to implement this principle include designing development to work with nature (thus improving water quality, reducing stormwater runoff, and contributing to improved water quality), supporting nature-friendly infrastructure, and preserving and enhancing urban habitat corridors.

by a lawn mower can be around 90 dB). The mental and physical health effects of exposure to prolonged or excessive noise range from stress, reduced productivity, and fatigue from lack of sleep to cardiovascular disease, cognitive impairment, and tinnitus.

Access to Healthy Foods

According to the National Center for Chronic Disease Prevention and Health Promotion, poor nutrition is one of four major risk factors for preventable chronic diseases (the others are tobacco use, lack of physical activity, and excessive alcohol use). A healthy diet helps children grow and develop properly and reduces their risk of chronic diseases, including obesity. Adults who eat a healthy diet live longer and have a lower risk of obesity, heart disease, type 2 diabetes, and certain cancers. Healthy eating can help people with chronic diseases manage these conditions and prevent complications (National Center for Chronic Disease Prevention and Health Promotion n.d.).

Healthy foods are fresh or minimally processed, rich in nutrients, and low in carbohydrates, cholesterol, and fats. In many urban and other areas across the nation (commonly referred to as *food deserts*), residents find it difficult to access afford-able or good-quality fresh food. Demographic analysis reveals that the residents of census tracts categorized as food deserts typically have lower education levels, lower incomes, and higher unemployment than other areas. Moreover, food desert tracts tend to have higher poverty rates and concentrations of minority residents than otherwise similar low-income tracts in urban and rural areas (Dutko, Ver Ploeg,

Table 11.3 Access to Healthy Foods

Policy Directions
Ensure that all people have access to healthy, locally produced food.
Support local and regional food production, processing, distribution, and consumption.
Encourage farmland conservation and sustainable agricultural practices that protect the air, water, soil, and habitat.

Applications
Increase the availability of healthy, locally produced food through sources such as affordable grocery stores and corner stores, farmers markets, and community gardens.
Partner with social service providers on programs to increase food access and security.
Revise zoning regulations to permit agricultural uses such as community gardens, urban farms, and accessory uses.

and Farrigan 2012). The absence of healthy food sources within food deserts is compounded by *food insecurity*, which is the lack of consistent access to food due to insufficient financial resources.[5]

Urban places such as Baltimore (Maryland), Cleveland (Ohio), and Minneapolis (Minnesota) and rural places such as Cabarrus County (North Carolina), Burlington and Chittenden County (Vermont), and Marquette County (Michigan) have implemented a range of policies and programs to strengthen local food systems and increase access to healthy foods.[6] Strengthening local food systems begins by increasing the amount of locally grown and produced food.[7] Strategies should focus on increasing the availability of healthy, affordable foods in food deserts and to food insecure populations.

Example: Bloomington, Illinois

Bloomington is a city with approximately 77,000 residents located in McLean County in northcentral Illinois. The *City of Bloomington Comprehensive Plan 2035* includes a Healthy Community Element with the vision that Bloomington "will provide healthy and active lifestyle choices for all." Access to healthy foods is one of seven guiding themes:

> Bloomington will become a food-secure community that promotes the ability to grow, consume, and distribute healthy, locally produced food. Our food system will benefit our community, our economy, and our environment.

Food system policies and actions are designed to encourage local food production, facilitate local food processing and distribution, and promote consumption of healthy, affordable, and locally produced food by all residents.

Public Safety

A key component of community health, public safety refers to the prevention and protection of people from crimes, disasters, and other potential dangers and threats. Community members expect their homes, neighborhoods, and surroundings in which they carry out their daily activities to be safe and secure. Public safety includes protection from domestic abuse and other forms of violence, as well as from injuries sustained in the home, moving about the community, or elsewhere.[8]

Addressing building and property safety and security, especially through codes and regulations, has traditionally been a core planning function of local governments. Crime and other physical safety threats are typically the responsibility of other local departments or agencies, including police, fire, emergency services, and emergency management. However, community planning and design has a major role to play in increasing the safety and security of the built environment. For example, crime prevention through environmental design (CPTED) is an approach to reducing crime and improving community safety by applying four principles: access control, surveillance, territorial reinforcement, and maintenance (National Crime Prevention Council 2009). Crime prevention extends beyond design of the built environment to addressing the root causes of crime, such as poverty, inequality, and dysfunctional family structures, which relate to the social determinants of health.

Mobility, Health, and Safety

Access to jobs, schools, shopping, recreation, entertainment, and services is vitally important for daily life. Yet the ways people get to work and services, which may include time spent in congestion, walking along streets with inadequate and unsafe pedestrian facilities, or lack of alternatives to personal automobile use, can cause stress and impact personal well-being. In 2020 an estimated 38,680 people, including pedestrians, bicyclists, and motorists, died in vehicular crashes in the United States (National Highway Traffic Safety Administration 2021). Being able to access destinations without danger and risk of injury is a public health and safety issue.

Vision Zero is a worldwide movement to reduce traffic collisions and give people the right to safe mobility, with the ambitious goal of achieving zero road facilities. Cities across the U.S. have adopted Vision Zero initiatives, including Denver, Los Angeles, New York City, Orlando, Philadelphia, San Antonio, and many more. The fundamental idea is that roads should be designed to be safe and secure for all users, through actions such as reducing vehicular speeds, redesigning streets for safety, and implementing safety improvements to priority corridors and intersections (Philadelphia 2020).

The design and operation of roadway and transit corridors, street, sidewalk, and bicycle networks, and other mobility facilities should prioritize safety and security for all users. Safe mobility is convenient, reliable, and free from risk of injury or crime. In addition, incorporation of street trees and other forms of green infrastructure into roadway corridors can help slow traffic speeds, manage stormwater, improve environmental quality, and make the experience more pleasant for pedestrians and bicyclists.

Disasters and Emergencies

Natural and human-made disasters pose major threats to public health and safety. The impacts of natural disasters are well-known and are addressed in Chapters 6 and 10. Human-made disasters can also cause injury, death, and severe disruptions to normal life. Examples include collapse of buildings and bridges, other infrastructure failures, acts of terrorism, and the spread of deadly infectious diseases facilitated by global travel.

To address these threats, communities should develop and maintain emergency preparedness and post-disaster recovery plans addressing both natural and human-made disasters. The COVID-19 pandemic illustrated the health, economic, and social costs of being unprepared for a major disaster. The comprehensive plan can identify risks, establish polices, and set the direction for action to respond effectively to different types of disasters. Topics to address in post-disaster recovery planning

Table 11.4 Public Safety

Policy Directions

Increase public safety through the reduction of crime and injuries.

Increase resilience to and prepare for the impacts of human-made and natural disasters.

Prioritize emergency preparedness and post-disaster recovery planning to minimize the impacts of natural and human-made disasters.

Applications

Implement approaches such as crime prevention through environmental design to reduce crime.

Address the root causes of crime through partnerships to improve education, increase economic opportunity, support families, and enhance other social services.

Develop policies, design standards, and regulations to increase the safety of the built environment, including roads and other mobility facilities.

Develop and regularly update emergency preparedness and post-disaster recovery plans to address basic human needs (such as shelter and food), as well as the restoration of damaged infrastructure, facilities, and services.

Example: Durham, North Carolina

The *Durham Comprehensive Plan* includes a Public Safety Element that addresses fire protection, emergency medical services, law enforcement, and emergency management. Key issues addressed by this element include (1) coordinating emergency services with growth; (2) coordinating public safety facilities with other municipal services and with services provided by adjacent jurisdictions, state, and federal agencies; (3) community involvement in public safety and crime prevention; and (4) reducing crime and increasing the perception of safety through design of the built environment. The element identifies level-of-service standards (including response times) for fire protection, emergency medical services, and law enforcement. It calls on the city to develop and maintain an emergency operations plan that defines responsibilities and establishes policies and procedures for collaborative action to respond to an emergency.

include, among others, restoration of medical facilities, damaged infrastructure systems, and other essential facilities and services; provision of temporary housing; and economic disruptions such as business closures and loss of jobs. Collaboration between planners, emergency managers, service providers, and others is critical to build capacity for effective response.

Summary

In the 21st century, public health has reemerged as foundational for planning and designing sustainable, resilient, and equitable communities. As exemplified by the social determinants of health, the planning profession has a key role to play in realizing the mission of public health: to fulfill society's interest in assuring conditions in which all people can be healthy. The comprehensive plan can set the direction for realizing the overarching goal of becoming a healthy community.

There is a growing awareness that health and wellness are affected by the natural environment, built environment, and other community systems. As demonstrated by stark disparities in life expectancy, health outcomes, and impacts of natural disasters on poor and disadvantaged communities, health equity is a fundamental concern. Health in All Policies is a collaborative approach that incorporates health considerations into policy development and decision-making across sectors and disciplines. Applying a health lens (along with the climate and equity lenses described in Chapters 6 and 9, respectively) can maximize the potential of the comprehensive plan to advance the well-being of all community members in all aspects of their lives.

Human health and the health of the environment are inextricably linked. Environmental health issues to address in the comprehensive plan include, among others, exposure to toxins and pollutants; the health benefits of contact with nature; the health effects of climate and climate change; and noise exposure.

Chronic diseases and conditions such as diabetes and obesity are a major health concern globally and in the United States. Two major risk factors for preventable chronic diseases – physical inactivity and poor nutrition – can be addressed by comprehensive plan goals and policies to promote active living and access to healthy, affordable foods. Public safety (the prevention and protection of people from crimes, injuries, natural and human-made disasters, and other potential dangers and threats) is another important health topic to address in the comprehensive plan.

Notes

1 A study by the Natural Center for Health Statistics found that life expectancy during the first half of 2020 declined by one year for the overall U.S. population, 1.9 years for the Hispanic population, and 2.7 years for the non-Hispanic Black population compared to 2019. Life expectancy for the population as a whole was at its lowest level since 2006 (Arias, Tejada-Vera, and Ahmad 2021).

2 A 2010 survey of local governmental planners found that 31 percent of draft or adopted comprehensive plans contained explicit goals, objectives or policies addressing public health while 69 percent did not (American Planning Association 2011).

3 The U.S. Department of Health and Human Services declared the opioid epidemic a public health emergency (2017).

4 The Health Assessment Lens was developed through grants from the Colorado Health Foundation and the American Planning Association. The Colorado Chapter of the American Planning Association worked with the Colorado Center for Sustainable Urbanism to develop and test initial drafts of the *Lens*. The final version of the Health Assessment Lens is included in *Creating Healthy Places Guidebook*, which was developed by students and faculty at the University of Colorado Denver's College of Architecture and Planning (Health + Design Initiative 2019).

5 The U.S. Department of Agriculture estimated that one out of nine U.S. households experienced food insecurity in 2018 (Coleman-Jensen et al. 2019).

6 These places were among 20 "communities of innovation" identified by Growing Food Connections, an initiative funded by the U.S. Department of Agriculture "to coordinate and integrate research, education, and planning and policy to build stronger community food systems" (Raja n.d.).

7 Locally and regionally produced food provides additional benefits by strengthening the economy and reducing reliance on long-distance shipping and transport.

8 According to the Center for Disease Control and Prevention's Injury Center, injuries and violence are the leading causes of death for children and adults 1–45 years of age in the United States.

References

American Planning Association (2011). *Comprehensive Planning for Public Health: Results of the Planning and Community Health Research Center Survey.* Prepared with support from the Centers for Disease Control and Prevention. Chicago, IL: American Planning Association.

American Planning Association, Planning and Community Health Center (2015). *Health in the Development Review Process.* Prepared with support from the Centers for Disease Control and Prevention. Chicago, IL: American Planning Association.

American Public Health Association (n.d.). Environmental Health. Accessed at https://www.apha.org/topics-and-issues/environmental-health

Arias, Elizabeth, Betzaida Tehada-Vera, and Farida Ahmad (2021). *Provisional Life Expectancy Estimates for January through June 2020.* Hyattsville, MD: National Center for Health Statistics Report No. 010.

Artiga, Samantha and Elizabeth Hinton (2018). *Beyond Health Care: The Role of Social Determinants in Promoting Health and Health Equity.* San Francisco, CA: Kaiser Family Foundation.

Colcombe, Stanley and Arthur F. Kramer (2003). "Fitness Effects on the Cognitive Function of Older Adults: A Meta-Analytic Study," *Psychological Science*, 14:2, pp. 125–130.

Coleman-Jensen, Alisha, Matthew P. Rabbitt, Christian A. Gregory, and Anita Singh (2019). *Household Food Security in the United States in 2018.* Washington, DC: United States Department of Agriculture, Economic Research Report Number 270.

Dutko, Paula, Michele Ver Ploeg, and Tracey Farrigan (2012). *Characteristics and Influential Factors of Food Deserts.* Washington, DC: United States Department of Agriculture, Economic Research Report Number 140.

Gorieb versus Fox (1927). 274 U.S. 603. Number 799. Washington, DC: U.S. Supreme Court.

Health + Design Initiative, with the Colorado Healthy Places Collaborative (2019). "Appendix A. Health Assessment Lens," in *Creating Healthy Places Guidebook.* Denver: University of Colorado Denver, College of Architecture and Planning, A1–A20.

Institute of Medicine (1988). *The Future of Public Health.* Washington, DC: National Academy Press.

Kirkby, MaryAnn. (1989). "Nature as Refuge in Children's Environments," *Children's Environments Quarterly*, 6, pp. 7–12.

National Center for Chronic Disease Prevention and Health Promotion (n.d.). Poor Nutrition Fact Sheet. Accessed at https://www.cdc.gov/chronicdisease/resources/publications/factsheets/nutrition.htm

National Crime Prevention Council (2009). *Best Practices for Using Crime Prevention Through Environmental Design in Weed and Seed Sites.* Arlington, VA: National Crime Prevention Council.

National Highway Traffic Safety Administration (NHTSA) (2021). *Early Estimates of Motor Vehicle Traffic Fatalities and Fatality Rate by Sub-Categories in 2020.* Washington, DC: NHTSA National Center for Statistics and Analysis.

Philadelphia, Pennsylvania (2020). *Vision Zero Action Plan 2025.* Philadelphia, PA: Vision Zero Task Force.

Raja, Samina, Principal Investigator (n.d.). Growing Food Connections. Support provided by the U.S. Department of Agriculture, National Institute of Food and Agriculture. Accessed at http://growingfoodconnections.org/

Repke, Meredith, Meredith S. Berry, Lucian Gideon Conway, Alexander L. Metcalf, Reid M. Hensen, and Conor N. Phelan (2018). "How Does Nature Exposure Make People Healthier? Evidence for the Role of Impulsivity and Expanded Space Perception," in *Public Library of Science* (PLOS One), 13:8, pp. 1–20.

Rudolph, Linda, Julia Caplan, Karen Ben-Moshe, and Lianne Dillon (2013). *Health in All Policies: A Guide for State and Local Governments.* Washington, DC and Oakland, CA: American Public Health Association and Public Health Institute.

The Robert Wood Johnson Foundation (2020). *Life Expectancy: Could Where You Live Influence How Long You Live?* Princeton, NJ: The Robert Wood Johnson Foundation.

U.S. Department of Health and Human Services (2017). *HHS Acting Secretary Declares Public Health Emergency to Address National Opioid Crisis.* Accessed at https://public3.pagefreezer.com/browse/HHS.gov/31-12-2020T08:51/https://www.hhs.gov/about/news/2017/10/26/hhs-acting-secretary-declares-public-health-emergency-address-national-opioid-crisis.html

Village of Euclid versus Ambler Realty Company (1926). 272 U.S. 365. Washington, DC: U.S. Supreme Court.

World Health Organization (1946). *International Health Conference* (held in New York). Geneva, Switzerland: World Health Organization.

World Health Organization (2018). *Climate Change and Health Fact Sheet.* Geneva, Switzerland: World Health Organization.

Chapter 12

Regional Connections

Local governments across the United States operate in a regional context. The practice of regional planning has a long history in the United States and continues to evolve in the 21st century (Piro, Leiter, and Rooney 2017). However, local governments have often not addressed relationships to the larger region in their comprehensive plans.

From a systems perspective, a community can be characterized as a system composed of interacting subsystems which are nested within a larger system (the region). Natural, built environment, and other community subsystems do not stop at municipal limits. For example, environmental issues pertaining to natural ecosystems and habitats, water and air quality, and climate transcend jurisdictional boundaries. Mobility networks are regional in nature, as are housing markets and economic interactions. Moreover, there is growing recognition that these systems extend beyond the region, and that local communities and regions are nested within an even a larger system – a region of regions, or *megaregion* (Barnett 2020; Figure 12.1).

This chapter addresses the connections between comprehensive plan goals, policies, strategies, and initiatives and those of adjacent jurisdictions and the region as a whole. Key topics addressed include (1) regional coordination and cooperation as an overarching theme that transcends jurisdictional borders, and (2) connections from the community systems covered in Chapters 6–10 (natural environment, built environment, social, and economic) to the larger region. Regional systems are influenced by federal and state policy frameworks and directives, in addition to connections with local jurisdictions (Figure 12.2).

DOI: 10.4324/9781003024170-14

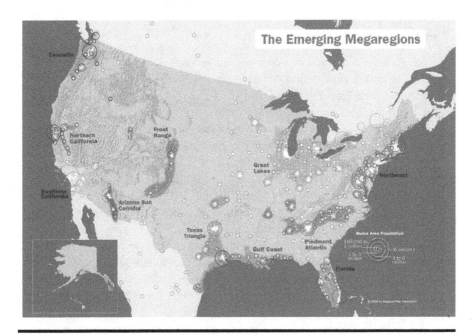

Figure 12.1 U.S. Megaregions

Source: Regional Plan Association.

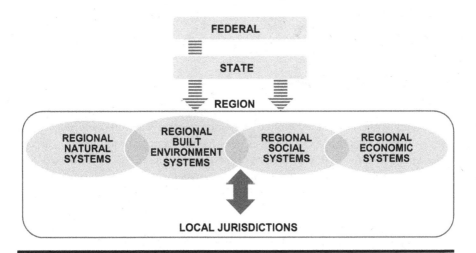

Figure 12.2 Regional Connections

Sustainability, Resilience, Equity

Think globally, act locally is a common adage related to sustainability. Local actions to reduce consumption of finite resources, recycle materials and waste, limit greenhouse gas emissions, and the like are more impactful if carried out at the regional scale. Planning for environmental, economic, and social sustainability requires an integrated approach that addresses complex, inter-dependent systems and issues that cut across scales from community to region, megaregion, and, ultimately, the planet as a whole. The regional scale is well-suited to provide a collaborative, cross-jurisdictional platform for planning and decision-making to increase sustainability.

Destructive storms, floods, wildfires, seismic events, and the like are not confined by jurisdictional boundaries. Magnified by climate change, the impacts of natural disasters are becoming increasingly severe and the geo-graphic areas affected growing in extent.[1] Cooperation and coordination among governments are needed to effectively prepare for, respond to, and recover from disasters. Again, the region is an appropriate scale for planning and decision-making to increase resilience.

Regional development patterns and the provision of infrastructure and ser-vices have historically promoted social inequities, based on economic status, race, ethnicity, and other factors. The results are evident in resource dispar-ities between center cities and surrounding communities in regions across the nation. In the 21st century, these dynamics are changing as poverty increases in suburban and rural parts of regions and urban areas experience gentrifi-cation and displacement of existing residents. Equity is a regional issue that requires commitment and solutions at the regional scale to address.

Inventory and Analysis

Inventories of existing conditions and trends too often end at the boundaries of the local jurisdiction undertaking the comprehensive planning effort. From a systems perspective, this approach does not account for relationships with adjacent jurisdictions and the region as a whole. These relationships can be addressed in a regional context section of the inventory and cross-referenced in other sections such as land use, mobility, housing, and natural systems. Relevant information includes:

- Plans prepared by the regional planning agency.
- Regional population and employment projections.
- Existing land use and development patterns, plans, and significant initiatives of adjacent jurisdictions.
- Major regional connections, such as transportation corridors, greenway and trail connections, and watersheds and riparian systems.

Regional Coordination and Cooperation

Issues that impact communities and the lives of community members transcend the boundaries of any one jurisdiction. Issue areas such as mobility, housing, infrastructure, and the environment are regional in nature and require regional collaboration (that is, coordination and cooperation) to address.

Regional coordination refers to aligning local planning provisions, including comprehensive plan goals, policies, and actions, with those of adjacent jurisdictions, the regional planning agency, and other agencies and organizations that operate at a regional or cross-jurisdictional scale. Examples include aligning local and regional land-use policies and providing seamless connections in the regional mobility network. A current regional plan or vision provides an invaluable framework for developing scenarios for future land use, mobility, and other community systems in the comprehensive plan that support a common direction for the region's future.

Coordinating local and regional projections minimizes the risk of planning at cross purposes due to inconsistent data (Godschalk and Rouse 2015). It is important not only to set a common baseline, but also to coordinate projections for future land use and development scenarios to be consistent between the local jurisdiction, region, and other local jurisdictions in the region.

Regional cooperation refers to working together on common initiatives, such as developing a regional open space network, establishing compatible performance standards along common borders, forming intergovernmental annexation agreements, or sharing of resources, facilities, and services. For example, a number of alliances have formed to address open space and natural resources at a regional scale.

Table 12.1 Regional Coordination and Cooperation

Policy Directions
Coordinate local and regional population, employment, housing, and other projections.
Coordinate with adjacent jurisdictions to address common issues in comprehensive plan development and implementation.
Cooperate with regional and local agencies and jurisdictions on initiatives that support common goals.

Applications
Establish common projections at the regional level that are allocated to local jurisdictions through a collaborative planning process.
Develop future scenarios in the local comprehensive plan that account for regional plans and visions.
Implement joint or multijurisdictional planning initiatives to address land use, mobility, open space, and other issues that transcend jurisdictional boundaries.
Pursue multijurisdictional opportunities to provide services and share resources, both to improve efficiency and reduce costs.

Examples include the Bay Area Open Space Council (California), Metro Denver Nature Alliance (Colorado), Chicago Wilderness (Illinois), Greater Baltimore Wilderness Coalition (Maryland), Houston Wilderness (Texas), and The Intertwine Alliance (Oregon and Washington).

Example: Asheville, North Carolina

Living Asheville, the Comprehensive Plan for Asheville, North Carolina, is organized around six themes that correspond to the six principles from the Comprehensive Plan Standards for Sustaining Places. Responsible Regionalism is one of these themes and includes a goal to "improve regional collaboration, and communication." The plan defines "regional governance relationships that are stronger than the sum of their parts" as the desired outcome for this goal, as measured by the number of organizations engaged in regional planning efforts and the degree of collaboration in planning and policymaking among local governments in the region. Strategies include supporting regional partnerships and initiatives on issues such as multimodal transportation, greenways, and economic development; city-county collaboration to address key issues identified in *Living Asheville*, such as accommodating regional affordable housing demand; and working with the state to ensure that regional funding opportunities are equitable for all jurisdictions.

Regional Natural Systems

Natural systems lend themselves to planning at the regional scale to minimize environmental harm and maximize the ecosystem services and benefits they provide for people and other species. Natural systems and processes (for example, topography, hydrology, vegetation and wildlife, climate, and air) do not conform to jurisdictional boundaries. Floodplains, wetlands, shorelines, and other sensitive resources typically are part of larger environmental systems at the regional scale and beyond. Key topics to address include regional open space planning, regional planning for water, and regional planning for climate change.

Regional Open Space Planning

Regional planning for parks and open space has a long history in the United States, dating back to Frederick Law Olmsted's *Emerald Necklace* plan for metropolitan Boston in the late 19th century. In the latter half of the 20th century, metropolitan planning organizations focused on regional transportation improvements, development patterns, and environmental issues, such as air and water quality, driven in large part by federal and state requirements and funding programs (Piro, Leiter, and Rooney 2017). Regional open space initiatives continued through the efforts of communities that acquired and maintained park and open space lands beyond their borders or collaborated to create greenways and trail systems across jurisdictional boundaries.

In the 21st century, open space has reemerged as a regional planning priority. Coordinated planning for open space at the regional scale makes sense, given that multiple agencies and organizations are responsible for managing different types of open space within the same region. For example, state and county-owned parks, educational and institutional campuses, natural areas managed by private land trusts, and other open space resources can be located next to or near parks managed by a city. A systems approach to regional open space planning seeks to integrate green spaces and connections with other local and regional systems, such as hydrology and stormwater management, mobility, and natural habitat, in order to generate multiple environmental, economic, and social co-benefits. Wildlife movement and migration patterns are important to understand and accommodate in regional open space systems, with the goal of maintaining functional landscape connectivity.[2]

Regional Planning for Water

Water is another natural resource that lends itself to planning at a regional scale. Watersheds, rivers, and groundwater do not observe jurisdictional boundaries. Supply sources may be located at great distances from end-users. How communities access, treat, and distribute water varies widely across the United States, with management responsibilities ranging from local governments to independent water districts to regional (and megaregional) authorities and agreements. The latter are prevalent west of the 100th Meridian – the dividing line frequently identified as separating areas of the United States with more precipitation to the east from drier areas to the west.

Different regions face different water planning challenges. For example, areas with low annual precipitation experience the reality of water as a finite resource. Western states, particularly those in the Colorado River basin, are under severe stress in balancing water availability with the demands of urban development, agriculture, and other uses. Water planning issues for midwestern and eastern states with more plentiful precipitation include floods, droughts, and water supply contamination. Many coastal communities face challenges of saltwater intrusion into freshwater systems, including groundwater supply sources.

Addressing the connections between local and regional water resource management in the comprehensive plan can help ensure consistent water supply to meet future demand, prevent water quality degradation, and promote collaboration among multiple agencies and service providers. The complexity and interrelationships of issues such as balancing water demands from different land uses, maintaining ecosystem health, water conservation and reuse, and wastewater and stormwater management require multidisciplinary and multijurisdictional collaboration at the local and regional scales and beyond.

Regional Planning for Climate Change

Climate change is causing increasingly severe natural disasters whose impacts extend beyond the boundaries of local jurisdictions to the regional and megaregional scales. Comprehensive plan strategies to reduce the potential impacts of natural disasters (referred to as hazard mitigation) should be coordinated with adjacent jurisdictions and regional planning agencies. For example, regional riparian and floodplain systems should be conserved to reduce property damage and provide natural flood control when a disaster strikes. Planning to prepare for, respond to, and recover quickly from natural disasters should similarly be coordinated at the regional scale.

Climate change is a global phenomenon driven in large part by greenhouse gas emissions from human activities. While local governments have a role to play in reducing greenhouse gas emissions from buildings, land uses, and other sources within their jurisdictions, the major contributors in urban regions typically are power plants and the regional transportation system, which require a multijurisdictional response to address. Therefore, the comprehensive plan should define policies and actions to mitigate climate change through a coordinated local and regional strategy.[3]

Table 12.2 Regional Natural Systems

Policy Directions

Collaborate with other local jurisdictions and agencies to conserve natural resource lands and protect critical areas that extend across municipal boundaries.

Coordinate local open space plans with plans of adjacent jurisdictions and the region.

Integrate local and regional planning for water supply and quality, stormwater, and wastewater management.

Coordinate local and regional planning for climate change.

Applications

Develop regional approaches and mechanisms to protect natural resources and systems, such as regional growth boundaries and intergovernmental transfer of development rights.

Implement joint or multijurisdictional greenway, trail, and other initiatives that meet local and regional open space needs.

Identify opportunities to share costs of acquiring, developing, operating, and maintaining parks, greenways, and other open space resources that extend across jurisdictional boundaries.

Identify opportunities to coordinate and share responsibilities for water supply, stormwater, and wastewater management to increase efficiencies and reduce costs.

Participate in regional disaster preparedness, response, and recovery planning.

Participate in regional initiatives to reduce greenhouse gas emissions.

Example: Portland, Oregon

The Intertwine Alliance in the Portland metropolitan region (which includes Vancouver, Washington) is a coalition of regional and local governments, nonprofits, institutions, businesses, and other organizations that work together to preserve and nurture a healthy regional system of parks, trails, and natural areas. The City of Portland and ten suburban communities actively participate in the coalition. Portland's *2035 Comprehensive Plan* specifically addresses coordination with the Intertwine Alliance in planning for trails and active mobility. Examples of Intertwine projects include a regional conservation strategy, a bi-state urban forest strategy, and Access Trails, a program to promote accessibility to the region's trails for people of all abilities (The Intertwine Alliance 2019).

Regional Built Environment Systems

Like natural systems, built environment systems extend beyond jurisdictional borders to connect to the region and beyond. Key regional built environment systems to consider in the comprehensive plan include land use and development, mobility, and infrastructure and services.

Regional Land Use and Development

Communities have different land use and development patterns determined in large part by their geographic locations and regional relationships. Central cities typically have regionally serving business districts, major employment centers, and dense patterns of residential, commercial, and mixed-use development. Surrounding suburban communities are more residential in character while the exurban fringes of the region and beyond are characterized by rural uses such as agriculture, low-density development, and undeveloped open space. Together, urban, suburban, and rural communities form a regional land-use pattern that provides places and choices for people to live, work, shop, acquire goods and services, and recreate.

Regional coordination in planning for land use and development provides many benefits for local communities and the region as a whole. Imbalances typically exist in the distribution of land uses and investments in different communities. These imbalances are reflected in regional inequities, including disparities in wealth and resources between different communities, as well as in strains on regional mobility systems, infrastructure, and services. Regional collaboration can help address these imbalances and facilitate the ability of each community to establish its identity and niche within the region, based on its assets and vision for the future set by the comprehensive plan.

Coordinating local and regional activity centers (locations with a high concentration of employment and commerce) with multimodal transportation investments makes it easier for residents to move through the region to access jobs, services, and recreational amenities (see Regional Mobility below). In general, coordinating local land-use plans with regional mobility networks improves mobility and accessibility for community members. Interjurisdictional collaboration results in more consistent land use and development patterns where adjacent municipalities share common borders. A regional approach to land use and development can also facilitate infill and redevelopment, reduce the fiscal impacts of growing outward from existing developed areas, and help maintain the character, economic viability, and lifestyles of rural communities.

Regional Mobility

Regional mobility refers to how residents, commuters, and visitors move through a region to access destinations using different modes of travel, including public transit, private vehicles, bicycles, micromobility options such as e-scooters, and (particularly to begin and end trips) walking. Community and regional mobility networks are complex systems comprising roadways of varying size and capacity; different types of public transit facilities and routes (bus, light rail, commuter rail, and others); bicycle lanes, routes, and trails; and pedestrian facilities, such as sidewalks, walkways, and trails. Interstate highways, intercity rail, and air service connect regions to other regions within a megaregion or beyond. *New mobility* (on-demand mobility services, such as rideshare and e-scooters, made possible by mobile technology) is disrupting established transportation practices and providing new options for residents to move about communities and regions.

Providing consistent travel options that are reliable, affordable, and equitable, including seamless connections from local to regional mobility systems and between different modes in these systems, is key to meeting the mobility and accessibility needs of community members. Integrating local and regional mobility in the comprehensive plan helps to achieve this consistency.

Local communities (with the possible exception of larger cities) have limited responsibility for the development, operation, and maintenance of regional mobility facilities and services. Therefore, collaboration with neighboring jurisdictions, transit agencies and other mobility providers, and regional, state, and federal agencies that provide funding for mobility investments is required to effectively integrate local and regional mobility planning. Regional planning agencies (in most instances serving as *metropolitan planning organizations*, or MPOs) develop long-range plans and transportation improvement programs that identify project priorities for federal transportation investments in the region. Local communities should participate in the regional transportation planning process and identify priority mobility projects in their comprehensive plans for inclusion in the MPO's transportation improvement program. Projects should be evaluated on how well they fulfill local and regional planning goals, for example: providing mobility options for poor and disadvantaged communities, supporting local and regional land-use plans, and reducing greenhouse gas emissions from the transportation sector.

Regional Infrastructure and Services

Essential infrastructure and services such as water, wastewater and stormwater management, solid waste, and public safety are typically the responsibility of local governments, independent authorities, and special service districts. In some cases, a regional agency may be responsible for providing services for an entire metropolitan area. Regional coordination and cooperation can increase efficiency, reduce costs, and facilitate more effective service delivery.

Forms of regional cooperation can range from sharing of resources (for example, facilities or equipment) to service consolidation to revenue-sharing agreements for regional facilities, infrastructure, and services. Some regions have multiple service districts providing functions such as water provision and fire protection. While consolidation of independent service districts may be controversial, it can increase capacity, eliminate redundancies, and result in more efficient, cost-effective services.

Capital-intensive infrastructure needs such as wastewater, stormwater, and solid waste management for urban areas can be most effectively provided by a regional agency. For example, the Milwaukee Metropolitan Sewerage District is responsible

Table 12.3 Regional Built Environment Systems

Policy Directions
Coordinate local and regional planning for land use, mobility, and infrastructure with the regional planning agency, local jurisdictions, and facility and service providers.
Coordinate regional investments in mobility and infrastructure systems with local and regional growth area designations.
Promote regional cooperation and sharing of resources in the provision of infrastructure, facilities, and services.

Applications
Develop joint or coordinated land use plans for areas along boundaries with adjacent municipalities.
Participate in developing the regional long-range transportation plan and incorporate relevant goals, polices, and projects into the comprehensive plan.
Enhance multimodal connections between local activity centers and regional destinations.
Identify opportunities to share and consolidate facilities and services to improve efficiency and reduce costs.
Ensure consistency between local capital improvement programs and regional infrastructure priorities.

for wastewater and stormwater management for 28 communities with a combined population of 1.1 million people in the Greater Milwaukee region. The district is nationally recognized for the use of green infrastructure at the regional scale to protect water quality and improve environmental quality while eliminating combined sanitary-storm sewer overflow.

Example: Roseville, Minnesota

The city of Roseville is an inner-ring suburb in the Twin Cities region of Minnesota. Many of the city's approximately 37,000 residents commute to other parts of the region for work or school. Roseville's location at the northern limits of Minneapolis and St. Paul means that Roseville experiences pass-through traffic traveling to and from these cities. Roseville is also home to Rosedale Center, one of the region's largest shopping malls and a major traffic generator. Recognizing these regional mobility influences, the transportation element of the *Roseville 2040 Comprehensive Plan* calls for coordinating transportation planning to ensure connectivity of regional routes. The plan references the *2040 Transportation Policy Plan* prepared by the Metropolitan Council (the regional planning agency) and describes the review process to ensure consistency between the city and regional plans. *Roseville 2040* endorses the *2040 Transportation Plan* goal of developing a reliable, affordable, and efficient multimodal transportation system, including transit, biking, and walking as alternatives to automobile use. Rosedale Center is a hub of region's first bus rapid transit line.

Regional Social Systems

People primarily experience social systems through interactions with family, neighborhood, and the larger community they are part of. Local social systems are impacted by patterns of discrimination and exclusion at the scale of the region as a whole, which manifest themselves in disparities in education, income, access to resources, and the like between different communities. Regional dynamics over time have perpetuated deep-seated social, racial, economic, and environmental inequities. In this context, it is incumbent upon local jurisdictions in their comprehensive plans to identify barriers and opportunities to overcoming structural inequality at the regional scale.

Housing is a key social system in which these dynamics are on display. Ensuring decent, affordable housing for all is a matter of equity, fairness, and inclusion. Because housing markets are regional in nature, addressing housing supply, demand,

and the needs of all community members requires regional solutions. The alternative is a disjointed, incremental approach in which perceived solutions in one jurisdiction can negatively impact other jurisdictions. To avoid such outcomes, local jurisdictions should participate in the development of a regional housing strategy, typically led by the regional planning agency, to evaluate housing conditions, identify housing needs, and set targets for fair share housing provision by communities. Housing goals, policies, and targets included in local comprehensive plans should be coordinated with and reflect the regional housing strategy.

Social systems (addressed in Chapter 9) encompass a network of facilities and services (collectively referred to as social infrastructure) provided by local governments, independent governmental agencies, nonprofit organizations, and more. Similar to the provision of physical infrastructure as discussed above, social infrastructure providers can benefit from sharing of facilities, resources, and coordinated program and service delivery.

Types of social infrastructure that serve a regional population include major educational and recreational facilities, museum and cultural facilities, performing arts venues, and so forth. Since construction, operation, and maintenance of these facilities can be expensive, some regions have developed intergovernmental agreements and revenue-sharing mechanisms to cover the costs. For example, the Allegheny Regional Asset District was established by Allegheny County, Pennsylvania (which includes Pittsburgh and 129 other municipalities) to support libraries, regional parks and trails, arts and cultural organizations, sports and civic facilities, and public transit through a one cent sales and use tax.

Table 12.4 Regional Social Systems

Policy Directions
Address regional inequities and disparities in the comprehensive plan.
Coordinate comprehensive plan goals and policies for housing with the regional housing strategy.
Coordinate local and regional planning for social infrastructure and services with the regional planning agency, local jurisdictions, and facility and service providers.

Applications
Incorporate fair share housing targets and other regional housing policies into the comprehensive plan.
Collaborate with the regional planning agency and local jurisdictions to plan for a jobs–housing balance across the region.
Identify opportunities to co-locate social infrastructure facilities and services and share resources to improve service and reduce costs.
Explore interjurisdictional agreements and regional revenue sources to support region-serving social infrastructure facilities.

Example: Minneapolis, Minnesota

Minnesota's Metropolitan Land Planning Act requires local jurisdictions to update their comprehensive plans every ten years and demonstrate consistency with the region's long-range plan. The housing policies in Minneapolis' comprehensive plan, *Minneapolis 2040*, were developed to follow the policy guidance of *Thrive MSP 2040*, the long-range regional plan for the more than 180 jurisdictions in the Twin Cities region. To better accommodate regional forecasts for population, households, and employment, the city revised its land use and zoning categories to accommodate new development in more compact urban communities with access to transit, improved walkability, and affordable housing, and to encourage density through good design. *Minneapolis 2040* includes a housing policy to allow up to three residential units on a lot in all single-family residential areas. This policy was subsequently implemented through a zoning revision, making Minneapolis the first major city in the nation to effectively prohibit single-family zoning.

Regional Economic Systems

The 21st-century economy has evolved to be regional, national, and global in scale. In response, local communities have moved away from competing with other local jurisdictions for businesses and jobs to working cooperatively to advance economic opportunity as a region. The economic competitiveness of regions depends upon factors such as key industry clusters; workforce education levels and skills; freight transportation and logistical links to the global economy; and quality-of-life factors such as access to parks, recreation, and cultural and natural resources. Economic competitiveness is enhanced when local communities share and leverage information to plan for economic growth, infrastructure, and the amenities needed to retain, attract, and grow businesses and a talented workforce at the regional scale (Metropolitan Council 2015).

Local economic initiatives such as green business development, workforce training, and investments in land and infrastructure are more effective if coordinated at the regional level. Replacing the old economic development model of competing to attract businesses through tax subsidies and other incentives, communities can build on their strengths and establish complementary niches in the regional economy through an asset-based economic development approach. For example, urban and rural communities can leverage and jointly market diverse historical, cultural, and natural resources to attract visitors and bring dollars into the regional economy.

Collaboration and partnerships between local communities, regional planning and economic development agencies, chambers of commerce, and other organizations involved in regional economic issues are important to enhance the strength and competitiveness of the local and regional economies. Similar to the role of long-range transportation plans prepared by MPOs to qualify for federal transportation funds, the U.S. Economic Development Administration requires regions to prepare *Comprehensive Economic Development Strategies* (CEDS) to qualify for economic development assistance (U.S. Economic Development Administration 2020). Local communities should coordinate comprehensive plan goals and policies for economic opportunity and resilience with strategies contained in the regional CEDS.

Taxation structures set by state statutes can create significant disparities between local jurisdictions in revenues and associated capacity to provide necessary infrastructure and services. This situation often results in fiscal imbalances, different levels of investment, and socioeconomic inequities between communities in the same region. Some regions have developed revenue-sharing agreements to share costs and benefits of regional economic growth more equitably among local communities. A well-known example is the Fiscal Disparities Program authorized by the Minnesota Legislature in 1971 for the Minneapolis-St. Paul metropolitan area. Administered by the Metropolitan Council, the goals of this program are to promote orderly and efficient growth, improve equity, strengthen economic competitiveness, and encourage land uses that protect the environment and contribute to livability (Metropolitan Council n.d.).

Table 12.5 Regional Economic Systems

Policy Directions

Collaborate with regional planning agencies, economic development organizations, and others involved in regional economic issues to strengthen local and regional economies through coordinated initiatives.

Address regional economic strategies in the comprehensive plan.

Address fiscal imbalances, differing levels of investment, and associated socioeconomic inequities among local jurisdictions in the region.

Applications

Develop and implement partnership initiatives to leverage resources and capitalize on the complementary strengths of local communities through asset-based economic development.

Partner with local school districts, colleges and universities, major employers, and other providers to develop a regional workforce development program.

Explore revenue-sharing or similar mechanisms to alleviate economic disparities among local jurisdictions and to finance region-serving infrastructure and facilities.

Example: Cincinnati, Ohio

Cincinnati is the center of a metropolitan region encompassing counties in three states (Ohio, Kentucky, and Indiana) with over two million residents. *Plan Cincinnati*, the city's comprehensive plan, is organized around five initiative areas. The goal of the first initiative area – Compete – is to "be the pivotal economic force of the region." Strategies include, among others, focusing growth and business recruitment on key economic sectors that reflect regional strengths; establishing clear roles for the city and regional economic development agencies in a streamlined and cohesive development process; and building on existing assets, such as Cincinnati's lifestyle, historic character, and cultural heritage. The plan identifies numerous local and regional partners across the public, private, and institutional sectors, thus positioning the region to increase its economic competitiveness through collaboration. Examples include Hamilton County, regional chambers of commerce, the Port of Greater Cincinnati Development Authority, colleges and universities, and the Cincinnati Area Board of Realtors.

Summary

A community's natural, built environment, social, and economic systems connect to the systems of neighboring communities and the region as a whole, and these connections must be considered in the comprehensive plan. Systems and issue areas such as land use, mobility, essential infrastructure and services, and economic development require coordination and cooperation between local communities and at the regional scale to address. Examples include coordination of local and regional planning projections; cooperative land-use planning, parks and open space development, and resource-sharing agreements between local jurisdictions; and participating in regional initiatives such as disaster preparedness planning, asset-based economic development, and fair share housing provision.

Natural systems and processes transcend jurisdictional boundaries, connecting local communities, regions, megaregions, and ultimately the entire planet. Key topics to address in the comprehensive plan include regional open space and natural resources, regional water resource management, and regional planning for climate change mitigation and adaptation.

Regional built environment systems include land use and development, mobility, and essential infrastructure and services. Regional social systems include housing and region-serving social infrastructure such as major educational, recreational, and cultural facilities. With regard to economic systems, interjurisdictional coordination and cooperation to strengthen regional competitiveness (as opposed to the old model of competing for businesses and jobs) is paramount to position local communities and regions to succeed in the global economy of the 21st century.

Deep-seated structural inequities (for example, patterns of discrimination and disparities in wealth and resources between different communities) require a regional response across all of these systems to address. The comprehensive plan can define how local communities will contribute and partner with others to build a more sustainable, resilient, and equitable regional future.

Notes

1 In October 2012, Hurricane Sandy affected 24 states, with the most severe impacts experienced in the Northeast Megaregion centered on New Jersey and New York.
2 In contrast to *structural connectivity*, which refers to the physical relationship between landscape elements, *functional connectivity* refers to the degree to which landscapes facilitate or impair the movement of organisms and processes (Meiklejohn, Ament, and Tabor 2010). Functional connectivity can be increased in urban landscapes by integrating trees, native plantings, and other green infrastructure elements into the built environment.
3 Many regional initiatives to address climate change have been undertaken across the nation with the participation of local jurisdictions. Two examples are *Vision 2040*, the long-range plan and sustainability strategy for the Puget Sound region in Washington state, and the *Climate Action Strategy* for the San Diego region in California (Piro, Leiter, and Rooney 2017).

References

Barnett, Jonathan (2020). *Designing the Megaregion: Meeting Urban Challenges at a New Scale.* Washington, DC: Island Press.

Godschalk, David and David Rouse (2015). *Sustaining Places: Best Practices for Comprehensive Plans*, Planning Advisory Service Report 578. Chicago, IL: American Planning Association.

Meiklejohn, Katie, Rob Ament, and Gary Tabor (2010). *Habitat Corridors & Landscape Connectivity: Clarifying the Terminology.* Bozeman, MT: Center for Large Landscape Conservation.

Metropolitan Council (2015). *Economic Competitiveness: Local Planning Handbook.* St. Paul, MN: Metropolitan Council.

Metropolitan Council (n.d.). Fiscal Disparities: Tax-Base Sharing in the Metro Area. Accessed at https://metrocouncil.org/Communities/Planning/Local-Planning-Assistance/Fiscal-Disparities.aspx

Piro, Rocky, Robert Leiter, and Sharon Rooney (2017). *Emerging Trends in Regional Planning*, Planning Advisory Service Report 586. Chicago, IL: American Planning Association.

The Intertwine Alliance (2019). *Strategic Plan 2019–2024.* Portland, OR: The Intertwine Alliance.

U.S. Economic Development Administration (2020). *Comprehensive Economic Development Strategy (CEDS) Content Guidelines: Recommendations for Creating an Impactful CEDS.* Washington, DC: U.S. Department of Commerce.

FORWARD TO IMPLEMENTATION

DOI: 10.4324/9781003024170-15

Part I of this book covers the process of creating a comprehensive plan that reflects the community's values, articulates a vision and goals for the future, and defines how to achieve the vision and goals through strategy and action. Part II covers the substantive contents of the plan that results from the process. Part III (this concluding section of the book) addresses how process and substance come together in a final comprehensive plan that is successfully implemented. It covers the characteristics of an effective comprehensive plan; the implementation component of the plan; and how to use and keep the plan up to date following adoption. The characteristics (for example, the plan's internal coherence and consistency, overall design, and how it is communicated to the public) are based on the two attributes – Consistent Content and Coordinated Characteristics – identified by the Comprehensive Plan Standards for Sustaining Places. David Godschalk, who led development of the standards, referred to these as "plan-making design standards" (Godschalk and Rouse 2015).

In the closing chapter, the authors speculate on the future of the comprehensive plan and its potential to address the major challenges facing communities in the 21st century.

The Importance of Implementation

"To plan is human, to implement divine" is an oft-repeated planning aphorism.[1] Irrespective of the effort that went into creating the comprehensive plan, its real-world impacts are measured by the extent to which it is implemented. Nonetheless, a review of contemporary practice reveals implementation to be the weakest component of the typical comprehensive plan.

Implementation is inherently difficult in a political environment with competing interests, needs, and priorities. Common obstacles include insufficient commitment by leadership and agencies responsible for carrying out the plan; limited community engagement and interest after the planning process concludes; and inadequate capacity and resources available for implementation. Moreover, the rapid pace of change in the 21st century necessitates ongoing monitoring and adaptation as conditions shift and new issues arise.

While a well-crafted comprehensive plan is no guarantee of ultimate success in realizing the community's vision and goals, it can position the local jurisdiction to overcome the above obstacles. Effective implementation begins with a section of the plan that defines action priorities, responsibilities, resource commitments, and a process to monitor progress in achieving desired outcomes. The full plan should transparently demonstrate how the vision, goals, and action priorities reflect community input during the planning process. It should be clearly written and illustrated to convey key concepts and recommendations; presented in accessible, user-friendly formats (both analog and digital); and effectively communicated to different audiences, including decision-makers and community members. Development and implementation of the comprehensive plan should be viewed as a continuous, iterative process. As part of this process, community engagement should continue after plan adoption by involving community members in implementing, updating, and amending the plan.

Overview of Chapters

Part III is organized into five chapters, as follows:

Chapter 13: Implementation. Chapter 13 introduces a model called *Levels of Implementation*, which illustrates the multidimensional scope of what is involved in successfully implementing a comprehensive plan. With community engagement as the foundation, the levels include regulations, public investments, alignment of departmental work programs, and external partnerships. The chapter describes how to incorporate these levels into an effective plan implementation section that translates the community vision and goals into directions for action.

Chapter 14: Consistency and Coordination. Chapter 14 addresses internal and external consistency and coordination, two key attributes of a successful comprehensive plan. Internal consistency and coordination refer to coherence and integration of the plan contents, including data sets and assumptions; the different topics addressed by the plan; and its goals, policies, and actions. It also covers consistency of other plans developed by the local government with the comprehensive plan. External consistency and coordination refer to alignment of the plan with regional, state, and federal planning processes and with plans, initiatives, and conditions in adjacent jurisdictions.

Chapter 15: Designing and Communicating the Plan. Communicating with diverse segments of the community is essential throughout the planning process, culminating in design and presentation of the final comprehensive plan to the public, community leaders, and decision-makers. Chapter 15 addresses the design of the plan in different formats; using clear and concise language, visuals, and techniques such as storytelling to convey information and ideas; and dissemination of the plan through different channels to generate interest and momentum for implementation.

Chapter 16: Maintaining and Updating the Plan. The comprehensive planning process does not end with plan adoption. Rather, an effective plan is used on an ongoing basis and regularly updated to guide policy and action. Chapter 16 addresses how to monitor implementation progress using benchmarks and indicators; periodically review and adjust the implementation program based on progress made; and update the plan to address changing conditions and new issues. It also describes the process of formally amending the plan.

Chapter 17: The Future of the Comprehensive Plan. The concluding chapter of the book provides thoughts on how comprehensive planning practice can evolve to help 21st century communities realize sustainable, resilient, and equitable outcomes.

Note

1 See, for example, Kayden (2014).

References

Godschalk, David R. and David C. Rouse (2015). *Sustaining Places: Best Practices for Comprehensive Plans* (PAS Report 578). Chicago, IL: American Planning Association.
Kayden, Jerold S. (2014). "Why Implementation Matters," in *Harvard Design Magazine*, 37. Boston, MA: Harvard University Graduate School of Design.

Chapter 13

Implementation

The real-world impacts of comprehensive plans are determined by the extent to which they are implemented. Successful implementation entails acting over time to realize the community vision and goals defined through the planning process. Too often, comprehensive plans fail to connect vision and goals to action. Common problems include a lack of implementation specifics (too little detail) or the inclusion of lengthy lists of policies and actions with limited guidance on how to prioritize them (too much). Looking to the future, communities need new approaches to prepare for and adapt to accelerating social, technological, economic, and environmental change.

An effective implementation program addresses these potential problems. Usually presented in a concluding chapter or section of the plan, the program must accomplish the following to maximize its effectiveness:

- Set priorities for action based on community engagement in the planning process.
- Identify resources to carry out the actions.
- Define policies to incorporate comprehensive plan goals into operations and decision-making.
- Establish accountability by specifying responsibilities, time frames, and measures of progress.
- Incorporate flexibility to adapt to changing conditions over time.

DOI: 10.4324/9781003024170-16

Levels of Implementation

Effective implementation begins with development of a cohesive framework of goals, polices, and actions through the planning process (described in Part I) and incorporation of the framework into the substantive components of the plan (described in Part II). The implementation section of the plan defines a game plan for deploying policy and action to realize the community's vision and goals. Successful implementation is a multidimensional process that encompasses a synergistic range of activities, participants, and relationships. The *Levels of Implementation* model shown in Figure 13.1 illustrates the scope of what is involved.[1] With community engagement as the necessary foundation, the levels are arranged by approximate degree of difficulty and cumulative impact from Level 1 (regulations) to Level 4 (external partnerships).

Foundation: Community Engagement

Community engagement is the foundation of the Levels of Implementation model. Meaningful engagement that extends from plan development into implementation builds support among community members for actions such as regulatory changes, capital investments, and new initiatives recommended by the plan. Early actions that produce tangible results can generate momentum and support for more resource-intensive projects that take longer to come to fruition. Providing regular updates on implementation progress and opportunities to participate in implementation activities are ways to engage the community on an ongoing basis.

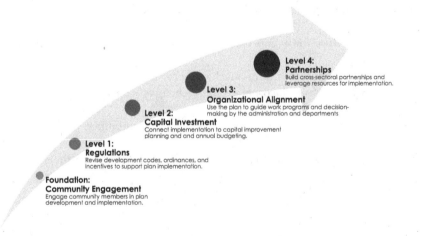

Figure 13.1 Levels of Implementation

Source: David Rouse and Garner Stoll.

Level 1: Regulations

Dating back to the *Standard State Zoning Enabling Act*, which called for zoning regulations "to be made in accordance with a comprehensive plan," zoning and land development regulations have been the primary mechanisms used to implement the plan (U.S. Department of Commerce 1926). Regulations, standards, and incentives have a major influence on the location, form, and character of new development and redevelopment and on the preservation of sensitive environmental resources. While regulatory changes are a key part of plan implementation (particularly in communities with a strong development market), they are not by themselves sufficient to realize desired plan outcomes.

Level 2: Public Investment

Public investment includes capital expenditures and budgetary allocations for projects and programs that support plan implementation. In addition to funding physical improvements such as parks, streets, and sidewalks that meet community needs, capital expenditures play an important role is shaping private sector investment. For example, infrastructure improvements such as water and sewer lines influence the pattern and density of new development, while public investments in parks, streetscape improvements, and the like can stimulate private investment in infill development areas. Coordinating capital investments with regulations (for example, by limiting infrastructure improvements to designated growth areas zoned for higher-density development) is more effective than using the tools separately.

The Government Finance Officers Association recommends using the comprehensive plan as a framework for capital project requests that are entered into the community's capital improvements program (Government Finance Officers Association n.d.). In the past, planning departments often played a lead role in capital improvement planning, a practice that is less common today.

Level 3: Organizational Alignment

Organizational alignment refers to integrating work programs and decision-making by the administration and line departments toward the common purpose of implementing the comprehensive plan. In practice, it is difficult to realize such alignment, as the innate tendency of departments with different missions and responsibilities is to operate independently. In a siloed organization, departments can view comprehensive plan implementation as the responsibility of the planning department and of limited relevance to their day-to-day activities. Using the goals and direction set by the comprehensive plan to guide operations and decision-making across the organization – from the manager's office to individual departments – is a powerful counterforce that can coordinate activities and resource commitments for effective implementation.

Organizational alignment begins by engaging departmental representatives in the planning process (for example, by serving on a technical advisory committee). Moving into implementation, comprehensive plan guidance can be operationalized in policies, procedures, and criteria for decision-making across the organization.

Level 4: External Partnerships

Consistent with the comprehensive plan's role as an official, long-range policy document, the first three levels are the responsibility of the local government. Successful implementation requires involvement of members of the community, nonprofits and civic groups, business and development interests, and external governmental agencies. It has become common for action plans to identify outside partners involved in particular actions, together with responsible parties (for example, lead and supporting departments) within the local jurisdiction. As noted, the foundation for engaging partners in implementation is established by public involvement in the planning process. Achieving broad consensus and support for the plan vision and goals can promote alignment of diverse community interests in a common direction and leverage funding and other resources for plan implementation.

Comprehensive plan implementation programs typically identify partnerships on a case-by-case basis. A more integrated approach would establish a structure for ongoing, cross-sectoral collaboration, such as a coalition of public, private, non-profit, and civic partners to coordinate resources in implementing plan priorities. While no good examples exist in contemporary comprehensive planning practice, Chattanooga Venture is an early example of a similar model. Chattanooga Venture was a public–private nonprofit created in 1984 to develop and implement a shared vision for the future of the city of Chattanooga, Tennessee (Cunningham 2008). Task forces comprising public and private sector partners were established to carry out projects that implemented the vision developed by community members. Chattanooga Venture is credited with spurring the revitalization of Chattanooga during the approximately ten years it was active.[2]

Levels of Implementation Example: Austin, Texas

The *Imagine Austin* comprehensive plan illustrates how the *Levels of Implementation* model can be applied in practice. It provides particularly strong examples of level 2 (capital investment) and level 3 (organizational alignment).

Foundation: Community Engagement. In Phase 3 of the comprehensive planning process, Austin's planning team synthesized policies and actions into eight programs and asked the community to rank their relative importance. Listed in order of priority based on responses from community members, the programs are:

1. Invest in a compact and connected Austin.
2. Sustainably manage Austin's water resources.
3. Grow Austin's economy by investing in the workforce, education, entrepreneurs, and local businesses.
4. Use green infrastructure to integrate nature into the city.
5. Grow and invest in Austin's creative economy.
6. Develop and maintain housing affordability throughout Austin.
7. Create a Healthy Austin program.
8. Revise the Land Development Code.

As of 2020, the city had used these programs to organize its implementation efforts since adoption of *Imagine Austin* in 2012.

Level 1: Regulations. Following plan adoption, the city launched an initiative to revise the city's Land Development Code, which was over 30 years old. This initiative proved difficult (possibly related to its low level of priority in the community survey) and the process was still underway in 2020.

Level 2: Capital Investment. Austin established a Capital Planning Office in 2010 (while the comprehensive planning process was underway) "to create a more robust, comprehensive and integrated Capital Improvement Program that supports the City's goals and priorities" (Austin n.d.a). This office works with city departments to develop an integrated capital improvement program that supports the goals and priorities defined by *Imagine Austin* and other adopted plans.

Level 3: Organizational *Alignment.* According to the city's website, "Austin is organizing its operations, core services, decisions, and investments around *Imagine Austin*" and implementation of its priority programs (Austin n.d.b). Eight interdepartmental work teams, each with a lead and contributing departments, were established following plan adoption to implement the programs. An indicators dashboard is used to track implementation progress.

Level 4: Partnerships. Imagine Austin identifies external partners for each of the eight priority programs. As is the norm in contemporary practice, it does not identify a structure or process for ongoing cross-sectoral collaboration to implement the plan.

The remainder of this chapter addresses the components of an implementation program in which the above levels work together to advance the plan vision and goals. It covers actions; policy guidance and decision-making; interdepartmental collaboration; engagement of external partners; funding and resources for plan implementation; and monitoring implementation progress.

Actions

An action is a task that is carried out within a specified time frame (as opposed to ongoing policy guidance and decision-making, addressed separately below). The substantive sections of the comprehensive plan make recommendations for policy and action to implement the community vision and goals (see Chapter 5). An effective implementation program distills and synthesizes these recommendations (which can be quite complex) into actionable directions for implementation, typically in the form of a matrix or table.

Action Types

While types of actions are characterized in various ways by different comprehensive plans, they can generally be divided into four categories: regulations, investments, initiatives, and planning.

Regulations

This category involves enacting revised or new ordinances, codes, standards, or incentives. In the past, comprehensive plans focused on revising the zoning ordinance and map to implement the future land-use plan, an example of *proscriptive regulations* intended to protect the public health, safety, and welfare (in this case, by restricting allowable uses and densities). Other examples include limitations on building in hazardous areas such as steep slopes and wetlands; setback requirements; and regulation of pollutants, light, and noise emissions.

The social and environmental impacts of Euclidean (use-based) zoning, such as racial segregation, automobile-oriented development, and increased greenhouse gas emissions, are well-documented (see Chapter 3). The *urban-to-rural transect* and other place-based typologies have emerged as alternatives, implemented through form-based codes and design standards. Form-based codes are an example of *prescriptive regulations* that define what should happen (in this instance, the physical form and character of new development) rather than what is prohibited from happening on a property. Other examples include landscape ordinances and inclusionary zoning requirements.

Incentives

Incentives provide inducements for new development that advances community goals such as affordable housing or energy-efficient development. Incentives most often take the form of density bonuses but can also include measures such as expedited development review and decreased infrastructure requirements (resulting in lower development costs). *Transfer of development rights* (TDR) is an incentive-based regulatory mechanism designed to protect valuable land by transferring development rights to property within a designated receiving area. To be effective, incentives must provide sufficient market return compared with conventional development.

Investments

This category involves capital expenditures and budgetary allocations by the local government and associated providers of public facilities and services. Expenditures on public buildings, infrastructure, land acquisition, and other capital needs are identified as projects in the capital improvements program, which should align with the community goals and priorities set by the comprehensive plan. A fiscally responsible program accounts for the construction, operations, and maintenance costs of capital projects and designates sustainable funding sources to support them over the entire project lifecycle. Too often, capital improvement programs allocate funding for initial project construction without considering the budgetary impacts of ongoing operations and maintenance or adequately addressing deferred maintenance needs associated with existing, aging infrastructure.

As with exclusionary zoning and housing practices (discussed in Chapter 3), capital improvement programs are part of the institutional structure that has promoted racial segregation and discrimination through disproportionate investment in rich and poor neighborhoods. To address this issue, the Baltimore City Department of Planning engaged a nonprofit research organization to conduct an equity analysis of the city's capital allocations over time (Baltimore Neighborhood Indicators Alliance 2019). The analysis revealed inequities related to race and income, life expectancy, and age (particularly neighborhoods with a high proportion of young children) and recommended using these factors to prioritize future capital investments.

In addition to capital expenditures, investment includes budgetary allocations to enhance existing or initiate new programs that implement comprehensive plan goals and priorities. Examples could include additional staff and fiscal resources to support housing, workforce training, and health and wellness programs, or higher levels of maintenance of public facilities such as parks. As with the capital improvement program, identifying funding sources for increased or new budgetary allocations is key to fiscal sustainability. Programmatic actions often entail collaboration between departments or with external partners, which can amplify the impact of existing resources and bring new sources to the table.

Initiatives

This category involves coordination and collaboration by different departments, agencies, or organizations. Initiatives range from discrete projects that conclude when specified objectives are met to new, ongoing programs, with internal and/or external cooperation to implement the comprehensive plan being the common denominator.[3]

Initiatives can overlap with other action categories. For example, an afford-able housing initiative could include regulatory changes such as inclusionary housing requirements or incentives, residential zoning modifications, and an acces-sory dwelling unit ordinance; capital and programmatic investments to increase housing supply; and more detailed planning (for example, a housing needs ana-lysis), implemented by cross-sectoral partnerships among agencies and organizations involved in housing issues. Such related actions are often listed separately in the action table. Addressing them as an integrated initiative can help focus plan imple-mentation on key priorities, create synergies, and attract resources from the different partners working the initiative.

Planning

This category involves the preparation of additional plans and technical studies needed to implement plan recommendations. By definition, a comprehensive plan is long-range, strategic, and general in nature. It is an "umbrella document" intended to guide more detailed planning and implementation efforts, helping to ensure that they support a common direction. More detailed plans include functional plans for community systems (for example, mobility, housing, and green infrastructure) and plans for subareas within the jurisdiction (for example, neighborhoods, districts, and corridors). Technical studies and analyses may be required before implementing other actions, such as recommended regulatory changes or capital investments.

Planning Action Examples: Burlington (Vermont), Philadelphia (Pennsylvania), and Las Cruces (New Mexico)

Burlington's *planBVT* identifies completion of several new or updated func-tional plans to implement comprehensive plan goals. New plans include an Integrated Water Quality Plan, Historic Preservation Plan, Arts and Culture Plan, and Economic Development Strategy. Updates include existing Open Space Protection and Urban Forestry Plans.

Philadelphia2035, the comprehensive plan for Philadelphia, defines a city-wide vision and policies for the city's development over a 25-year period. *Philadelphia2035* provided a framework for subsequent preparation of more detailed subarea plans for 18 districts by the Philadelphia City Planning Commission.[4]

The *Elevate Las Cruces Comprehensive Plan* calls for a transfer of develop-ment rights (TDR) technical study to identify potential sending and receiving areas (rural and urban place types, respectively). This study is the first step in enacting a TDR ordinance to support implementation of the place-based *Elevate Las Cruces* Future Development Map.

The Action Table

Actions are commonly presented in a matrix or table displaying information such as relevant goals and strategies, action types, time frames, responsibilities, and funding sources. *Goals and strategies* indicate what each action aims to accomplish. Including *action types* allows similar actions (for example, regulatory changes or capital investments) to be grouped for implementation purposes. *Time frames* provide guidance on how implementation is phased over the time horizon of the plan; a typical breakdown is short-term (0–2 years), mid-term (2–5 years), and long-term (5+ years). Identifying *responsibilities* (lead and supporting departments or agencies; external partners) establishes accountability for implementation. *Funding sources* should be determined for short-term actions at a minimum. Identifying potential funding sources for mid- and long-term actions can be used to develop an overall fiscal strategy to support plan implementation.

The action table is a useful way to organize complex information to guide implementation and can be used by staff as a checklist to track progress over time. To the extent possible, the table should be simplified and integrated, for example, by combining related actions in a broader initiative. Most importantly, given real-world constraints on staff capacity and funding available for implementation, priorities need to be established and clearly presented in the plan.

Setting Priorities

The action table is a useful tool to establish accountability (particularly compared with comprehensive plans that provide little or no detail on concrete steps to be taken to implement the plan). Its format can, however, be daunting for the user, raising the questions of where to begin and how to secure the resources needed to implement a long list of actions. An effective implementation program, therefore, defines what should be done first, in the form of a focused set of actions that address the community's priority issues and can be undertaken with available capacity.

Various methods can be used to set priorities for action. First and foremost, they should derive from the community priorities identified through the planning process. Feasibility – what can realistically be accomplished given staff capacity, fiscal limitations, political and legal factors, and the like – is a key consideration in setting priorities. A feasibility assessment can be conducted to finalize the list of short-term actions (to be undertaken within the coming year) and to determine the specifics of how they are executed (project management and staffing, work plan, and budget). Actions that require more substantial effort to implement can be deferred to subsequent years and incorporated into annual work programs as resources become available.

Because priority actions by definition are carried out in the early stages of plan implementation, they should act as catalysts that generate momentum for further action and system change. As an example, high-visibility, easy-to-implement public realm interventions using a tactical urbanism approach can demonstrate tangible results and lead to more substantial investments.

Implementable Comprehensive Plan Example: Jeannette, Pennsylvania

Developed by the Pennsylvania Department of Community and Economic Development, the "implementable comprehensive plan" is based on the idea that the success of a comprehensive plan is measured not by the length or quality of the plan document, but by its real-world results. This approach identifies five keys to a plan that can be implemented:

1. Focus on relevant, real issues.
2. Organize the plan the way officials and citizens think.
3. Devise practical and workable recommendations.
4. Recruit partners and create capacity to implement the plan.
5. Get local ownership of the plan and commitment to implement it (Pennsylvania Department of Community and Economic Development 2020).

Retooling Jeannette, the comprehensive plan for a city of approximately 9,000 residents in southwestern Pennsylvania, is an example of this approach. The *Retooling Jeannette* planning process began with a community meeting in which residents identified issues, hopes, and ideas for the future of Jeannette. A steering committee distilled the results into four themes: Fighting Blight, Vibrant Downtown, Positive Impressions, and Welcoming Gateways and Corridors. These themes drove the remainder of the planning process, including a multi-day community design workshop in which community members worked with subject matter experts to define issues and brainstorm solutions.

The resulting comprehensive plan document was organized around the four themes, identifying a vision, goals, objectives, strategies, and action steps for each. The plan also identified short-term actions to start implementation, called "the top 10 things to do in next six months." An example is to "create a community appearance working group and select one easy demonstration project to complete, such as planting street trees along a major corridor." Several of the actions focus on building capacity for implementation; for example, reactivating the city's planning commission (which had lapsed in prior years) to lead plan implementation.

Accounting for Uncertainty

One limitation of the action table format is the linear approach implied by dividing implementation into sequential time frames. In reality, implementation is an iterative process that requires ongoing monitoring, review, and adjustment as conditions change. In the 21st century, the uncertainty created by emerging issues and drivers of change has made this process even more challenging.

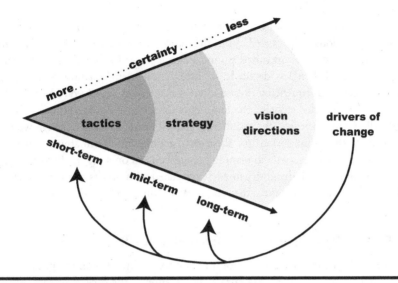

Figure 13.2 "Cone of Uncertainty" Strategic Framework
Source: Adapted from Webb (2019).

How might comprehensive plan implementation better account for the uncertainty of future change? Figure 13.2 illustrates a strategic framework that might be used to inform plan implementation over time. Adapted from work by the Future Today Institute, this framework integrates short-, medium-, and long-term thinking to deal with increasing uncertainty (Webb 2019). In the short term (when conditions are most certain), the focus is on tactics (priority actions) to catalyze desired systems change. As uncertainty increases in the medium term, the focus shifts to strategies to achieve plan goals. Longer-term time horizons address strategic directions set by the plan vision and the potential disruptive effects of future drivers of change.

The framework shown in Figure 13.2 differs from a traditional implementation timeline in two important respects:

1. In contrast to the traditional practice of checking action items off of a list before moving to the next one, it requires simultaneous consideration of short-, medium-, and long-term time frames. For example, short-term tactical interventions and mid-term strategy development could anticipate projected long-term impacts of drivers of change such as climate change or autonomous vehicles.

2. The "Cone of Uncertainty" continually advances in time, requiring periodic resets (for example, annual progress reviews) to recalibrate the vision and iterate new strategies and actions as implementation moves forward and conditions change.

If this framework were applied to the action table format, the most detail would be developed for actions to be carried out in the more certain, near-term future. The mid-term time frame would be organized around strategic priorities for which implementing actions are identified in less detail; basic information such as action type, potential funding sources, and sequencing (for example, other actions that need to be carried out first) might be provided. Finally, the long-term time frame would emphasize broader strategic directions to realize the vision and goals. Future drivers of change would be monitored for their implications for short-term actions, mid-term strategy, and long-term vision. Exploratory scenario planning could be used on a regular basis to identify and prepare for potential disruptive impacts associated with drivers of change, including shocks such as pandemics, natural disasters, and economic recessions.

Policy Guidance and Decision-Making

Effective implementation depends not only on action, but also on integration of the comprehensive plan into the organizational culture of the local government. This can be accomplished by institutionalizing policies, practices, and processes to guide ongoing decision-making, administration, and operations. Examples include criteria to evaluate development applications, capital investments, budget allocations, and the like for consistency with the comprehensive plan; new work groups, processes, or other forms of interdepartmental collaboration; and strategic planning efforts by the administration and line departments. Less tangibly but with potentially significant impact, leadership can promote an entrepreneurial mindset within the organization to encourage initiative in advancing plan goals and priorities.

Modified or new policies, practices, and processes should be put in place in the short-term time frame in order to operationalize plan implementation. For example, the *Elevate Las Cruces* comprehensive plan calls for the development of "new administrative forms, guides, and other educational resources or processes to effectively implement updates to the Las Cruces land development code." *Elevate Las Cruces* also recommends project prioritization criteria (community benefit and operational) for use by the city in its annual capital improvement programming process. Community benefit criteria, which relate to goals and objectives contained in the comprehensive plan and other policy plans, include public health and safety, economic development, land development and growth, community reinvestment, and quality of life. Operational criteria include budget impact, cost-sharing, regulatory compliance, leveraging other projects based on timing or location, and public interest (identified needs that may not be referenced in a plan).

Collaboration and Partnerships

Collaboration and partnerships are essential to effective plan implementation. As noted, departments such as public works, parks and recreation, and transportation have separate missions and work programs, which can work at cross-purposes to the systems approach inherent in an effective comprehensive plan. To illustrate this point, consider the *public realm*: places that are accessible to all community members, such as streets and sidewalks; parks, natural areas, and trails; and civic buildings and spaces.

Viewed as a system, the public realm comprises many subsystems, such as parks and recreational facilities, public rights-of-way, and stormwater management facilities. In a typical municipal organization, these subsystems are managed separately by different departments. External agencies and organizations, such as other governmental entities, institutions, and nonprofits, also manage components of the public realm.

Landscape architect and planner David Barth advocates planning the public realm as a *plexus* – "an interwoven combination of parts or elements in a structure or system" – in order to generate greater environmental, economic, and social benefits (Barth 2020). From this perspective, the comprehensive plan implementation program can identify collaboration and partnership opportunities to maximize the benefits that the public realm provides for the community.

Public Realm Collaboration Examples: Portland (Oregon) and Atlanta (Georgia)

Portland's *Citywide Systems Plan*, which is part of its *2035 Comprehensive Plan*, was developed by a cross-departmental team led by the Bureau of Planning and Sustainability. The plan calls for coordinated planning, management, and investment in city-maintained physical systems that provide services for the public. These systems include transportation; water, wastewater, and stormwater utilities; parks and recreation; and other assets such as city buildings, police and fire stations, and technology. While the systems are addressed in separate chapters of the plan, the overall intent is to coordinate the provision of facilities and services by different bureaus. For example, Portland Parks & Recreation and the Bureau of Transportation work together to provide "an interconnected, multi-modal transportation and recreation system."

Collaboration with external partners can amplify the benefits of the public realm. Portland's *Citywide Systems Plan* identifies the need to cooperate with other providers of facilities and services for systems such as water, transportation, and parks and recreation.

The PATH Foundation, a nonprofit whose mission is to develop a system of interconnected greenway trails throughout the Atlanta, Georgia metro area, is an example of the potential impact of partnering with external organizations. Since 1990, PATH has worked with Atlanta and other local governments to develop over 290 miles of multi-use trails.[5]

Collaboration and partnerships can be structured around cross-cutting themes identified through the comprehensive planning process. For example, many contemporary plans identify community health as a guiding principle. Numerous factors influence the health of communities and individuals. Collectively referred to as the social determinants of health, these include, among others, design of the built environment, housing and economic stability, access to healthy food, social integration and support systems, and access to health care (see Figure 11.1). Professional disciplines whose work impacts the social determinants of health include public health, urban planning and design, parks and recreation, social services, health care, transportation, civil engineering, and more. Bringing together agencies and organizations involved in these various disciplines (many of whom do not normally interact) to work on joint projects and initiatives is a powerful way to advance the community health goals of the plan.

Funding and Resources

A comprehensive plan cannot be successfully implemented without sufficient funding, staff capacity, and other resources. Given the constrained fiscal environment and competing priorities that are typical of local governments, it is important to consider where these resources come from when developing the plan implementation program. It is particularly important to establish their availability for short-term actions that generate momentum for further progress.

While public finance is a complex field, in basic terms, it involves management of revenues and expenditures by a local government. It is not necessary or appropriate to address the details of public finance in the comprehensive plan. Rather, the bottom line is that all implementation actions – whether requiring capital investment, staff commitments, outside consulting services, ongoing operations and maintenance, or other initial or recurring costs – fall into the expenditure category and must have sufficient revenues to support them. From this perspective, it is important to understand the local fiscal context, constraints, and opportunities to confirm that capacity exists or can be developed to support plan implementation over time. Ideally, an analysis should be conducted to address the financial feasibility of comprehensive plan actions and the long-term fiscal sustainability of the community (that is, the costs of providing infrastructure and services versus revenues generated by existing and new development). The municipal finance officer/department is a key partner to engage both in conducting this analysis and to bring the perspective of fiscal sustainability to the planning process.

While financial feasibility is critical to successful implementation, it should not constrain the ambition and potential of the comprehensive plan to realize the community vision and goals. A strong plan with a compelling vision can be used to secure philanthropic funding, leverage resources from external partners, and attract private investment – highlighting the value of identifying actions that may not be feasible to implement in the short term, but which could have a high impact if resources become available in the future.

Implementation Funding Examples: Flint (Michigan) and Memphis (Tennessee)

Imagine Flint and *Memphis 3.0* are examples of comprehensive plans that address funding and cost considerations related to implementation.

Imagine Flint Master Plan. The implementation chapter of this plan groups actions into three cost categories: (1) actions primarily involving internal staff time with limited outside funding required ($), (2) actions requiring outside consulting services or relatively minor investment in infrastructure or project development ($$), and (3) actions requiring significant investment in infrastructure or project development ($$$). While the plan does not specify funding sources for these categories, order-of-magnitude cost estimates can be useful for planning operating and capital budgets.

Memphis 3.0 Comprehensive Plan. This plan calls on the City of Memphis to establish a Community Catalyst Fund using initial seed funding and annual general fund allocations. The purpose of the fund is to target investment and incentives to key areas identified in the comprehensive plan, with the intent of leveraging additional funding from private and philanthropic sources. Funding for the Community Catalyst Fund was included in the city's first annual budget following plan adoption.

Monitoring Implementation Progress

A methodology or system to monitor and assess progress in realizing the desired outcomes of the comprehensive plan is the final ingredient in an effective implementation program. This system should be designed to track progress in carrying out the action plan (*implementation monitoring*) and in achieving plan goals and objectives (*performance monitoring*). A well-designed action table or similar tool can be used to monitor implementation progress (for example, whether actions have been started, are in process/what remains to be done, or have been completed). Indicators, benchmarks, and targets can be identified in the comprehensive plan to monitor implementation performance. *Indicators* are quantitative measures of social, environmental, and economic conditions and trends that relate to plan goals and objectives. *Benchmarks* are standards or criteria against which progress toward plan goals and objectives can be measured. *Targets* are aspirational levels of achievement for a specific goal or objective, often tied to a defined time frame. Monitoring implementation progress is addressed in more detail in Chapter 16.

Monitoring Example: Memphis, Tennessee

To serve as a bridge from developing the comprehensive plan to its real-world application, monitoring should connect to the community goals and priorities identified during the planning process. The *Memphis 3.0 Comprehensive Plan* assigns monitoring responsibility to the Office of Comprehensive Planning using indicators identified through the scenario planning phase of the process. This phase engaged community members in exploring community values and trade-offs associated with three future growth scenarios (trend, growth in the core and along major corridors, or growth around neighborhood centers). The resulting indicators are grouped into three categories: land (for example, new residential development, changes in access to parks and open spaces, and new investments in anchors and anchor neighborhoods), connectivity (for example, transit frequency, changes in access to walkable and bikeable areas, and reduced travel-to-work time), and opportunity (for example, new tax revenues, residential access by affordability, and changes in household poverty). The plan charges the Office of Comprehensive Planning with tracking progress using these indicators and producing annual plan reviews and updates.

Summary

A comprehensive plan is effective only when implemented; otherwise, it is relegated to the proverbial shelf (or server). Effective implementation begins by identifying a compelling vision and goals through community engagement in the planning process. The implementation section of the plan specifies how strategies and actions are deployed over time to realize the vision and goals.

A complex and multidimensional endeavor, implementation involves a range of activities, participants, and relationships. The Levels of Implementation model is a useful construct to illustrate the scope of an effective implementation program. With community engagement as the foundation, the levels include revising development codes, ordinances, and incentives; using the plan to guide capital improvement planning and annual budget allocations; aligning internal work programs and decision-making; and leveraging additional resources by engaging external partners in implementation efforts. A successful implementation program applies these levels in complementary, synergistic ways to achieve desired outcomes.

Actions are the core of the implementation program. They are often presented in the form of a table or matrix that identifies action types, time frames, responsible departments or agencies, external partners, and potential funding sources. Action types include regulatory changes, capital and budgetary investments, project and program initiatives, and more detailed plans and studies. Short-term, catalytic actions should be identified to generate momentum for further action. While a table or matrix format is a useful way to organize complex information into an actionable guide for implementation, new approaches are needed to account for the uncertainty of change, particularly beyond the short-term time frame.

Other components of an effective implementation program include policies, practices, and processes to guide operations and decision-making; collaboration and partnerships; identification of sufficient funding, staff capacity, and other resources; and a monitoring system to track progress in achieving desired plan outcomes. Implementation is a dynamic process that requires ongoing review, evaluation, and adaptation to changing conditions (see Chapter 16).

Notes

1 The Levels of Implementation model was developed by David Rouse and Garner Stoll, former City of Austin Deputy Planning Director and project manager of the *Imagine Austin* Comprehensive Plan.
2 For a detailed accounting of Chattanooga Venture's role in revitalizing the city, see Cunningham (2008, pp. 241–267).
3 In the latter case, development and launch of a new, ongoing program could be identified as an action in the action table.
4 Prior to the 2011 adoption of *Philadelphia2035*, subarea plans were prepared independently at the neighborhood level.
5 More information is available on the PATH Foundation website at https://www.pathfoundation.org/our-story.

References

Austin, Texas (n.d.a). *About Capital Planning Office.* Accessed at http://www.austintexas.gov/department/capital-planning/about

Austin, Texas (n.d.b). *Priorities.* Accessed at https://www.austintexas.gov/department/priorities

Baltimore Neighborhood Indicators Alliance (2019). *Equity Analysis of Baltimore City's Capital Improvement Plan, FY2014-FY 2020.* Baltimore, MD: City of Baltimore.

Barth, David L. (2020). *Parks and Recreation System Planning: A New Approach for Creating Sustainable, Resilient Communities.* Washington, DC: Island Press.

Cunningham, Storm (2008). *reWealth! Stake Your Claim in the $2 Trillion redevelopment Trend That's Renewing the World.* New York, NY: McGraw Hill.

Government Finance Officers Association (n.d). *Best Practices: Master Plans and Capital Improvement Planning.* Accessed at https://www.gfoa.org/materials/master-plans-and-capital-improvement-planning

Pennsylvania Department of Community and Economic Development (2020). *Planning Series #3: The Comprehensive Plan in Pennsylvania,* Eighth Edition. Harrisburg, PA: Governor's Center for Local Government Services.

U.S. Department of Commerce (1926). *A Standard State Zoning Enabling Act.* Washington, DC: U.S. Department of Commerce.

Webb, Amy (2019). "How to Do Strategic Planning Like a Futurist," in *Harvard Business Review,* 7 (July). Boston, MA: Harvard Business Publishing.

Chapter 14

Consistency and Coordination

The complexity of issues and challenges faced by 21st-century communities requires attention to consistency and coordination in planning in order to achieve more successful outcomes. Consistency in comprehensive planning can be described as establishing a standard foundation for all facets of a plan, its implementing actions, and related plans. Coordination involves working together with other agencies and localities on planning issues that transcend organizational or jurisdictional boundaries.[1]

In Part II, the 21st-century comprehensive plan is presented as an integrated document, organized around interconnected systems. This approach requires internal consistency and integration of plan content, as well as consistency of other plans and zoning regulations with the comprehensive plan. In addition, an effective comprehensive plan is coordinated with planning at other levels of government.

Consistent Content and Internal Integration

To support an integrated approach, assumptions, information, and expectations must be reliable and consistent across systems and issues addressed by the comprehensive plan and its resulting goals, policies, and actions. This means, at a minimum, using consistent information and data throughout plan development. Common baseline information, forecasts, models, and scenarios should be used for all plan components. Data derived from federal, state, regional, or other sources may need to be adapted to make it appropriate for the local context. Geographic information systems (GIS) can be used to organize disparate data sets into consistent formats.

DOI: 10.4324/9781003024170-17

In the past, when comprehensive plans consisted of discrete elements and data availability was limited, different information was often used for the different planning topics addressed by the plan. For example, one set of information and assumptions could be used for land use, another set for transportation, and yet another for housing. Supplemental functional plans (for example, economic development, parks and recreation, or natural resource conservation) could also be developed with information that was inconsistent with or even independent of the data and assumptions used for the comprehensive plan.

To reiterate, land-use information and assumptions must be consistent with those used for housing, which must be consistent with those used for mobility and the economy, and so forth. This emphasis on consistency can be especially challenging when different teams are working on different aspects of the comprehensive

---

Consistency Example: Renton, Washington

Renton is a city of approximately 100,000 residents located in the growing Puget Sound region of Washington. Renton uses a common set of growth targets based on a buildable lands analysis as assumptions for the various systems addressed by its comprehensive plan: land use, mobility, wastewater treatment, and utilities (Figure 14.1). The city's growth targets are the result of a countywide allocation process involving King County and all 39 municipalities in the county. In addition, the countywide growth targets are consistent with the *Regional Growth Strategy* adopted by the four-county Puget Sound Regional Council, the metropolitan agency. The *Regional Growth Strategy* and its related multicounty planning policies serve as the core for the region's integrated long-range sustainability strategy for growth management, mobility, and economic opportunity (Puget Sound Regional Council).

	Housing Target	Employment Target
2012-2035 Growth Target per 2014 Buildable Lands Report	14,050	28,755
Growth Capacity Estimated 2012 BLR and Land Use Element Update	15,351-16,741	26,090-31,076

Figure 14.1 City of Renton Growth Targets

Source: City of Renton, Washington.

plan (for example, if consultants with special expertise are retained to develop the mobility or housing component of the plan). In such circumstances, it is imperative to establish upfront the information and assumptions to be used to develop the plan, so that team members do not develop work programs using independent data and forecasts.

Consistency in Plan Content

As described in Part I, the comprehensive planning process involves the development of a shared community vision, supported by goals, objectives, policies, and actions to realize the vision. It is imperative that these plan components be fully consistent with one another. Goals define desired future outcomes in support of the vision. Objectives introduce measurable targets or intentions in support of the goals. Policies define principles or criteria to guide ongoing decision-making, while actions are discrete tasks carried out during plan implementation. Policies and actions support and must be consistent with the vision, goals, and objectives for effective implementation.

The vision statement provides the guiding direction for all plan components. It is good practice to reference the vision throughout the plan, for example when presenting the goals and objectives, as well as policies and actions. The vision should be the point of reference for the substantive components of the plan, whether organized into elements, systems, or cross-cutting themes. Consistency and integration can be particularly powerful when plan content is organized around themes from the vision statement. Irrespective of plan organization, a systems approach requires acknowledging and leveraging key interrelationships among the community systems addressed by the plan. Planning provisions for natural, built environment, social, and economic systems must be mutually reinforcing and consistent (as opposed to working at cross purposes, as can happen when the plan is organized into discrete elements).

Consistent Content Example: City of Fairfax, Virginia

The City of Fairfax, with a population of just under 25,000, is located in the Washington, DC metropolitan area. As with other incorporated Virginia municipalities, the city is an independent jurisdiction within Fairfax County. The city's *2035 Comprehensive Plan* establishes a consistent set of goals, objectives, and policies based on the plan's vision. The vision serves as the foundation of the plan and is based on common assumptions related to community conditions, major issues, and impacts. Consistency is reflected throughout the provisions of the plan, including sections on hazards abatement, human services, community appearance, transportation network, and land use. In addition, the plan calls for consistency of development regulations and zoning with the comprehensive plan.

Consistency of Other Jurisdictional Plans with the Comprehensive Plan

In its role as the broadest and most inclusive prepared by a local government, the comprehensive plan may be viewed as the "umbrella" plan for the jurisdiction's "family" of plans. As noted in Chapter 13, other types of local plans include functional plans and subarea plans. Functional plans address a single planning topic (for example, housing), or a set of related topics (for example, a water resources management plan that covers water supply, water distribution, stormwater, and wastewater management). They provide more detail on the topic or topics addressed, including specific implementation actions and projects. The list of topics addressed by functional plans prepared by local jurisdictions across the country is quite extensive. Examples include air quality, arts and creativity, climate action, community design, energy, equity and diversity, green infrastructure, historic preservation, public health, mobility or new mobility, and many more.

Subarea plans include neighborhood plans, district plans, corridor plans, transit-oriented development plans, development project plans, and the like. These too can vary in scope. For example, neighborhood plans can address multiple community systems at the subarea scale, resembling a localized version of the jurisdiction-wide comprehensive plan. In other instances, subarea plans may address key planning topics or issues, such as economic opportunity or mobility. District plans are commonly prepared for downtowns, other mixed-use/commercial areas, or manufacturing/industrial areas. Some subarea plans focus on areas surrounding transit stations or stops. Development project plans are prepared by a developer or consortium of developers for sites ranging from small, single parcels to multiple parcels assembled into large tracts. It is important that development project plans be reviewed for consistency with the comprehensive plan, ideally beginning with informal consultation and review of sketch plans early in the process.

It is commonplace for jurisdictions (particularly larger ones) to have many adopted plans, which can create complications for community members, businesses, staff, and decision-makers. Questions may arise regarding which plans are relevant when a proposal comes forward for jurisdictional consideration. Where plans have been prepared and adopted independently of each other, there is the risk of conflict and incompatibility between different plans, policies, and provisions.

A best practice is to have the comprehensive plan, as the umbrella plan, serve as the policy framework for all plans developed by the jurisdiction. The role of functional and subarea plans is to develop more detail on how the policy framework applies to the topic, issues, or subarea addressed by the plan. If a functional or subarea planning process results in proposed changes to existing comprehensive plan policies or development of new ones, the comprehensive plan policy framework can be amended as part of the adoption action for the functional or subarea plan.

Plan Consistency Example: Norfolk, Virginia

The Plan Integration for Resilience Scorecard is a methodology that enables a community to evaluate the consistency of its plans in reducing vulnerabilities to hazards (Berke et al. 2015, Malecha et al. 2019).[2] For example, a subarea plan may encourage investment in an area that a local hazard mitigation plan identifies as a flood zone. The Scorecard can be used to (1) evaluate community plans for how well they target a community's most vulnerable areas, (2) identify conflicts between plans, and (3) resolve conflicts across plans to reduce hazard vulnerabilities.

The Scorecard was pilot tested in Norfolk, a coastal city on the Chesapeake Bay that is experiencing more frequent flooding because of sea-level rise and storm surge (DeAngelis et al. 2021). Evaluation of Norfolk's comprehensive plan, *Vision 2100* climate adaptation plan, and other functional and subarea plans revealed a number of inconsistencies. For example, the comprehensive plan does not include policies to relocate essential public facilities outside of areas identified by *Vision 2100* as being at long-term risk from sea-level rise and flooding. Outcomes of the evaluation included comprehensive plan amendments, regulatory changes, and infrastructure investment policies to address identified gaps and inconsistencies.

Subarea Planning Example: Raleigh, North Carolina

As described in Raleigh's *2030 Comprehensive Plan,* the city has used subarea planning for several decades. The comprehensive plan identifies four types of subarea plans – neighborhoods, small areas, corridors, and watersheds – that are viewed as critical extensions of the citywide comprehensive plan. Subarea plans provide additional details and specifics on how the comprehensive plan applies in 22 subdistricts of the city. Raleigh's small area planning process is community driven, allowing for more in-depth local analysis, local adaptation of the comprehensive plan policies, and more tailored implementation actions. Each subarea plan has its own unique features. Actionable recommendations are included, ranging from urban design guidelines to updated mobility strategies.

Regulatory Consistency with the Comprehensive Plan

For the benefit of community members, staff, decision-makers, developers, and other professionals who use the comprehensive plan, zoning and development regulations should be fully consistent with the comprehensive plan (particularly its goals and policies). Consistency between the zoning code and comprehensive plan is a requirement of a number of state planning statutes. In many parts of the country, however, the zoning code and the comprehensive plan may have significant inconsistencies, especially where they are developed, updated, or amended through separate processes and schedules. The likelihood of inconsistencies between the comprehensive plan and zoning and development regulations is even greater in jurisdictions where the plan is considered to be an advisory rather than a binding document.

As described in Chapter 13, zoning and development regulations are primary tools used to implement the vision, goals, and strategies defined by the comprehensive plan. It is important that this relationship be understood by community members and that the comprehensive planning and zoning update processes be coordinated. Ideally, the zoning and development regulations should be revised concurrent with the comprehensive planning process (perhaps starting midway in the process after the community vision and goals have been established) or immediately following plan adoption. It can be problematic for all concerned if too much time elapses between adoption of the comprehensive plan and initiation of the zoning update process.

External Consistency and Coordination

Developing and implementing comprehensive plan goals, policies, and actions involves consistency and coordination across multiple agencies and organizations, including external governmental structures. As described in Chapter 13, effective implementation depends upon expanded and new partnership relationships. Partners can include federal and state agencies, regional planning bodies, local jurisdictions, special service districts (such as water providers and school districts), nongovernmental organizations, academic and philanthropic institutions, and others. Aligning programs, processes, and projects of these diverse entities is a powerful way to implement the comprehensive plan. Coordination can also include resource sharing with other agencies and jurisdictions to support plan implementation (Piro, Leiter, and Rooney 2017).

Consistency with Planning Processes at Other Levels of Government

Federal policy directives are in place for planning topics such as transportation, affordable housing, and environmental protection. Compliance with these directives is a requirement of many federal grant programs.

State planning legislation varies across the United States. State statutory provisions range from detailed requirements and mandates to more general advisory and enabling guidance. Regional plans vary from region to region but also provide guidance and direction for local planning.

All relevant federal, state, and regional planning expectations should be identified at the beginning of the comprehensive planning process. Moreover, it is good practice to identify provisions in the comprehensive plan document that comply and conform with guidance and directives established at all levels of government.

A number of states and regions have processes in place for review of local plans to demonstrate consistency with state or regional planning expectations. New Jersey and Washington are examples of processes that have been developed in response to state planning guidance. New Jersey's cross-acceptance process promotes consistency between municipal, county, regional, and state plans (New Jersey State Office of Planning Advocacy n.d.). Washington's process focuses on the certification review of local plans by regional organizations in the state (State of Washington 1990). The

---

Regional Consistency Examples: Central Puget Sound, Washington and Twin Cities, Minnesota

Central Puget Sound is an example of region that certifies the comprehensive plans of local cities and counties. When the review process was first implemented, formal certification applied to compliance of the transportation element of the local comprehensive plan with the regional transportation plan. Other local plan elements were also reviewed for consistency with the regional plan. As transportation and mobility planning at the regional and local levels have become more integrated with planning for other systems, the region's certification process has evolved. Now when local plans are amended or updated, their policies are reviewed for consistency with the full policy framework in the long-range regional growth management, mobility, and economic plan. The Executive Board of the Puget Sound Regional Council, which oversees the consistency review of local plans, ties plan certification to eligibility to compete for federal transportation and economic development funds managed by the region (Puget Sound Regional Council 2020).

The Metropolitan Council for the seven-county Minneapolis-St. Paul (Twin Cities) region has developed a review process for coordinating regional and local planning among the region's municipalities and counties. The Council maintains regional plans for mobility, wastewater, and parks. It then develops "systems statements" that inform local governments of expectations for local programs and plan amendments. Once a regional plan has been updated or adopted, Council staff are made available for local planning assistance. Assistance includes guidance on how policy plans for regional systems apply to local jurisdictions, review of proposed amendments and updates to local comprehensive plans, provision of examples and best practices from around the region, and more. The overall process is a cycle of regional plan updates that are followed by assistance to localities for local plan updates (Metropolitan Council, n.d.).

Minneapolis-St. Paul (Twin Cities) region is an example of a process developed and adopted by a regional agency in consultation with its member jurisdictions. The Twin Cities approach involves regular cycles of regional plan updates followed by comprehensive plan updates by local jurisdictions.

Coordination with Plans of Adjacent Jurisdictions

Planning issues transcend jurisdictional limits and should be addressed by adjacent local governments in a coordinated manner. For example, an arterial roadway in a regional mobility network should be consistent in function across boundaries between neighboring jurisdictions. Other examples include compatible land uses and connected open space networks where jurisdictions share a common border. At a minimum, comprehensive plans should acknowledge common borders and issues that transcend boundaries. Regular consultation with neighboring communities on planning issues is advisable. A good practice is to include representatives from adjacent localities in the comprehensive planning process.

Consistency and coordination should extend to special districts, which are separate units of government that provide one or more essential public services for the community. Examples of facilities and services provided by these districts include schools, water supply, wastewater, stormwater, fire protection, public health, and transit. Special districts can provide their services within a single local jurisdiction, for several adjacent jurisdictions, or for a defined region. Some states have statutes providing for more than 100 different types of special service districts. Coordination between local jurisdictions and special service districts is key to ensure that planning assumptions and service provision by special districts are compatible with and support implementation of the comprehensive plan.

Interjurisdictional Coordination Example: Manatee County, Florida

Comprehensive plans in Florida are required to have an element addressing interjurisdictional coordination. The Intergovernmental Coordination Element of the *Manatee County Comprehensive Plan* addresses consistency with the plans of municipalities and adjacent counties. In addition, the element provides guidance for coordination with special districts and agencies, including the school board, fire districts, county sheriff's office, state agencies, utility districts, the port authority, and the airport authority. The county works with municipalities to coordinate performance standards for facilities and services. Collaborative efforts include facility maintenance, annexation, service delivery (including parks), and mitigation of development impacts. The county evaluates development proposals for significant impacts on municipalities, adjacent counties, the region, and the state, to ensure compatibility and consistency at the local, regional, and state levels. A conflict resolution process is included in the element.

Summary

Consistency and coordination are key attributes of the 21st-century comprehensive plan. Consistency refers to internal integration of the contents of the plan, including vision, goals, policies, actions, and sections addressing community systems and related topics. All plan components should be developed using common assumptions and data sets. Consistency also refers to alignment of zoning, development regulations, and other plans prepared by the local government with the policy framework established by the comprehensive plan. An update to the zoning ordinance to make it consistent with the comprehensive plan should be initiated concurrently with the comprehensive planning process or immediately following plan adoption. Prepared on an ongoing basis as part of plan implementation, subarea and functional plans apply the policy framework in more detail to specific geographic areas, community systems, or planning topics.

For comprehensive plans to be most effective, they also require coordination with neighboring communities and organizations and agencies at the regional, state, and federal levels. As described in Chapter 12, regional coordination is particularly important because planning systems and issues transcend jurisdictional boundaries. Regions such as Central Puget Sound in Washington State and Twin Cities (Minneapolis-St. Paul) in Minnesota provide good models for coordination between regional and local governments. Engaging multiple partners in the comprehensive planning process – including other local jurisdictions, special service districts, regional agencies, and nongovernmental organizations and institutions – is a powerful way to align programs and leverage resources for successful implementation.

Notes

1 Regional coordination is addressed in detail in Chapter 12.
2 The Plan Integration for Resilience Scorecard was developed by the Department of Homeland Security, Science and Technology Coastal Resilience Center of Excellence and its partner, the Institute for Sustainable Communities at Texas A&M University.

References

Berke, Philip R., Newman, Galen, Lee, Jaekyung, Combs, Tabitha, Kolosna, Carl, and Salvesen, David (2015). "Evaluation of Networks of Plans and Vulnerability to Hazards and Climate Change: A Resilience Scorecard," Chicago, IL: *Journal of the American Planning Association*, 81:4, pp. 287–302.

DeAngelis, Joseph, Johamary Pena, Alexsandra Gomez, Philip Berke, and Jaimie Masterson (2021). *Building Resilience Through Plan Integration* (PAS Memo). Chicago, IL: American Planning Association.

Malecha, Matthew, Masterson, Jaimie Hicks, Yu, Siyu and Berke, Philip (2019*). Plan Integration for Resilience Scorecard Guidebook: Spatially Evaluating Networks of Plans to*

Reduce Hazard Vulnerability - Version 2.0. College Station, TX: Institute for Sustainable Communities, College of Architecture, Texas A&M University.

Metropolitan Council (n.d.). Community Policies & Planning: Coordinating Regional and Local Plans. Accessed at https://metrocouncil.org/Communities/Planning.aspx

New Jersey State Office of Planning Advocacy (n.d.). State Plan – Cross Acceptance. Accessed at https://nj.gov/state/planning/state-plan-cross-acceptance.shtml

Piro, Rocky, Robert Leiter, and Sharon Rooney (2017). *Emerging Trends in Regional Planning*, Planning Advisory Service Report 586. Chicago, IL: American Planning Association.

Puget Sound Regional Council (2020). *Vision 2050: A Plan for the Central Puget Sound Region*. Seattle, WA: Puget Sound Regional Council.

Washington, State of (1990, subsequently amended). "Statewide Consistency," Chapter 47.80.070(3); "Comprehensive Plans, Transportation Guidelines, and Principles," Chapter 47.80.026. Olympia, WA: Revised Code of Washington.

Chapter 15

Designing and Communicating the Plan

Successful implementation requires that the final plan be designed in accessible, user-friendly formats and its contents communicated to the public in a clear and engaging manner. Contemporary plan formats go beyond the traditional paper document (and its digital successor, the online file) to encompass interactive, web-based platforms and other means of connecting with diverse audiences. Effective communication is critical throughout comprehensive plan development, adoption, and implementation. A persuasive plan communicates its vision, goals, and policies in ways that inform, inspire, and motivate the community to take action.

The Comprehensive Plan Document

Digital technology has minimized the need for the printed edition, the de facto format of the 20th-century comprehensive plan. Nevertheless, the comprehensive plan document continues to have an important role to play, primarily in digital form that is accessible through a website. Transparently documenting the planning process, information base, technical analyses, and outcomes enables public understanding of the plan and how it reflects community input during the process. It also provides access to the full contents of the plan for staff and others engaged in implementation, as well as community members interested in specific topics.

The comprehensive plan document can be organized in many different ways. The following are the contents of a prototypical document.

Summary. A well-written and visually compelling summary, suitable for dissemination as a standalone product, is essential to communicate key content, concepts, and recommendations of the plan.

DOI: 10.4324/9781003024170-18

Introduction. The introductory chapter provides background information such as the purpose of the comprehensive plan, the community context, and the motivation for planning (for example, key issues and priorities). It should also provide an overview of the plan contents (often framed as a guide on how to use the plan).

Planning Process. This section describes the steps in the planning process, the methods used to engage the community, and how the results shaped plan directions and priorities. Infographics are useful to visually represent information about the process and input received from participants.[1]

Existing Conditions and Trends. This section provides an overview of the factual basis of the plan, described by the Comprehensive Plan Standards for Sustaining Places as "an evidence-based description and analysis of current conditions and the best possible projection of future trends, such as land use, development, environmental factors, the economy, and population changes" (Godschalk and Rouse 2015). It is customary to summarize key information, findings, and implications for planning in this section and refer to technical appendices, a separate report (sometimes called a "data book"), or online database for details.

Vision and Guiding Principles. This section describes and illustrates the community's desired future based on community engagement in the planning process. It often identifies overarching principles or themes intended to guide efforts to realize the vision.

Goals and Policies. The substantive core of the 20th-century comprehensive plan typically consisted of elements with goals, objectives, and policies for planning topics such as land use, transportation, and housing. Particularly in states with strong planning systems, such as California and Washington, 21st-century comprehensive plans can be similarly divided into elements specified by state legislation. Contemporary plans are, however, more commonly organized around systems or themes that cut across multiple topics (see Chapter 5). Regardless of organizational structure, this section of the plan provides policy guidance for plan implementation.

Implementation. This section describes how the plan will be implemented. As described in Chapter 13, its contents include actions, time frames, responsibilities, funding sources, and measures to evaluate progress in achieving the desired outcomes. A detailed action table or matrix can be provided in an appendix for use by staff to monitor implementation.

Subarea Planning. As a rule, the comprehensive plan establishes the all-inclusive policy direction for jurisdiction-wide decision-making, as well as for more detailed planning at the subarea scale as part of implementation. However, some comprehensive plans include additional sections addressing smaller areas or districts within the jurisdiction. These sections identify geographically specific issues, priorities, and projects for more in-depth planning and project development during implementation.

Appendices. The complexity and length of the comprehensive plan document is a significant barrier to its dissemination and use. As noted, the length of the full document can be reduced by summarizing technical information and providing details in supporting appendices or reports.

Example: Stearns County, Minnesota

The *Stearns 2040 Comprehensive Plan* is an example of a contemporary approach to organizing the comprehensive plan document. Table 15.1 compares the contents of the plan to the sections of the prototypical document described above. The five pillars articulate the county's overarching values and vision for 2040. The core of the plan consists of five chapters identifying focus areas, goals, and policies for each pillar (Figure 15.1 shows examples of the focus areas). The implementation chapter identifies a series of six "land use decision factors" (formatted as checklists) to determine if a proposed project aligns with the comprehensive plan. A technical appendix provides detailed information about the county's natural resources, parks, and open spaces.

Table 15.1   *Stearns 2040 Comprehensive Plan* Document

Stearns 2040 Plan Organization	Prototypical Document Section
Introduction	Introduction
What is a Comprehensive Plan?	
The Five Pillars	Vision and Guiding Principles
The Planning Process	Planning Process
The Public Engagement Process	
Emerging Trends	Existing Conditions and Trends
Plan Components (Pillars)	Goals and Policies
Agriculture	
Living	
Nature	
Business	
Connectivity	
Implementation	Implementation
Natural Resource Manual	Appendix

The Comprehensive Plan Online

Digital technology, and the Internet in particular, have transformed planning practice and how community members engage with the comprehensive plan. A user-friendly website should be established early and kept current throughout the planning process. In addition to communicating information about the plan (for example, opportunities for community engagement and the results of engagement activities), the website can incorporate interactive features (for example, online

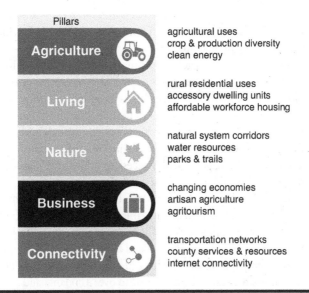

Figure 15.1 *Stearns 2040 Comprehensive Plan* **Pillars and Focus Areas**
Source: Stearns County, Minnesota.

surveys) to garner public input. At the conclusion of the process, a well-designed website can transition to a platform that makes the final plan accessible to the public. Following plan adoption, the website should be maintained and regularly updated to provide information on implementation progress.

As noted, digital technology has changed how people access and process information. To keep pace, the online plan should go beyond the digital equivalent of a paper document (a web landing page with a link to a lengthy file) to provide easy ways to navigate the key content and concepts of the plan. At a minimum, the website should consist of a simple landing page that orients the user to the plan and provides links to the full plan, individual chapters or sections, and related resource materials. A well-designed website integrates text and visual images, with the former provided as concise summaries that link to more detailed information for those who are interested. It also facilitates seamless navigation between the different components of the plan.

Examples of Online Formats: Huntsville (Alabama), Minneapolis (Minnesota), and Flint (Michigan)

Online formats are evolving as digital applications become more sophisticated. Huntsville's *Big Picture Comprehensive Master Plan* is noteworthy for its well-designed landing page, comprising brief text accompanied by visual images. The page provides a welcoming statement that defines the purpose of the plan, followed by a quote by the mayor on its importance for Huntsville's future. Users can explore the plan contents by clicking on four tabs – Principles, Policies, Places, and Process – each with links to more detailed information.

The landing page for the *Minneapolis 2040 Comprehensive Plan* invites the user to explore goals and topics, two of the three major components of the plan. The goals and topics provide links to policies, the third major plan component. Each of the 100 policies supports one or more goals and topics. Links provide for easy navigation among the three interrelated components. A menu along the left side of the page provides access to additional plan details, such as the planning process and a pdf of the full plan.

The *Imagine Flint* website features an ArcGIS StoryMap that summarizes the components of the plan in text, maps, and images.[2] The StoryMap format allows the user to scroll through topics such as The Purpose of the Plan, An Introduction to Flint, A Vision for Flint, and the Place-Based Land Use Plan. Three-dimensional renderings and photographs illustrate what different place types look like. A translation feature enables the text to be translated to over 100 languages.

Communicating the Plan

Communication is key throughout the comprehensive planning process, culminating in presentation of the final plan to the community. The plan contents are inherently complex, technical, and difficult to grasp. Effective communication translates this complexity into terms that community members can understand and relate to their own experience. The plan should be written in simple, clear language; avoid planning jargon, buzzwords, and acronyms; and use images, figures, and other visual aids to present key information and concepts.

Weaving stories into the plan narrative can connect with people in ways that objective presentation of planning information and concepts cannot (Walljasper 2018). Artful storytelling can communicate how the plan will affect the day-to-day lives of community members. "Person-oriented narratives" have been used in scenario planning to characterize the impacts of change from different scenarios on fictional characters from the community (Zapata 2007). Similar techniques can be applied to the comprehensive plan by telling stories of how community members will benefit if the plan is implemented and the vision realized. Stories are particularly powerful coming from actual voices within the community rather than from city officials, planners, or subject matter experts.

Most people will likely access the comprehensive plan online, where it will compete for attention with all that the Internet has to offer. This underscores the importance of a landing page with concise and compelling text and visuals that draw users into the website. It is also important to recognize that different people connect with different communication styles; some prefer reading, others listening, and others seeing. Alternative formats such as videos, podcasts, and posters can be provided to fulfill these preferences.

In today's digitized society, information is distributed through multiple channels, from traditional media such as newspapers, television, and radio to social media, community blogs, and online streaming services. To reach a broad spectrum of community members, the plan should be communicated through channels that people are comfortable with and use in their daily lives (Kirkhaug 2016). Analog as well as digital means of communication are required to reach people who lack reliable broadband service or are otherwise uncomfortable using the Internet. Printed copies of the full plan, summary, and other supplementary materials should be made accessible to those who require them. Plan communications should also address the needs of persons who have visual or hearing impairments or speak languages other than English.

Example: *places2040* Plan for Lancaster County, Pennsylvania

Lancaster County is known for its scenic landscapes, productive farmland, and the cultural heritage of its Amish and Mennonite communities. The county's comprehensive plan, *places2040*, is an example of creative plan formatting and communication based on shared community values. It replaced the county's previous comprehensive plan, which comprised separately prepared elements.[3]

The new plan is framed as the story of a voyage – "our journey" – taken by participants in the planning process. County residents are identified as the most important participants; others include county government, local municipalities, and partner organizations and agencies. The plan highlights how collective community voices identified eight priorities for Lancaster County's future. The priorities are integrated into five crosscutting "big ideas" and 26 policies that form the core of the plan. Scenario planning was used to define a "roadmap to the future" (a future land-use and transportation map depicting the big ideas and policies). Continuing the analogy to a journey, the final section of the plan (Moving Forward Together) addresses how the plan will be implemented.

Summary

To be effective, the final plan must be well designed, presented in accessible, user-friendly formats, and communicated in clear, persuasive ways that connect with diverse audiences. The Internet has changed how people access and use information, making it even less likely that they will read lengthy documents (the comprehensive plan format of the past). Nevertheless, the full plan must be made available online and as hard copies for those who need them. Doing so provides a transparent record of the planning process and its outcomes, as well as access to complete plan contents for those engaged in implementation or otherwise interested. The length of the plan document can be reduced by providing detailed information in appendices or separate technical reports. A clear and compelling summary should be prepared for widespread distribution as a standalone product (for example, a brochure or poster with strong text and visuals).

In today's world most people will likely access the comprehensive plan online. An engaging, easy-to-navigate website should be maintained throughout the planning process, transitioning to a platform that makes the final plan accessible to the public. The website landing page should be simple and straightforward to use, with concise text and strong visual images inviting users to click on links to access more information.

Regardless of format, plan communications should translate complex, technical planning information and concepts into terms (narrative text, infographics, and images) that people can understand and relate to their own experience. The ancient art of storytelling is a powerful way to convey the plan's relevance to people's needs and aspirations for the future. In conclusion, a human-centered design approach should be used to develop, design, format, and communicate the plan from the perspective of its users – the community members who will ultimately be affected by its implementation.[4]

Notes

1 The planning process section could follow the introduction or be included in an appendix.
2 StoryMap is a web-based application developed by Esri that enables storytelling using maps, narrative text, images, videos, and other media. The *Imagine Flint* StoryMap was developed by Houseal Lavigne Associates (accessed at https://www.imagineflint.com/pages/imagine-flint-interactive-plan).
3 *Greenscapes*, the green infrastructure element of Lancaster County's previous comprehensive plan (which is provided as a case study in Chapter 6), is incorporated by reference into *places2040*.
4 A definition of *human-centered design* is provided in Chapter 2.

References

Godschalk, David R. and David C. Rouse (2015). *Sustaining Places: Best Practices for Comprehensive Plans*, Planning Advisory Service (PAS) Report 578. Chicago, IL: American Planning Association.

Kirkhaug, Trine Rydningen (2016). *Communication in Urban Planning: How Quality of Communication Can Facilitate Constructive Citizen Participation*. Trondheim, Norway: Norwegian University of Science and Technology.

Walljasper, Jay (2018). "Planning and the Art of Storytelling," *Planning Magazine*, 86:8. Chicago, IL: American Planning Association, pp. 28–31.

Zapata, Marissa A. (2007). "Person-Oriented Narratives: Extensions on Scenario Planning for Multicultural and Multivocal Communities," in Lewis D. Hopkins and Marisa A. Zapata (eds.), *Engaging the Future: Forecasts, Scenarios, Plans, and Projects*. Cambridge, MA: Lincoln Institute of Land Policy. pp. 261–282.

Chapter 16

Maintaining and Updating the Plan

The comprehensive planning process continues beyond formal adoption of the plan. After adoption, attention turns to implementation, monitoring progress, and updating the plan on a regular basis to keep pace with change. Implementation is an ongoing endeavor, involving continued community engagement, execution of work program responsibilities by departments and agencies within the local jurisdiction, and partnerships with external agencies, institutions, nonprofit organizations, and others. This chapter addresses monitoring progress made in implementing the comprehensive plan goals, policies, and actions. It also provides guidance for regularly reviewing, updating, and amending the plan.[1]

Monitoring Implementation and Performance

There are two main types of progress monitoring: implementation monitoring and performance monitoring. *Implementation monitoring* tracks progress made in implementing actions identified in the comprehensive plan. *Performance monitoring* measures whether implementation is realizing the plan goals and objectives.

Implementation Monitoring

Implementation monitoring can be a relatively simple auditing process that tracks whether plan strategies and actions are being carried out. Chapter 13 addresses the importance of identifying priorities, timelines, responsible parties, and required

DOI: 10.4324/9781003024170-19

resources, typically in the form of an action table or matrix. The action table is a useful checklist for staff to use in implementation monitoring.

Implementation monitoring also involves tracking the extent to which ongoing operations, programs, and decision-making follow the guidance set by comprehensive plan goals and policies. For example, if a goal calls for improving the quality of the community's water supply and waterways, are decisions made on proposed capital investments, regulatory changes, development projects, and the like fulfilling this policy? Planning staff should identify and report on relevant comprehensive goals and policies for items brought to elected officials and other decision-makers for review and determination.

Implementation Monitoring Example: Springfield Township, Ohio

Springfield Township is a community of approximately 15,000 residents located in the Akron metropolitan area in northeastern Ohio. The Implementation and Monitoring section of the *Springfield Township Comprehensive Land Use Plan* focuses plan implementation monitoring on 22 actions. Examples include actions to revise zoning regulations, enact sustainable development practices, develop special area plans, create mixed-use zoning districts, develop access management plans for certain corridors, and acquire additional park and open space lands. The city uses a checklist in its annual review of implementation progress, which then informs setting priorities and identifying resource commitments for the coming year. The annual reviews are part of a process that includes more in-depth five-year reviews to ensure that goals and policies continue to be relevant, given likely changes in trends. This process, in turn, informs periodic updates to the comprehensive plan.

Performance Monitoring

Performance monitoring is used to measure progress in achieving plan goals. In so doing, it helps determine how effectively plan implementation is turning community aspirations and potential into reality. For example, the plan may include a goal, objectives, and strategies that advance alternatives to driving alone (such as walking, bicycling, rideshare, and transit use) in order to reduce transportation-related contributions to air pollution and climate change. Performance monitoring can be used to determine whether a shift to other modes of travel is actually occurring and whether the result is a measurable reduction of air pollutants and greenhouse gas emissions. Performance monitoring is conducted using benchmarks and indicators.

Benchmarks. A benchmark is a standard or criterion used to measure whether plan goals are being realized. A benchmark can be a target to work toward, a reference point that allows for comparison with other (peer) communities or a national standard, or both. An example of a target is the amount of future growth that occurs as infill and redevelopment within existing developed areas. The Comprehensive Plan Standards for Sustaining Places are an example of a reference point (in this case, a national standard for comprehensive planning practice) against which local plans can be measured.

Indicators. An indicator is a measure used to track progress toward reaching a target. For the infill/redevelopment growth target, the indicator is the percentage of growth that occurs in developed areas over time, which provides information on whether the target is being achieved. Indicators can be identified through the comprehensive planning process (for example, the inventory and analysis, development of goals and objectives, and evaluation of future scenarios), thus promoting integration, consistency, and continuity from plan development to implementation.

Indicators can be complex or simple to measure. For example, air quality assessment involves a number of standards (referred to as the National Ambient Air Quality Standards) for the measurement of air pollutants that include carbon monoxide, lead, nitrogen dioxide, ozone, particulate matter, and sulfur dioxide (U.S. Environmental Protection Agency n.d.). Population, unemployment, and poverty rates are examples of simple indicators derived from readily available data sources. Walking access to parks is an intermediate example that can be measured using geospatial analysis to determine park locations and walksheds (defined by a comfortable walking distance to each park along the surrounding street/sidewalk network).[2]

Planning Issues – Land Use/Zoning

- The region has strong agricultural zoning in place and permits a range of densities in the growth areas. Further analysis will determine up-to-date capacity for future housing units.

- Region has been directing growth into designated areas, promoting mixed-use development, and appears to have sufficient capacity.

- The quality and compatibility of growth with existing character is a concern.

- The Donegal region has limited commercial and industrial land use, limiting region's tax base.

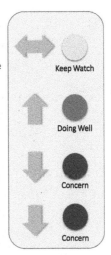

Keep Watch

Doing Well

Concern

Concern

Figure 16.1 Community Indicators Summary Example

Source: Wallace Roberts & Todd, LLC.

In the information-rich age of cloud computing and the Internet, which allow for compilation and analysis of complex data sets, it should be kept in mind that benchmarks and indicators will be used to communicate and report on plan implementation progress. Results of technical analyses should be translated into clear, understandable, and compelling terms for community members and decision-makers. Figure 16.1 provides an example of summarizing indicators related to land use and zoning as key findings for presentation to the public.[3]

A useful approach is to identify a manageable set of benchmarks for community systems and associated goals, each with a primary indicator to measure performance. Table 16.1 provides selected examples of indicators that could be used to measure the performance of different community systems and subsystems.

Table 16.1 Community System Indicator Examples

System	Indicator Examples
Natural Environment	Acres of habitat preserved or restored
	Acres of contaminated lands (brownfields)
	Amount of impaired waterbodies
	Per capita levels of air pollutants and greenhouse gas emissions
	Acres of parks and open space per 1,000 residents
Built Environment	Acres of rural or resource lands converted to urban uses
	Percentage of development occurring as mixed use
	Acreage/percentage of impervious surface
	Mode split among travel options
	Per capita energy consumption
Social Systems/Healthy Communities	Community facilities and services within a ten-minute walk
	Percentage of households with housing costs greater than 28 percent of income
	Annual income needed to afford market-rate rent
	Mortality/morbidity rates by zip code
	Frequency of use of an equity lens or health impact assessment in reviewing plan, program, and project proposals
Economic Systems	Per capita income
	Percentage of employed persons earning a living wage
	Percentage of green business and jobs
	Poverty rate
	Households with/without broadband Internet access

Community Indicators Example: Lincoln-Lancaster County, Nebraska

The City of Lincoln and Lancaster County use community indicators to monitor implementation of their joint comprehensive plan (Lincoln and Lancaster County 2020). The process tracks 36 benchmarks across six categories: growth, economy, environment, housing, transportation, and recreation. An indicator, or primary data source, is identified for each benchmark. Four general criteria are used to select the indicators: validity, understandability, reliability, and availability.

The city and county publish an annual *Community Indicators Report* to track changing community conditions and assess whether the assumptions in the comprehensive plan are valid and its goals are being achieved. Key observations and implications (what does it mean?) are provided for each indicator. The city and county update their comprehensive plan on an ongoing basis in coordination with the community-indicators process.[4]

Engaging the Community in Plan Implementation

Community engagement does not end with adoption of the comprehensive plan. An effective planning process continues to engage community members in plan implementation, progress monitoring, and regular updates and amendments to the plan. There are multiple ways to engage community members in implementation. A number of communities have established committees to provide overall guidance and coordination of implementation activities, a role similar to that played by a community advisory committee during comprehensive plan development. Partnerships can be formed with external organizations and groups to align work programs and leverage resources for plan implementation. Task forces and working groups can be established to support plan initiatives. Community members can be engaged in development of subarea, functional, and other plans that implement the comprehensive plan policy framework.

Regularly communicating implementation progress is key to successful community engagement. Many communities publish annual reports that recap progress made in implementing the comprehensive plan during the previous year. Annual reports should be supplemented by communications and opportunities for engagement throughout the year. In addition to more frequent reporting, a variety of online, interactive tools can used to inform and engage the public on an ongoing basis. Where plan implementation is demonstrating success, the community can be engaged in celebrating achievements. Where implementation efforts have not met expectations (for example, when targets have not been met or priority actions have not been carried out), the implementation team should acknowledge the situation, identify contributing factors, and invite community input in determining course corrections.

Examples of Community Engagement in Implementation: Topsham (Maine) and Portland (Oregon)

Topsham is a small town (population of 8,784 at the 2010 census) located in the Portland-South Portland-Biddeford, Maine metropolitan statistical area. The implementation section of the *Topsham Comprehensive Plan Update* begins with the following statement:

> The implementation of a Comprehensive Plan takes an all-hands-on deck, coordinated effort of staff, committees, elected officials, and community service groups working together to move the visions and goals of the plan into action.

The plan identifies appointment of a Comprehensive Plan Implementation Committee as the first implementation priority following plan adoption. The committee's role is to advocate for the plan, oversee implementation activities, and provide coordination support. The committee includes community members who were intimately involved in the comprehensive planning process and representatives of town committees and boards that play a direct role in plan implementation.

The City of Portland, Oregon's Department of Planning and Sustainability developed an online tool it called the "Comprehensive Plan Map App" for the *2035 Comprehensive Plan*. The Map App was used in the planning process to communicate how the plan and its recommended changes to land use, transportation, and infrastructure contribute to meeting community goals (Rouse and McElvaney 2015). The city has used the Map App since plan adoption to invite the public to review and provide input on planning proposals (for example, draft policy plans, changes to zoning and development regulations) that relate to comprehensive plan implementation.

Plan Reviews, Updates, and Amendments

The comprehensive plan is a dynamic tool whose implementation applies the community vision and goals on an ongoing basis. It should be a point of reference for the mission and work programs of local governmental departments and agencies, for engagement with the community, and for collaboration with outside partners and allied groups, as well as a tool for evaluating development applications and other proposals requiring review and approval.

To keep the comprehensive plan current and relevant, procedures should be in place to guide regular reviews, updates, and amendments to the plan. Progress reviews should be conducted annually. Amendments allow existing plan provisions to be modified or new ones added in response to progress review findings or other changed circumstances. A regular process should be established for when amendments are developed and considered between updates. Updates involve a more thorough review and revision process to address new circumstances and issues that have arisen since the last full plan was adopted.

Plan Reviews and Updates

Communities are continually changing places in which new issues and needs can arise, new facilities and services can come online, other conditions can change, and unanticipated events (for example, economic shocks, natural disasters, and pandemics) can occur – all of which require an adaptive approach to plan implementation. The need for flexibility is compounded by the accelerating rate of social, technological, economic, and environmental change in the 21st century. Regular plan reviews and updates help to keep the comprehensive plan current and responsive to change.

Various approaches are used to determine the timing and extent of updates to the comprehensive plan. Some states address the frequency of updating comprehensive plans in their planning statutes. Where state guidance is lacking, many local jurisdictions have identified update schedules tailored to their situations. A common best practice is to conduct progress reviews annually, a more in-depth (midpoint) review and update every five years, and a full plan update every ten years.

Annual Review. The annual review allows a community to assess progress made during the prior year in (1) carrying out actions, projects, and programs identified in the plan (implementation monitoring) and (2) achieving goals and benchmarks set by the plan (performance monitoring). The results are used in determining implementation priorities and resource commitments for the coming year. Proposed amendments to be considered in the next plan amendment cycle can also be identified in the annual review. The annual review should be coordinated with the jurisdiction's capital improvement and annual budget processes.

Midpoint Review. It is advisable to conduct a more in-depth review of implementation progress midway between adoption of the most recent plan and the next scheduled full plan update (that is, every five years for a ten-year cycle). The midpoint review provides an opportunity to "reset" plan implementation based on an assessment of accomplishments, challenges, and relevant trends and changes in the period since plan adoption. The midpoint review can be used to determine plan amendment proposals that are best brought forward before the next update, as well as issues to be addressed in the update. It can also identify preliminary work and scoping that could be done in advance of the next update process.

Full Plan Update. As noted, best practice calls for the community to conduct a full plan update every ten years. The update should begin with an assessment of the previous comprehensive plan: what has been successfully accomplished, what remains to be done, what is out-of-date, and what has changed since its adoption. The planning and community engagement process described in Part I should be used to carry out the update.

Plan Amendments

Proposed revisions or additions to the comprehensive plan should be approached in a manner that is transparent, engages the public, and is easily understood by community members and decision-makers. A best practice is to create a single unified amendment docket on an annual schedule. The docketing process can include (a) time for proposed amendments to be submitted, (b) time for review of amendment proposals and selection of those to undergo further review and consideration, (c) time for gathering information and community comment, and (d) time for crafting recommendations, deliberations, and official action.

Proposed amendments may originate from community members and groups, property owners, staff, or elected officials. The time allowed to submit proposed amendments can be several months in duration with a clearly communicated deadline or be more limited in extent (for example, three to four weeks). Selecting which amendment proposals will be considered in the current cycle can similarly occur over a period of several weeks to a month. The selection process should be transparent and based on established criteria.

Once the proposals for a given amendment cycle have been identified, sufficient time should be allotted for developing informational materials and soliciting comments on the requests. Public engagement should occur throughout this step, through means such as written comments, online input, community forums, and public meetings. This step concludes with crafting of staff recommendations addressing conformance of proposals with the comprehensive plan and transmittal to decision-makers for consideration. The procedures for deliberation and action by decision-makers should also include the opportunity for genuine community engagement.

A similar, parallel docketing process should be developed for amendments to zoning and development regulations, including rezoning proposals for sites and districts. A primary purpose of this approach is to ensure that the comprehensive plan, zoning code, and development regulations remain consistent with one another. Modifications and additions to the comprehensive plan must be reflected in all local planning and decision-making tools, including regulations and zoning. Regular, coordinated cycles for plan and regulatory amendments, with clearly defined review procedures and criteria, promote transparency, consistency, and certainty and allow all interested parties to participate.

Plan Amendment Process Example: Washington State

Since the 1990s, the State of Washington has provided direction to local governments for regular and orderly amendments and updates to comprehensive plans. The process creates predictability, certainty, and efficiency and promotes authentic public engagement and transparency in decision-making.

Washington's planning statutes limit "updates, proposed amendments, or revisions of the (municipal or county) comprehensive plan" to "no more frequently than once every year" (State of Washington 1990). This model lends itself to adaptation by local governments elsewhere in the country.

The legislation allows for exceptions to the once-a-year requirement in specific circumstances (for example, adoption of a subarea plan for which an environmental review of cumulative impacts has been completed). The capital facilities element can also be amended concurrently with the adoption of a municipal or county budget. The legislation calls for local jurisdictions to develop and "widely disseminate" public participation programs are that must be followed for all plan amendments and updates (State of Washington 1990).

Summary

All communities – large or small, rural or urban, or with other distinguishing characteristics – should view their comprehensive plan as a dynamic resource and tool to realize a more successful and sustainable future through implementation. Keeping the plan current and relevant requires ongoing monitoring of progress, including implementation monitoring to determine whether actions identified by the plan are being carried out and performance monitoring to determine if plan goals are being achieved. A well-designed action table or matrix from the comprehensive plan can be used as a checklist for implementation monitoring. Performance monitoring is conducted using benchmarks (targets) and indicators (measures to track progress in achieving the targets).

Successful implementation requires ongoing communications and engagement of community members. To keep the plan up-to-date, reviews should be conducted annually to assess progress and determine implementation priorities for the coming year. Annual reviews should be coordinated with the capital improvement and budget processes. Best practices call for more in-depth reviews every five years and a major plan update every ten years. Establishing a reliable process and schedule for plan reviews and updates benefits all community members, including neighborhood and civic groups, the business community, institutional and nonprofit participants, and decision-makers. Plan amendments should similarly be carried out using a consistent and predictable process with clear criteria to promote transparency, authentic public engagement, and certainty.

Notes

1 The components of a robust implementation section of the comprehensive plan are discussed in detail in Chapter 13.

2 A partnership of the Trust for Public Land, National Recreation and Park Association, and Urban Land Trust, the ten-minute walk campaign has set a national target of

ensuring that all people have safe, easy access to a quality park within a ten-minute walk of home by 2050 (https://10minutewalk.org/).

3 This example is taken from a public presentation by the firm Wallace Roberts & Todd, LLC for the *Donegal Regional Comprehensive Plan*, a comprehensive plan for East Donegal Township, Marietta Borough, Mount Joy Borough, and the Donegal School District in Lancaster County, Pennsylvania.

4 In 2021, the City and the County were developing a new comprehensive plan to replace the *Lincoln-Lancaster County 2040 Comprehensive Plan*, the subject of the 2020 *Community Indicators Report*.

References

Lincoln and Lancaster County, Nebraska (2020). *Lincoln-Lancaster County Community Indicators Report*. Accessed at https://www.lincoln.ne.gov/City/Departments/Planning-Department/Planning-Reports

Rouse, David and Shannon McElvaney (2016). *Comprehensive Planning and Geodesign*. PAS Memo. Chicago, IL: American Planning Association.

U.S. Environmental Protection Agency (n.d). NAAQS Table (National Ambient Air Quality Standards). Accessed at https://www.epa.gov/criteria-air-pollutants/naaqs-table

Washington, State of (1990). "Comprehensive Plans – Review Procedures and Schedules – Amendments" in *Growth Management – Planning by Selected Counties and Cities*. Chapter 36.70A.130. Olympia, WA: Revised Code of Washington.

Chapter 17

The Future of the Comprehensive Plan

Comprehensive planning is analogous to a journey – through the planning process and on to implementation – taken collectively by a community in search of a better future. In many ways, the authors of this book have been on a journey as well. We began our journey with the American Planning Association's Comprehensive Plan Standards for Sustaining Places, a widely recognized benchmark for excellence in comprehensive planning. We reviewed dozens of plans from the second decade of the 21st century to understand the current state of practice. While we found many excellent examples, we concluded that the comprehensive plan must evolve to help communities address challenges such as climate change, socioeconomic inequality, and accelerating technological change.

Just as the planning process can take twists and turns due to unanticipated developments, the scope of this book changed as the events of 2020 unfolded. The COVID-19 pandemic, systemic racism highlighted by the deaths of Black Americans at the hands of law enforcement officers, and the divisiveness that tears at the fabric of American society all raise the question as to whether the comprehensive plan (a product of 20th-century planning practice) is up to the challenges of the 21st century. Our answer is a qualified yes. At its best, comprehensive planning can exemplify democratic engagement in charting a course for the future. However, it must be taken to a new level to meet the pressing needs of today and tomorrow.

This chapter begins with a summary of the current state of comprehensive planning practice. It then provides thoughts about what the comprehensive plan might become in the future to yield truly sustainable, resilient, and equitable outcomes. These thoughts are offered not as predictions, but with the hope of making a small contribution to inspiring a new generation of comprehensive plans that make a difference in the lives of people and communities.

The Comprehensive Plan Today

The framework established by the *Comprehensive Plan Standards for Sustaining Places* (Standards) encapsulates the evolving state of comprehensive planning practice (Godschalk and Rouse 2015). The components of this framework are at various levels of development and expression in contemporary plans, from well-established to still in their infancy. Drawing on the Standards framework, this book is organized around four major areas of comprehensive planning practice: (1) the planning process (Part I), (2) the substance of the plan (Part II), (3) implementation (Part III), and (4) the attributes of the plan (also in Part III). The following text briefly recaps the current state of practice for each of these four areas.

Planning Process

A primary goal of the planning process used to develop contemporary plans is meaningful involvement of a diverse spectrum of community members. The process is driven by community engagement: from identification of shared values and important issues in Phase 1, to articulation of a vision and goals for the future in Phase 2, to development of strategies, policies, and actions to realize the vision and goals and address the issues in Phase 3. Increasingly sophisticated tools are being used to involve the community, such as online engagement platforms and scenario planning exercises. Equity has emerged as a fundamental principle, underscored by the need to engage historically underserved, underrepresented groups in the planning process. The Standards call for community engagement to continue in implementation, which is not yet prevalent in practice.

Plan Substance

The substantive content of the comprehensive plan is changing in response to 21st-century challenges. Contemporary plans have evolved from a focus on land use and physical development (the norm for 20th-century plans) to address social, economic, and environmental issues related to community sustainability, resilience, and equity. In contrast to 20th-century plans, which were organized around discrete elements addressing conventional planning topics such as land use and transportation, contemporary plans are organized around systems or cross-cutting themes identified through community engagement. Examples include mobility, health, equity, and resilience in response to climate change. While most comprehensive plans identify equity as a vision component, goal, or guiding principle, the extent to which intent is being converted into policy and action that significantly affect structural racism and socioeconomic inequality is not yet apparent.

Implementation

The typical 20th-century comprehensive plan provided limited direction for implementation. As specified by the Standards, current best practices call for plans to identify actions, time frames, responsibilities, and metrics to measure progress in achieving desired outcomes. Plan implementation programs have moved beyond the traditional focus on zoning and development regulations to a more integrated approach encompassing capital investments, annual budget allocations, interdepartmental collaboration, and engagement of external partners. Implementation is viewed as an ongoing process that involves monitoring of progress, periodic evaluations, and adjustment of the implementation program based on the evaluation. While contemporary plans increasingly incorporate these practices, more work is needed to fully translate them into results through on-the-ground implementation. Issues include the need to set priorities, begin with what is feasible, engage community members, and account for the uncertainty of future change.

Plan Attributes

Contemporary practice emphasizes effective communication in designing and presenting the plan to connect with people, including community members, business owners, and decision-makers. Going beyond the standard printed document of the 20th century, contemporary plans use innovative new formats that integrate visual images, infographics, and other ways of conveying information and ideas. The plans are presented on digital and online platforms that people are comfortable navigating in the age of the Internet. A user-friendly, accessible website is used for ongoing communications and engagement during the planning process, to present the final plan to different audiences, and to keep the community updated on implementation progress.

The Comprehensive Plan of the Future

To achieve sustainable, resilient, and equitable outcomes, the comprehensive plan of the future must build on the above trends in contemporary practice and take them in new directions. Given the unprecedented challenges facing humankind in the 21st century and their profound implications for local communities, its success will be measured by real-world impacts through implementation. To maintain its position as the leading local governmental policy document, the comprehensive plan must help communities prepare for and adapt to the disruptive effects of social, technological, environmental, and economic drivers of change in an uncertain world.

There are many ways of framing what the comprehensive plan of the future could be. We offer five interrelated themes to illustrate key directions in which comprehensive planning practice may and must evolve to yield truly sustainable, resilient, and equitable outcomes.

1. **Equity and Engagement**
The comprehensive plan of the future will advance the principle of interwoven equity by giving voice to and providing for the needs of all community members.

America's enduring legacy of racial injustice and the current trend of increasing socioeconomic inequality are unsustainable and antithetical to the ideal of a healthy, prosperous, and resilient community. For this ideal to be realized, the comprehensive plan of the future must prioritize equity throughout the planning process, in the comprehensive plan that results from the process, and in its implementation. This means engaging all segments of the community – especially those previously excluded – in the planning process in ways they find accessible, comfortable, authentic, and transparent. It means applying an equity lens to plan development and the goals, strategies, policies, and actions that result. Finally, it means carrying the equity lens through to plan implementation by using fairness and equity – who benefits and whose needs are met – as fundamental criteria to prioritize action and monitor results.

2. **Climate Change Mitigation and Adaptation**
The comprehensive plan of the future will set the direction for communities to address climate change, the existential environmental threat of the 21st century.

Similar to the principle of interwoven equity (with which it is inextricably connected), combatting climate change must be integrated into the comprehensive plan of the future through goals, policies, and actions that address both mitigation and adaptation. To address mitigation, the comprehensive plan of the future must go beyond net-zero carbon emissions (the current benchmark) to *climate-positive* planning and design of land use and development patterns, buildings, and mobility and infrastructure systems.[1] To address adaptation, plans must promote *climate-resiliency* as a guiding principle through the planning, design, and integration of natural, built environment, social, and economic systems.[2] The impact of community-wide goals, policies, and actions addressing climate change will be magnified through implementation at the microscale (neighborhood and site applications) and macroscale (the region and beyond, through coordination and cooperation across jurisdictional boundaries and levels of government).

3. **Systems Thinking**
The comprehensive plan of the future will embed systems thinking in the planning process, the substance of the plan, and plan implementation.

Systems thinking in contemporary practice is reflected in the organization of the comprehensive plan around community systems but is not yet operationalized in policy and implementation. The comprehensive plan of the future must complete the evolution away from the siloed elements of the 20th-century model to an integrated systems approach. This approach will be manifested by plan formats, policies, and actions that recognize the complex interrelationships between different community systems and subsystems. The concept of leverage points – places to intervene in a system to change its behavior – should be used to prioritize and target interventions for effective implementation (Meadows 2008).[3] The increasing power of technology and availability of data will enable use of key indicators to model system behavior, monitor implementation progress, and adaptively manage the community's response to change.

4. **People-Centered Technology**
The comprehensive plan of the future will harness technology to engage and serve the needs of the community.

Rapid technological change is transforming society, the economy, and the environment, with profound implications for local communities. The accelerating pace of technological development (for example, fifth generation and beyond wireless technology, quantum computing, and artificial intelligence) makes it impossible to predict the ultimate impacts on local communities with any degree of certainty. It is clear, however, that planning can help communities prepare for and adapt to change, and that the comprehensive plan can help guide the use of technology to serve the needs of people.[4] Toward this end, the comprehensive plan of the future should use technology to involve people in democratic processes that define community priorities and develop solutions to address them (Cohen 2015; van den Bosch 2018). The planning process will be transformed by engagement methods such as gamification, three-dimensional visualizations, and real-time analysis of the impacts of scenarios generated by community members. Technology will enable new approaches and tools to turn the community's vision and goals into reality through effective implementation (the next and concluding theme).

5. **Effective Implementation**
The comprehensive plan of the future will apply new approaches and tools to translate the community's vision and goals into measurable results through implementation.

Successfully meeting the challenges faced by 20th-century communities depends on effective implementation. The comprehensive plan of the future should replace the current practice of developing an implementation program at the end of the planning process with a strategic focus on implementation throughout the process, resulting in a plan that is feasible to implement.[5] New implementation models (for example, flexible regulatory approaches that replace outdated land-use requirements and adaptive infrastructure standards that account for climate change projections) must be developed to address the uncertain impacts of future change. The traditional future land-use map (which contemporary plans are replacing with form or place-based maps) will see further evolution into new ways of spatially representing community systems, dynamics, and change over time. As noted, technology will enable more effective monitoring of progress and adjustment of implementation activities to achieve community goals. Finally, the comprehensive plan of the future must use new governance approaches to realize desired outcomes. Examples include integrated operational and decision-making platforms, public–private partnership structures to leverage resources for plan implementation, and more robust mechanisms for regional coordination and cooperation.

Conclusion

The above themes are not intended to be an exhaustive list. Rather, they illustrate the potential of the comprehensive plan of the future to help local communities realize transformative change. Other themes could be added, for example:

> The comprehensive plan of the future will catalyze cross-sectoral collaboration and resource commitments to improve community health and equity by addressing the social determinants of health.

Our hope is that the themes stimulate further ideas, discussion, research, and practice applications to inform the next generation of comprehensive plans.

In closing, some may question whether local comprehensive plans can have transformative effects given the global trends and challenges of the 21st century. Consider, however, the thousands of communities across the United States that prepare and maintain comprehensive plans. Consider further the potential impacts if these communities were to develop and implement a new generation of plans, and what might happen if communities around the globe adopted similar approaches. Planning is at its core an optimistic profession based on the notion that it is possible to change the world for the better. As the long-range policy document for local governments, the comprehensive plan is uniquely positioned to help communities realize sustainable, resilient, and equitable outcomes. The challenge and opportunity for planners and the communities they serve is to transform this potential into reality through a new model of comprehensive planning for the 21st century.

> Never doubt that a small group of thoughtful, committed, citizens can change the world. Indeed, it is the only thing that ever has.
> (Margaret Meade)

Notes

1 Climate-positive solutions go beyond achieving net zero carbon emissions to remove additional carbon dioxide from the atmosphere.
2 A climate-resilient community anticipates, prepares for, and adapts to changing climate conditions. It can also withstand, respond to, and recover rapidly from disruptions caused by these climate conditions (Mullan 2018).
3 See discussion of systems thinking in Chapter 1).
4 This role is essential given dystopian scenarios of a future characterized by stark inequality, a lack of personal privacy, and reduced human autonomy in a world where technology is controlled to benefit the socioeconomic elite (see, for example, West and Allen 2020).

5 A comparable approach has been proposed for parks and recreation system planning (Barth 2020). This approach involves the development of a "preliminary implementation framework" early in the planning process to initiate discussion of possible implementation strategies and funding sources.

References

Barth, David L. (2020). *Parks and Recreation System Planning: A New Approach for Creating Sustainable, Resilient Communities*. Washington, DC: Island Press.

Cohen, Boyd (2015). *The 3 Generations of Smart Cities*. Fast Company. New York, NY: Mansueto Ventures LLC.

Godschalk, David and David Rouse (2015). *Sustaining Places: Best Practices for Comprehensive Plans* (PAS Report 578). Chicago, IL: American Planning Association.

Meadows, Donella, edited by Diana Wright (2008). *Thinking in Systems: A Primer*. White River Junction, VT: Chelsea Green Publishing.

Mullan, Michael (2018). *Climate-Resilient Infrastructure*. OECD Environment Policy Paper 14. Paris, France: Organization for Economic Cooperation and Development.

van den Bosch, Herman (2018). *Smart City Tales*. Accessed at https://www.dropbox.com/s/c9f1v4od86ibaa3/2018%2007%2030%20Smart%20City%20Tales.pdf?dl=0

West, Darrell M. and John R. Allen (2020). *Turning Point: Policymaking in the Era of Artificial Intelligence*. Washington, DC: Brookings Institution Press.

Appendix A

Comprehensive Plan Standards for Sustaining Places

The Comprehensive Plan Standards for Sustaining Places were developed by the American Planning Association as a framework for use by communities seeking to integrate sustainability into their comprehensive plans. The Standards provide a concise guide to contemporary comprehensive planning practice, including the planning process, the content and attributes of the plan that results from the process, and implementation. This appendix provides the complete list of principles, processes, attributes, and best practices for each from PAS Report 578, *Sustaining Places: Best Practices for Comprehensive Plans* (Godschalk and Rouse 2015). Additional details, including definitions of the 85 best practices, are provided in the report.

Principles

1. *Livable Built Environment.* Ensure that all elements of the built environment, including land use, transportation, housing, energy, and infrastructure, work together to provide sustainable, green places for living, working, and recreation, with a high quality of life.
   1.1 Plan for multimodal transportation.
   1.2 Plan for transit-oriented development.
   1.3 Coordinate regional transportation investments with job clusters.
   1.4 Provide complete streets serving multiple functions.
   1.5 Plan for mixed land-use patterns that are walkable and bikeable.

1.6   Plan for infill development.
1.7   Encourage design standards appropriate to the community context.
1.8   Provide accessible public facilities and spaces.
1.9   Conserve and reuse historic resources.
1.10 Implement green building design and energy conservation.
1.11 Discourage development in hazard zones.

2. *Harmony with Nature.* Ensure that the contributions of natural resources to human well-being are explicitly recognized and valued and that maintaining their health is a primary objective.
   2.1   Restore, connect, and protect natural habitats and sensitive lands.
   2.2   Plan for the provision and protection of green infrastructure.
   2.3   Encourage development that respects natural topography.
   2.4   Enact policies to reduce carbon footprints.
   2.5   Comply with state and local air quality standards.
   2.6   Encourage climate change adaptation.
   2.7   Provide for renewable energy use.
   2.8   Provide for solid waste reduction.
   2.9   Encourage water conservation and plan for a lasting water supply.
   2.10 Protect and manage streams, watersheds, and floodplains.

3. *Resilient Economy.* Ensure that the community is prepared to deal with both positive and negative changes in its economic health and to initiate sustainable urban development and redevelopment strategies that foster green business growth and build reliance on local assets.
   3.1   Provide the physical capacity for economic growth.
   3.2   Plan for a balanced land-use mix for fiscal sustainability.
   3.3   Plan for transportation access to employment centers.
   3.4   Promote green businesses and jobs.
   3.5   Encourage community-based economic development and revitalization.
   3.6   Provide and maintain infrastructure capacity in line with growth or decline demands.
   3.7   Plan for post-disaster economic recovery.

4. *Interwoven Equity.* Ensure fairness and equity in providing for the housing, services, health, safety, and livelihood needs of all citizens and groups.
   4.1   Provide a range of housing types.
   4.2   Plan for a jobs/housing balance.
   4.3   Plan for the physical, environmental, and economic improvement of at-risk, distressed, and disadvantaged neighborhoods.
   4.4   Plan for improved health and safety for at-risk populations.
   4.5   Provide accessible, quality public services, facilities, and health care to minority and low-income populations.
   4.6   Upgrade infrastructure and facilities in older and substandard areas.
   4.7   Plan for workforce diversity and development.

4.8 Protect vulnerable populations from natural hazards.

4.9 Promote environmental justice.

5. *Healthy Community.* Ensure that public health needs are recognized and addressed through provisions for healthy foods, physical activity, access to recreation, health care, environmental justice, and safe neighborhoods.

5.1 Reduce exposure to toxins and pollutants in the natural and built environments.

5.2 Plan for increased public safety through reduction of crime and injuries.

5.3 Plan for the mitigation and redevelopment of brownfields for productive uses.

5.4 Plan for physical activity and healthy lifestyles.

5.5 Provide accessible parks, recreation facilities, greenways, and open space near all neighborhoods.

5.6 Plan for access to healthy, locally grown foods for all neighborhoods.

5.7 Plan for equitable access to health care providers, schools, public safety facilities, and arts and cultural facilities.

6. *Responsible Regionalism.* Ensure that all local proposals account for, connect with, and support the plans of adjacent jurisdictions and the surrounding region.

6.1 Coordinate local land-use plans with regional transportation investments.

6.2 Coordinate local and regional housing plan goals.

6.3 Coordinate local open space plans with regional green infrastructure plans.

6.4 Delineate designated growth areas that are served by transit.

6.5 Promote regional cooperation and sharing of resources.

6.6 Enhance connections between local activity centers and regional destinations.

6.7 Coordinate local and regional population and economic projections.

6.8 Include regional development visions and plans in local planning scenarios.

6.9 Encourage consistency between local capital improvement programs and regional infrastructure priorities.

Processes

7. *Authentic Participation.* Ensure that the planning process actively involves all segments of the community in analyzing issues, generating visions, developing plans, and monitoring outcomes.

7.1 Engage stakeholders at all stages of the planning process.

7.2 Seek diverse participation in the planning process.

7.3 Promote leadership development in disadvantaged communities through the planning process.

7.4 Develop alternative scenarios of the future.

7.5 Provide ongoing and understandable information for all participants.

7.6 Use a variety of communications channels to inform and involve the community.

7.7 Continue to engage the public after the comprehensive plan is adopted.

8. *Accountable Implementation.* Ensure that responsibilities for carrying out the plan are clearly stated, along with metrics for evaluating progress in achieving desired outcomes.

8.1   Indicate specific actions for implementation.

8.2   Connect plan implementation to the capital planning process.

8.3   Connect plan implementation to the annual budgeting process.

8.4   Establish interagency and organizational cooperation.

8.5   Identify funding sources for plan implementation.

8.6   Establish implementation indicators, benchmarks, and targets.

8.7   Regularly evaluate and report on implementation progress.

8.8   Adjust the plan as necessary based on the evaluation.

Attributes

9. *Consistent Content.* Ensure that the plan contains a consistent set of visions, goals, policies, objectives, and actions that are based on evidence about community conditions, major issues, and impacts.

9.1   Assess strengths, weaknesses, opportunities, and threats.

9.2   Establish a fact base.

9.3   Develop a vision of the future.

9.4   Set goals in support of the vision.

9.5   Set objectives in support of the goals.

9.6   Set polices to guide decision making.

9.7   Define actions to carry out the plan.

9.8   Use clear and compelling features to present the plan.

10. *Coordinated Characteristics.* Ensure that the plan includes creative and innovative strategies and recommendations and coordinates them internally with each other, vertically with federal and state requirements, and horizontally with plans of adjacent jurisdictions.

10.1 Be comprehensive in the plan's coverage.

10.2 Integrate the plan with other local plans and programs.

10.3 Be innovative in the plan's approach.

10.4 Be persuasive in the plan's communications.

10.5 Be consistent across plan components.

10.6 Coordinate with the plans of other jurisdictions and levels of government.

10.7 Comply with applicable laws and mandates.

10.8 Be transparent in the plan's substance.

10.9 Use plan formats that go beyond paper.

Appendix B

Comprehensive Plans Cited

This appendix provides a list of comprehensive plans cited in this book. Covering a range of types and sizes of local governmental jurisdictions, these plans are representative of comprehensive planning practice in the second decade of the 21st century. Figure B.1 shows the geographic distribution of the jurisdictions across the United States.

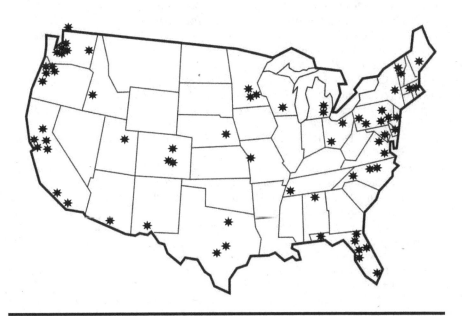

Figure B.1 Locations of Comprehensive Plans Cited

Alachua County, Florida (2019). *Alachua County Comprehensive Plan.*

Albany, New York (2012). *Albany 2030: Your City, Your Future*

Allentown, Pennsylvania (2019). *Allentown Vision 2030 Comprehensive Plan and Economic Development Plan.*

Asheville, North Carolina (2018). *Living Asheville: A Comprehensive Plan for our Future.*

Aurora, Colorado (2018). *Aurora Places: Planning Tomorrow's City.*

Austin, Texas (2012). *Imagine Austin Comprehensive Plan.*

Bloomington, Illinois (2015). *City of Bloomington Comprehensive Plan 2035.*

Boston, Massachusetts (2017). *Imagine Boston 2030: A Plan for the Future of Boston.*

Burlington, Vermont (2019). *planBVT Comprehensive Plan.*

Butte County, California (2010). *General Plan 2030.*

Cambridge, Massachusetts (2019). *Envision Cambridge* and *New Mobility Blueprint.*

Cheney, Washington (2011). *Comprehensive Plan.*

Cincinnati, Ohio (2012). *Plan Cincinnati: A Comprehensive Plan for the Future.*

Clay County, Florida (2018). *2040 Comprehensive Plan.*

Colorado Springs, Colorado (2020). *PlanCOS.*

Durham, North Carolina (2005). *Durham Comprehensive Plan.*

Eagle, Idaho (2017). *City of Eagle Comprehensive Plan.*

East Donegal Township, Pennsylvania (2011). *Donegal Regional Comprehensive Plan.*

Essex, Vermont (2016). *2016 Essex Town Plan.*

Eugene, Oregon (2016). *Envision Eugene Comprehensive Plan.*

Fairfax (City), Virginia (2020). *2035 Comprehensive Plan.*

Fairfax County (2017a). *Policy Plan: The Countywide Policy Element of The Comprehensive Plan for Fairfax County, Virginia.*

Fairfax County (2017b). *Tysons Urban Center Plan.*

Flint, Michigan (2013). *Imagine Flint: Master Plan for a Sustainable Flint.*

Fort Walton Beach, Florida (2018). *Comprehensive Plan 2019–2029.*

Hillsborough County City-County Planning Commission (2016). *Imagine Hillsborough 2040.* Hillsborough County, Florida.

Huntsville, Alabama (2018). *Big Picture Comprehensive Plan.*

Inglewood, California (2020). *General Plan, Environmental Justice Element.*

Jeannette, Pennsylvania (2017). *Retooling Jeannette Comprehensive Plan.*

Kansas City, Missouri (1999). *FOCUS (Forging Our Comprehensive Urban Strategy) Kansas City Comprehensive Plan.*

Lancaster County, Pennsylvania (2009). *Greenscapes: The Green Infrastructure Element of the Lancaster County Comprehensive Plan.*

Lancaster County, Pennsylvania (2011). *Donegal Region Plan for East Donegal Township, Marietta Borough, Mount Joy Borough, and Donegal School District.*

Lancaster County, Pennsylvania (2012). *Blueprints: The Water Resources Element of the Lancaster County Comprehensive Plan.*

Lancaster County, Pennsylvania (2015). *Lancaster County: A Changing Place, 2000–2015.*

Lancaster County, Pennsylvania (2018). *Places2040: A Plan for Lancaster County.*

Las Cruces, New Mexico (2020a). *Elevate Las Cruces Comprehensive Plan.*

Las Cruces, New Mexico (2020b). *Elevate Las Cruces Comprehensive Plan, Volume III: Scenario Planning Initiative.*

Las Cruces, New Mexico (2020c). *Elevate Las Cruces Comprehensive Plan, Volume IV: Community Participation Program.*

Lincoln and Lancaster County, Nebraska (in process 2021). *Plan Forward Lincoln-Lancaster County 2050 Comprehensive Plan.*

Long Beach, California (2019). *City of Long Beach General Plan.*

Manatee County, Florida (2020). *Manatee County Comprehensive Plan.*

Manitou Springs, Colorado (2017). *Plan Manitou: Community Master Plan and Hazard Mitigation Plan.*

Memphis, Tennessee (2019). *Memphis 3.0 Comprehensive Plan.*

Miami-Dade County (2019). *Comprehensive Development Master Plan.*

Minneapolis, Minnesota (2018). *Minneapolis 2040- The City's Comprehensive Plan.*

Multnomah County, Oregon (2016). *Multnomah County Comprehensive Plan.*

Olympia, Washington (2019). *Olympia Comprehensive Plan.*

Palo Alto, California (2017). *City of Palo Alto 2030 Comprehensive Plan.*

Philadelphia, Pennsylvania (2011). *Philadelphia2035 Comprehensive Plan.*

Portland, Oregon (2018). *Comprehensive Plan.*

Portsmouth, Virginia (2018). *Build One Portsmouth.*

Raleigh, North Carolina (2020). *2030 Comprehensive Plan Update.*

Renton, Washington (2015). *City of Renton Comprehensive Plan.*

Roseville, Minnesota (2020). *2040 Comprehensive Plan Update.*

Sacramento County, California (2017). *Sacramento County General Plan.*

Sahuarita, Arizona (2019). *Aspire 2035: Sahuarita's General Plan.*

Salt Lake City, Utah (2015). *Plan Salt Lake: Salt Lake City Citywide Vision.*

San Diego County, California (2020). *San Diego County General Plan: A Plan for Growth, Conservation and Sustainability.*

Seattle, Washington (1994). *Towards a Sustainable Seattle: City of Seattle Comprehensive Plan.*

Seattle, Washington (2019). *Seattle 2035 Comprehensive Plan.*

Springfield Township, Ohio (2010). *Springfield Township Comprehensive Land Use Plan Update.*

Stearns County, Minnesota (2020). *Shape 2040 Stearns.*

Stockton, California (2018). *Envision Stockton 2040 General Plan.*

Thurston County, Washington (2014). *Comprehensive Plan.*

Tigard, Oregon (2018). *Tigard Comprehensive Plan.*

Topsham, Maine (2019). *Topsham Comprehensive Plan Update.*

Index

Note: **Bold** page numbers refer to tables; *italic* page numbers refer to figures and page numbers followed by "n" denote endnotes.